"A lively personal examination of what it means to choose a life partner (regardless of race or age or sex)."
—Marilyn Murray Willison, *Washington Post Book World*

MAY 2004

"*What Is Marriage For?* fills a gap in the literature of marriage history . . . Scholars, law clerks and judges, journalists, politicians and concerned citizens, all caught up in the same-sex marriage debate, will find Graff's book invaluable."
—Paul Kafka, *San Francisco Chronicle*

"[A] fascinating journey across time, religions, cultures and forms of economic organization, demonstrating that marriage is a historically contingent institution, that its rules, rituals and purposes have changed dramatically over time, that no one can make any claim about its core essence . . . This is an important book."
—Nancy Polikoff, *Women's Review of Books*

"I found myself devouring Boston-based journalist E. J. Graff's intriguing new book . . . While many members of the gay community (like me) debate the rather mundane question, 'Why can't we get married, too?' Graff poses a far more elemental, a far more provocative question: What is marriage for?"
—Michael Hemmes, *Gay Chicago Magazine*

"This book is a must-read for anyone genuinely interested in placing the same-sex marriage debate in its broader historical context."
—Beth Robinson, attorney for the plaintiffs,
Baker et al v. State of Vermont

"In this important book, E. J. Graff shows us how very different the history of marriage is from what most people believe it to be. *What Is Marriage For?* will give everyone new and more thoughtful insights into the battles being fought over same-sex marriage today."
—Dan Foley, co-counsel in *Baehr v. Miike*,
the same-sex marriage suit conducted
in Hawaii Circuit Court

What Is Marriage For?

What Is **Marriage** For?

E. J. GRAFF

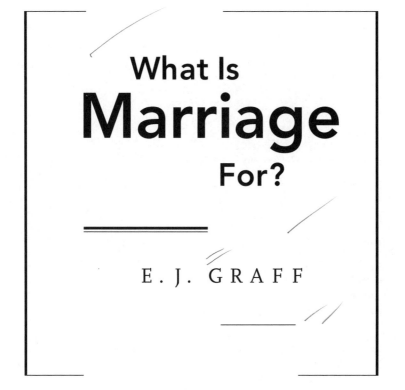

Beacon Press
Boston

TO MADELINE

Beacon Press
25 Beacon Street
Boston, Massachusetts 02108-2892
www.beacon.org

Beacon Press books
are published under the auspices of
the Unitarian Universalist Association of Congregations.

09 08 07 06 05 04   8 7 6 5 4 3 2 1

This book is printed on acid-free paper that meets the uncoated paper
ANSI/NISO specifications for permanence as revised in 1992.

Text design by Charles Nix
Composition by Wilsted & Taylor Publishing Services

Foreword adapted from Richard Goldstein, "The Radical Case for Gay Marriage," which first
appeared in the *Village Voice*, September 3–9, 2003. Used by permission of the author.

Library of Congress Cataloging-in-Publication Data

Graff, E. J.
    What is marriage for? / E. J. Graff.
        p.   cm.
    Includes index.
    ISBN 0-8070-4135-1 (pbk.)
    1. Marriage.   2. Same-sex marriage.   I. Title.
HQ734.G716   1999
306.81—dc21   98-54818

Contents

RICHARD GOLDSTEIN

Foreword

The Radical Case for Gay Marriage:
Why Progressives Must Join This Fight

For some Democrats, gay marriage is the political equivalent of doggie doo. James Carville has identified it as one of those "icky" issues his party should shy away from. But the times won't allow it. The Massachusetts Supreme Judicial Court has weighed in on the issue, calling for an end to marriage discrimination based on sexual orientation. In New Jersey, a lawsuit is under way that's expected to yield the same result. A proposed constitutional amendment to ban recognition of same-sex marriage is regularly discussed everywhere from the U.S. Senate to the popular media. This wedge issue has been wedged, and the only question is the fundamental one when it comes to human rights: Which side are you on?

Usually progressives can be counted on to prod the Democrats, but not this time. Carville's comment has gone virtually unanswered by the Left. There's been no crush of Hollywood celebs at fund-raisers for this cause. The radical cadres that march against globalization and war haven't agitated against the proposed gay-marriage amendment. "There is virtually no opposition from progressive groups," says Evan Wolfson of the advocacy group Freedom to Marry. "The problem is a failure to speak out and get involved." From a movement noted for its passion about social justice, this lack of ardor demands to be addressed.

Mind you, plenty of progressives, queer and otherwise, have enlisted in this fight. NOW has filed amicus briefs in several marriage cases. The Leadership Council for Civil Rights circulated a letter among its members opposing the amendment. But there is dissent in each of these organizations, and the divisions are sufficiently deep that activists have had to present two options: If you can't support same-sex marriage, surely you can see the danger in an amendment banning it. This approach has been fruitful, but the larger problem remains. "Whether it's due to a failure of progressives to connect the dots or a failure of gay groups to ask for their help," says Wolfson, "there's a curious silence."

Why the reticence? In part, it's because the Right has attached this issue to fears about the future of the family, and some progressives are all too willing to fall for that line. In part, it's a question of style. Ever since the days of Emma Goldman, marriage has been icky for radicals. Their image of gay culture as a "site of resistance" is threatened by the thought that these sexual outlaws might hew to the narrow if not the straight. Underlying these concerns is the fundamental reason why many feminists and sex radicals are cool to gay marriage. They worry about the unintended consequences.

"In seeking to replicate marriage," Judith Levine wrote recently in the *Voice*, "reformers may stall the achievement of real sexual freedom and social equality for everyone." Queer theorist Michael Warner regards marriage as part of a larger push toward gay "normalcy," and he sees this trend as a threat to the variety that has flourished in the queer community, "with its ethical refusal of shame or implicitly shaming standards of dignity." Warner calls marriage "selective legitimacy."

Both feminism and gay liberation have developed a potent critique of matrimony, exposing its relationship to repression and patriarchal privilege. Activists who cut their teeth on this reasoning are guided by it (and anyone headed for the altar would be well advised to check it out). But as E. J. Graff reveals in this smart and profoundly progressive volume, institutions change, and—thanks largely to agitation by radicals—marriage today is (or can be) different from the prison many older feminists escaped. Yet these memories of underdevelopment color the reaction of some progs.

I want to argue that their critique of gay marriage is shortsighted in several respects. Even when it is correct—as in its claim that

marriage is organized to bolster the socio-marital order—it ignores the human capacity to transform an oppressive institution.
As for the notion of normalcy, it simplifies the reasons why lesbians and gay men might want their relationships to carry the same
legal weight as heterosexual ones. Major questions of civic equity
and social prestige are on the line; this is much more than a flight
from the creative anarchy of queer life. What gays are fighting for is
the option to marry, not the obligation to do so—and choice, as all
progressives should know, is the essence of freedom. In that sense,
there's a connection between same-sex marriage and abortion
rights. That's why both issues are central to the culture wars.

If the Right succeeds in barring gay marriage, the fallout will do
much more to set back sexual freedom than any wedding vow. The
proposed amendment stipulates that no state constitution can be
read in a way that extends the "incidents" of marriage to same-sex
couples. In other words, all domestic-partner arrangements and
civil-union statutes that come by court order will be voided. Only
laws that emanate from legislatures or policies enacted by private
companies would be valid. The result would be a patchwork of procedures varying so dramatically that no unmarried couple could be
sure of the right to inherit assets, retain custody of children, carry
a partner's health insurance, or even visit a loved one in the hospital. (It's worth noting that even in New York City the tradition of
forcing lovers to identify themselves as siblings in order to be with
their mates in the intensive-care unit is still alive.)

The panic over gay unions obscures this hidden agenda, but rest
assured, the real object of the Right's campaign is straights who
stray. The same people who are agitating for the amendment don't
intend to stop there. The next thing they will go after is what they
call "divorce on demand." Feminists who recoil at the thought of
supporting marriage rights should consider what America will be
like if everyone except homosexuals is coerced into matrimony.

And that's just the start. In weakening the role of the judiciary, a
federal marriage amendment would be a powerful tool in halting
the advance of civil rights. All potential victims of discrimination
should be aware that, for the first time ever, the Constitution would

restrict the ability of judges to fight inequality. What's more, courts stacked with conservatives could strike down decisions that have nothing to do with marriage, applying the logic of this amendment just as liberal judges have used the Bill of Rights to establish many of the liberties we enjoy today. The principle so eloquently articulated by Justice Anthony Kennedy in his 2003 ruling against sodomy laws—that the Constitution allows each generation to expand the terrain of freedom—will be effectively moot once that process has been abridged.

What stops some lefties from applying their libertarian instincts to this issue? The most inexcusable reflex is the one that casts gay marriage as a bourgeois exercise in assimilation. It hardly helps that the loudest voices on this issue belong to gay conservatives who have framed it in similar terms. The media abet this image by focusing on gay couples who can afford to travel to Canada to wed legally, or who are tony enough to qualify for nuptial notices in the *New York Times*. To focus on poor people in a gay story is rare enough; but to show such folks fighting for marital benefits threatens the upbeat image of gays that the mainstream media feel compelled to project. Same-sex marriage activists aren't much more discerning. As a result, those gays who get to speak don't look like working stiffs.

But there are many more poor queer families than meet the media's eye, and they are the ones who stand to gain the most from marriage rights. As things are, they may not qualify for public housing; family courts may not accept their claims of domestic abuse; hospitals can—and regularly do—dismiss their right to make medical decisions on behalf of a loved one; they lack the standing to sue for a partner's wrongful death; they can't count on a partner's social security benefits; and even when private pensions are passed along, the tax-exempt status is lost if the recipient is an unmarried mate.

Child custody, always a perilous pursuit for gay couples, is an almost Sisyphean task for the queer poor, especially in Southern or Midwestern states with laws and policies denying legal recognition to domestic partnerships. It isn't widely known that 34 percent of lesbian and gay couples in the South are raising kids. That's more than in any other region, but not by much; about a third of lesbian households in America contain children. (Among gay men, it's a fifth.) Census data also suggest that lesbians of color are more likely than white dykes to have kids at home. In other words, same-sex marriage is a black, working-class, women's issue, despite its palmy facade.

But doesn't this argue for a system in which benefits aren't tied to marriage at all? "Even as we support legalizing same-sex unions," Katha Pollit writes, "we might ask whether we want to distribute these rights and privileges according to marital status. Why should access to health care be a by-product of a legalized sexual connection, gay or straight?" Wouldn't we all be better off if everyone raising a child were entitled to the same break? And why not allow people to structure their intimate lives as they choose, without sacrificing security? Generations of radicals have imagined a world in which the norm-making rules of matrimony are suspended—or at least loosened to suit the way people actually live. This is a struggle worth waging. Why do radicals assume it will be hindered if gay people can wed?

It's understandable that advocates for gay marriage would portray it as a tribute to normalcy, and in the short term it probably will look like that. But as gay people grow accustomed to this option they will shape it to suit their particular needs. You'll see leather weddings, boi-on-boi unions between queers of the opposite sex, trans matches that defy the boundaries of gender—all of a piece, with rice-throwing, trip-to-Niagara realness. Queers won't stop being queer just because they can get hitched. The tradition of open relationships won't cease to exist, nor will the boundless exploration of identity and desire. Marriage won't change gay people but merely affirm them as they are—and that, in all its profane glory, isn't so different from what straight people have become.

The vogue for white weddings notwithstanding, most young heterosexuals entering the state of matrimony have very different expectations than their parents did. Some take their vows as a statement of eternal fidelity, others regard them as the affirmation of a loving but not necessarily lifelong bond; some are laying the groundwork for having children, while others are focused on fitting their kids from prior unions into a new whole. For each of these strategies, there are couples that mean to accomplish the same goals without hitching up. The growing range of options both within and outside marriage is a reality not just in the United States but across the Western world, and the law is evolving accordingly. The Right's anxiety about gay unions has everything to do with this new flexibility. The more patterns of intimacy change, the more conservatives rush to keep the form of marriage the same.

It's debatable whether allowing gay people to wed will open the floodgates to legal recognition for other relationships. But certainly civil unions present a model that can be broadly applied. I'm not thinking of Republican senator Rick Santorum's specter of incest and polygamy, but of the elderly who live together and don't want to sully the memory of their deceased spouses with another formal marriage. Civil unions might suit them, along with siblings who want to commemorate their bond (and join their assets). Down the road we may see groups of people sharing the custody of children, or geriatric communes seeking a legal tie. Each of these contingencies will involve its own process of agitation, and it will be up to society to accept or reject each claim. But the result could be a menu of possibilities, ranging from trial unions to so-called covenant marriages that are very difficult to dissolve. People may elect to pass from one category to another as their attitudes change. This begins to look like the kind of world radicals want to see—a world of choice.

Gay marriage won't bring that about; nor will banning gay marriage prevent it. But the outcome of this struggle could determine whether America will adhere to a rigid code of intimacy, enforced by a system of penalties and stigma, or evolve toward the democratic vistas our poets have foreseen. "The greatest lessons of

Nature," wrote Walt Whitman, are "the lessons of variety and freedom." America, Whitman believed, was the ultimate repository of
that principle. If we see gay marriage in that light—as an emblem
of variety and freedom manifest in love—we can understand why
the Right feels compelled to crush it. And we can see why the Left
must defend it, if only for its potential as a radical act.

Introduction

Every family is full to the brim with marriage stories that are intriguing or shocking, heartwarming or startling. Mine is no exception. My mother's parents, for instance, married secretly; this was in the depths of the Depression, and as my grandmother-to-be Rebecca and my grandfather-to-be Al were the main support of their families, they felt too responsible to their impoverished families to move out, and so told no one they were married for many months. My mother, like so many in the late 1950s, married just days before she turned 21. And in the 1970s, again like so many in her cohort, she divorced just before she turned 40. My other grandfather, several years after divorcing his first wife, married a second. Her Irish family rejected him, a divorced Jew, and when his second wife died he remarried his first. One of his sons, my uncle, married a black woman and (depending on who's telling the story) either drifted or was pushed away from our family. All these stories were shaped by the social forces of their time, such as the Depression, antisemitism, racism, postwar marriage hysteria—not to mention forces of *all* time, like the desire for sex, children, and companionship.

And me? Early in my thirties, I married the woman I adore.

Or did I? Can two women get married? I wasn't at all sure. As a discontented daughter of 1970s cornfield suburbs, I'd always intended to evade marriage's confining traditions, disdaining those who dreamed of being brides. Had I fallen in love with a man, I assumed I would have refused legal marriage, remaining (like most

[*xvii*]

of my friends) in what social scientists call a "consensual union." And ever since, at age fifteen, I realized that my heart was drawn to other girls, I'd assumed I was an outsider to the institution that had shaped the lives of everyone else in my family—that I could be a critical observer, nothing more.

And so, after Madeline and I had our ceremony (attended by family and friends), I became urgently determined to understand what we had done. Had our ceremony had anything to do with marriage—and if so, what? What did it mean that, after untold millennia in which marriage has meant Boy + Girl = Babies, every postindustrial nation is beginning to publicly discuss opening the institution to couples like Madeline and myself—just as so many people are holding a mass civil disobedience action against legal marriage, having sex and babies outside its walls? Is marriage a worthy or useful goal—or a way of forcing people to squeeze their lives and dreams into too-small boxes? Is civil marriage, which locks private affections into an intimate relationship with the state, an institution I wanted to enter? Is marriage a patriarchal hangover, useful only to those who want to assign each womb to some male owner? What, to put it simply, is marriage *for*?

That large question was the one I had to answer, I quickly realized, if I was to understand whether marriage was an institution in which I belonged. And so my search dragged me through history, anthropology, sociology, law, opinion, and literature. Along the way, I turned up far more questions than I had when I began. The history of the family has become a popular academic discipline. There's an enormous amount of freshly harvested data—accompanied by extremely heated discussions about how to interpret that data. I am hardly qualified to form an opinion on so many of the things that preoccupy scholarly debate, such as whether parents loved their children less in, say, 1258 than in 1958, the year I was born. What this book does report, however, is something that every scholar makes clear: marriage and the family have been in violent flux throughout history, the rules constantly shifting to fit each culture and class, each era and economy.

And that flux itself is startling enough—as startling and intrigu-

ing as the individual marriage stories in my own, or anyone's family. And so, in this book, my hope is to entertain and inform by il-
lustrating (selectively, not comprehensively) just how widely the
marriage battles have ranged—showing that, contemporary discussion to the contrary, marriage is anything but "traditional."
The book will draw only from the West, and not Asia, Africa, or the
pre-colonial Americas, since this is the tradition in which I live and
in which today's marriage debates are raging. (In scholarly terms,
the Romans, early Hebrews, and Africans who were imported into
American slavery—all of whose marriages this book glances at
briefly—cannot really be counted as part of the Western mainstream; I use their marriages only as a kind of contrast, for some
extra illumination of the peculiar twists and turns of marriage in
the West.)

But with or without a look at those contrasting societies, the
West's marriage history is plenty contentious. When you've listened mainly to the American shouting matches over whether the
death of Ozzie and Harriet is good or bad, it's disorienting to discover the depth and variety in marriage's historical shifts—which
include the weird demographic blip of the 1950s, when people like
my mother and father suddenly married at much younger ages and
had more children, going against history's trends. Although people throughout history have been sure that they'd know a marriage
if they saw one, its exact borders have been so slippery as to garner
thousands of pages of commentary from lawyers and scholars, rabbis and monks.

Marriage, in other words, turns out to be a kind of Jerusalem, an
archaeological site on which the present is constantly building over
the past, letting history's many layers twist and tilt into today's
walls and floors. As with Jerusalem, many people believe theirs is
the one true claim to this holy ground. But like Jerusalem, marriage has always been a battleground, owned and defined first by
one group and then another. While marriage, like Jerusalem, may
retain its ancient name, very little else in this city has remained the
same—not its boundaries, boulevards, or daily habits—except the
fact that it is inhabited by human beings. And yet marriage exists

in every recorded society. The institution may at different times be put to different uses—uses I've grouped by chapter: *Money, Sex, Babies, Kin, Order,* and *Heart.* And yet marriage has outlasted its many critics (critics ranging from Plato and Jesus to Engels and Ann Lee)—and has outlasted, as well, the doomsayers of so many eras who post marriage's obituary notice every time society talks about changing its marriage rules.

When hearing this book's title and central question, people often laugh with something between amusement and discomfort, as if I'd exposed their secret frustrations. Sometimes their answers are wistful (one divorced man, aiming at irony and missing, said, "It's for everyone but me"), sometimes light-hearted ("For the presents"), sometimes practical ("I needed dental insurance")—but almost everyone's answers are personal. That surprised me, since my main goal was to look at marriage's public policy purposes. But those answers kept reminding me that public and private are not separate: they are, rather, twin sides of a single Moebius strip. How history has shifted its answers about marriage's public purposes has everything to do with individual marriages' shifting inner lives. To return to my metaphor, if public policy has altered the position of this Jerusalem's streets and walls, then the space in which we (the married, the unmarried, the all-but-married) live our daily lives has shifted as well.

And it's in those shifts that I found the answer to my private question: why do so many same-sex couples suddenly feel we can make a public claim to this institution—and why are those claims being taken seriously (in many different forms) in legislatures and courts as remote from one another as Hawaii, Vermont, Alaska, the Netherlands, Finland, France, and South Africa? The answer is also the answer to many other questions, such as, Why are so many of my cohorts cohabiting rather than registering with the state? Why are so many people divorcing and remarrying rather than putting up with relationships that chafe them raw? Why do wives no longer take second-class status for granted but argue for full equality? Why is contraception—so recently considered immoral, illegal, and unmentionable—almost universally accepted now just as rates of adoption and IVF-assisted births are skyrocketing?

While it will take the entire book to attempt to answer those questions adequately, the short answer is that marriage transformed dramatically in the nineteenth century. With capitalism, marriage stopped being the main way that the rich exchanged their life's property, and that the rest of us found our life's main co-worker. That change—the death of "traditional" marriage, which had dropped ill in the mid-eighteenth century and breathed its last by the 1920s—was so dramatic that it set off changes in every other philosophy of marriage: what makes sex sacred or even acceptable; what children need to grow up well; how far in or out of their kinship circle (whether defined by tribe, religion, race, ethnicity, or class) people are expected or allowed to marry; what marriage rules are required to keep social order; and how important it is to consult your own heart.

Of course, not everything can be reduced to economics—which is why this book is filled with marriage battles between the Romans and the early Christians, the radical Protestants and the sixteenth-century Catholics, the Comstock reactionaries and the Sanger insurgency, and so much more.

You may soon notice that this book often looks at marriage from the vantage point of women. That's because I wanted to overcome a bias that struck me as especially odd: leaving aside advice books, much that is written about marriage is quite clearly by, about, and for *men*. (One respected sociologist actually suggested that women marry young and stay married to avoid accumulating ex-boyfriends and ex-husbands, which would put them at a higher risk for murder. Does he really think abuse is so inescapable that women better just pick one abuser and try to avoid antagonizing him?) The history of marriage looks slightly different from a female point of view. For one thing, it soon becomes clear that many of the nineteenth-century changes that led to today's marriage battles are changes in the status of *women*: whether sex must lead instantly to babies, or whether contraception should be legal; whether married women should be free to own property, or to have custody of their children, or to hold jobs. And once men and women are equal, choosing their jobs (both within and outside marriage) as earner, nurturer, cook, or household handyperson based on their desires and talents and circumstances rather than on sex, then what bars two men or two women from marrying?

That may seem like a large intellectual leap; I hope it will seem so no longer by the time you finish this book. What's more important to notice is that the philosophy of marriage that's based on equality, freedom, and the integrity of the individual conscience is under siege. Plenty of people want to run other people's sexual and emotional lives, refusing to trust each of us to our own conscience. In 1998 the Southern Baptist Convention reminded women that they belong at their husband's heel, not by his side—and condemned Disney for recognizing same-sex couples, presumably because we're too equal. The man who bombed an Atlanta abortion clinic also bombed an Atlanta lesbian bar. Feminism and same-sex marriage, as this book will argue, are directly linked—and the latter is a more widely acceptable target for attack. It's hard for most people to argue directly against the idea of female equality: too many girls have now grown up playing soccer and would laugh at any hint that they can't be doctors, pilots, biologists, mothers, CEOs. Instead, many of those who oppose female equality aim their harsher language at lesbians and gay men—and same-sex marriage—calling *us* unnatural, just as our great-grandmothers were called unnatural for wanting to own property or use contraception.

While writing, I have kept on my desk a crumbling little book, about six inches high and one inch thick, titled *Marriage: Its History, Character, and Results; Its Sanctities, and Its Profanities; Its Science and Its Facts. Demonstrating Its Influence, as a Civilized Institution, on the Happiness of the Individual and the Progress of the Race.* Glancing every day at this thundering nineteenth-century tome, which reads now as so ridiculous, has kept me a little cautious—reminding me that any assertions I make about the meaning of marriage will also, surely, quickly become dated. I have tried, therefore, to keep my ranting to a minimum, concentrating instead on pointing readers to the historical surprises that have so often made me gasp. Which does not mean I have written a history of marriage: the subject is too vast for that. Rather, I have tried to offer up its most interesting twists and turns. In doing so, I hope this book shows you how your ancestors' marriages have been startling and intriguing, foreign and frankly strange—and that its look at marriage in the past illuminates your own.

ONE:

Money

_____

Who marrieth for love without money hath good nights and sorry days.

—English proverb (1670)

What is earned in bed is collected in widowhood.

—Medieval folk saying

Children are so much the goods, the possessions of their parents, that they cannot, without a kind of theft, give themselves away without the allowance of those that have the right in them.

—Eighteenth-century British advice manual

What is the difference in matrimonial affairs, between the mercenary and the prudent move? Where does discretion end, and avarice begin?

—JANE AUSTEN, _Pride and Prejudice_ (1813)

"Now, let me recommend to you," pursued Stryver, "to look it in the face. Marry. Provide somebody to take care of you. Never mind your having no enjoyment of women's society, nor understanding of it, nor tact for it. Find out somebody. Find out some respectable woman with a little property— somebody in the landlady way, or lodging letting way—and marry her, against a rainy day. That's the kind of thing for you. Now think of it, Sydney."

"I'll think of it," said Sydney.

—CHARLES DICKENS, _A Tale of Two Cities_ (1859)

OFTEN WHEN I TELL PEOPLE I'M WRITING A BOOK called *What Is Marriage For?*, they answer: toaster ovens and silverware. Or, getting dental benefits. Or, passing on property. While they may be joking, they're also correct. Whether through the kind of dowry that today's middle-class parents pass on in wedding gifts and home down payments, or the corporate mergers of medieval aristocratic families that might have taken years to negotiate, or the small businesses launched when two well-trained vineyarders joined their complementary skills and marriage portions, marriage has always been a key way of organizing a society's economy. Or to put it more bluntly: marriage is always about money.

How visible (or rather, how openly acknowledged) that link is—and just how tightly or loosely it's enforced—varies from one economy to the next. It's no coincidence that a world in which one's financial prospects have come dramatically unmoored from one's marriage prospects—in which how you make your living is separate from where you make your bed—is a world whose marriages much more easily unravel. And it's no coincidence that a world in which each individual can (and must) make his or her own financial future—men and women equally exploiting their own brains, brawn, or brio—is a world in which two people of one sex claim the freedom to marry.

Money is one of this society's most clandestine and volatile subjects, certainly more so than sex. (Would you find it easier to ask a new friend about sex life or income? Psychologists, at least, find the latter far more taboo.) In this, we're quite different from most societies. In "traditional" marriage—that is, marriage in most societies across culture and history—people talk first about money, assuming that after the important financial matters are arranged, the couple can work out such details as sex and affection and maybe even love.

How did marriage get turned on its head? How is it possible that today we talk first, last, and endlessly about the heart, considering it somewhat rude (almost until the wedding day) to talk directly about something so private as finance—an attitude almost directly the opposite of our ancestors'? That question is the main subject of this chapter, which traces lightly the economic history of marriage. The short answer is: Today, your financial future is no longer so completely determined by how you marry. That fact, which we take for granted, has been a social earthquake that over several centuries has shuddered deeply into the foundations of marriage, transforming it into the institution we know today. Thus, alongside the nineteenth century's accelerating capitalism (which made it possible for each of us to earn our livings, separate from our families) came accelerating changes in our marriage ideals—changes we'll see throughout this book. All these changes, from the debates over such "unnatural" proposals as mother-custody and contraception to debates over no-fault divorce and same-sex marriage, grow from money's weakening link. Precisely because we can each make our own living, with or without our families of origin, with or without a spouse, we have vastly more choice in matters of the heart.

We could probably date the conception of "modern" marriage at around 1850, with its gestation through the Gilded Age, and its birth about 1920. Not coincidentally, serenading that pregnancy and birth has been a steadily rising chorus of outcries about the death of marriage and the family. By the 1920s every third magazine article seemed to be titled "Will Modern Marriage Survive?" Of course, reports of marriage's death have been greatly exaggerated: even laying aside the peculiar 1950s (which none of "the family's" doomsayers foresaw), marriage remains outrageously popular, divorce statistics and all. And yet money still can't quite be separated from marriage; today's couples are necessarily financially intertwined in ways large and small. Although it may not define our lives entirely, the last half of this chapter looks at how and why marriage remains a financial contract enforced by the state. Or to put it in terms of this book's guiding question, this chapter closes with a look at what (in money's terms) marriage is for today—and at why same-sex couples now belong. But that's jumping ahead of our story, which begins long before Adam Smith's invisible hand started to remold marriage into the institution we now know.

Exchanging It: The Marriage Market

Just about every human language has words for the various portions exchanged or promised in the marriage transaction: bride price, dowry, dower, *antefactum, arras, asura, biblu,* bridewealth, *chidenam, coemptio, coibche,* curtesy, *dahej, desponsatio,* dower, *donatio ante* or *propter nuptias, dos ex marito, exovale, faderfio, hedna, lobola, loola, maritagium, matan, meta, metfio, morgengabe, mohar, mundium, nedunia, nudunnu, pherne, proix, stridhan, sulka, tercia, tinól, tinnscra, titulo dotis, vara-dakshina, yautaka.* Exactly in what directions that alphabet of money will travel when a couple marries—and whether as cash, cattle, cowrie shells, farm implements, furniture, houses, labor, land, linens, orchards, pigs, plate, quilts, or some other gift—varies among cultures and classes. Usually social systems have either dowry or bridewealth. Dowry travels from the bride's family to the groom or his father, while bridewealth or bride price travels from the groom's family to the bride or her father. Almost always, there are other gifts or feasts traveling in additional directions as well, whether they be farm service owed to the new brother-in-law, or mementos given to every wedding guest. Some of that money is compensating one family or the other for the loss of a worker; some is celebratory potlach; some is roped off as "dower" to guarantee the bride support when she's deserted or widowed—when, in other words, she's a dowager. As one historian puts it, "marriage for love has traditionally been assumed to be the dubious privilege of those without property." Without the marriage exchange, most traditional economies would cease to turn.

The rules in these exchanges are so varied and intricate that any informed anthropologist or historian will wince at how this brief section simplifies them into a few principles. But anyone within any given group knows how their own system works—and finds that system quite "natural." Everyone knows that exactly what changes hands when two people marry must be explicitly haggled over by the families involved and discussed all over town. If, for instance, a young premodern French bourgeois made her debut and was not married within the year, there'd be some nasty gossip about . . . the size of her dowry. Of one particular seventeenth-century match, one pair of historians write, "It did not matter that anyone of good society in Annecy was capable of providing a fairly exact assessment of the two [orphaned and sole heirs] young people's 'expectations' (each had 70,000 livres in property) or that their marriage had been taken for granted by everyone for ages: the actual finalization of the marriage took many long months." "Finalization" is a softer word for *haggling*—exactly what would go to whom, and when. During most of the history of the West, the engagement feast was when the two families finished negotiations and finally signed, witnessed, and notarized the marriage contract (and perhaps let the two start living together). The marriage ceremony itself was usually when money (or its stand-in, the ring) actually changed hands, a ceremony that was—at least in classes where enough money changed hands for this to matter—for many years overseen by a notary, not a priest.

All this sounds abominably mercenary and soulless now, so much so that we may feel smugly superior to this prostitution of something so sacred and personal as one's life partner. But for thousands of years, the marriage bargain your parents made for you was more comparable to today's college education than to today's marriages. Any responsible middle- or upper-class parent (or class aspirant) will at his child's birth start worrying about, and maybe saving for, tuition, often with some investment from the grandparents. It's all very well to say *you can be anything you want to be when you grow up,* but achieving that will be a lot harder if you go to your local community college than if you go to Yale. In fact, for the first twenty or so years that women could take a college education for granted, it was still seen as a dowry: she was there to get not a career but her "MRS" degree.

In the same way, traditionally one's offspring would have a much better chance of marrying, and therefore living, well in every sense if they brought a hefty marriage portion. Perhaps no era's parents can guarantee their children's future—charm, talent, smarts, looks, luck, and effort all matter on the career market as on the marriage market—but parents rightly worry about giving their children the best possible start.

Of course, your parents and siblings cared about your marriage not just for your sake, but also for their own. It's hard to imagine now how fully your marriage could define the future of all your relatives and allies—who they would socialize with, who they could call on in hard times, who would be able to present them at Court, which cows would be left for their own inheritance. "Many marriages have been, as everyone knows, causes of a family's ruin, because concluded with quarrelsome, litigious, proud, or malevolent individuals," wrote one fifteenth-century Tuscan. Not an individual—*individuals.* That marriage was a critical group merger was simply common wisdom. Every marriage was such an important shift in the social and economic landscape that when Florence put a cap on dowries, it was essentially an antitrust law. (Those good free-market capitalists the Medici revoked the cap, stating that "marriages must be free, and everyone should be free to endow his daughters, sisters, and other female relatives as he sees fit and as he likes, because one must be able to arrange his affairs in his way." Move over, Steve Forbes!) And so your marriage choice was not simply your own. Your family and friends were your board of directors, experienced people with a direct stake in guiding you to a successfully concluded merger. Breach of contract suits were seriously enforced because not just emotions and reputations but money and property—very serious things indeed—had been painstakingly engaged, and while negotiations had been going on the merchandise (not just the girl but property on both sides) had been taken off the market during selling season.

In other words, for most of history the phrase "a good marriage" meant something more like the phrase "a good education" or "a good job" than the shimmering rainbow of emotions that phrase implies today. Sure, marriage—like education or work—brought emotional satisfaction, but how could that satisfaction be disentangled from other, more practical rewards? Not without reason did people talk about marriage markets, marriage brokers, and marriage bargains: marriage was society's economic linchpin. For millennia, until there was a marriage contract—*cartas de arras, ketubah, pacta dotalia*—ensuring the new family's future against penury and starvation, nobody married.

If nobody could marry without money, and if large amounts of money changed hands at marriage, society cared about dowries in a way far more urgent than we might think from its quaint, white-lace associations. Not only did every marriage bargain reshuffle social and economic power, but without marriages there would be no legitimate babies and the state (or religion) would collapse for lack of citizens or parishioners. "It is a matter of state concern that women should have secure dowries," one Roman legal scholar wrote. Medieval peasant widows contributed to funds for poor girls' dowries, as philanthropists in our time might adopt an inner-city class and guarantee their college tuitions. In 1425 the city of Florence—concerned that, after several plagues, there weren't enough marriages and births—launched a savings-bond institution (the Monte delle Doti, or Dowry Fund) in which a family could invest for a daughter's future dowry with returns of up to 15.5 percent compounded annually, with both capital and interest paid to the husband after consummation (and immediately taxable). Eighteenth-century Spanish legislation tried to limit dowry to no more than twelve times the annual income of the head of household. And suits over dowry—either because the cooking pot, two carpets, and six shillings were never paid, or because the silk promised to be worth 900 florins was assessed at only 750 florins—fill every era's records. The economic world simply couldn't keep turning if the marriage bargain wasn't kept.

Not only did societies worry explicitly over the size and transfer of marriage payments, but—naturally—so did families. Dante famously noted that fathers in his time were appalled by the birth of a daughter—already anxious, in an era of extreme dowry inflation (much like tuition inflation at prestigious American colleges today), about how they would raise the fortune needed to marry a girl off. No wonder a Florentine father started sweating at each daughter's birth, aware that he might have to liquidate goods from an entire mercantile voyage in order to marry off Maria, and knowing that the higher his daughter's dowry (which everyone in town would know) the higher his credit rating and status could rise. Meanwhile, Maria's younger sisters had to be prepared to end up in convents, which required far smaller dowries, unless there came a dowry-bequest from some widowed aunt or godmother's will—known to us as the fairy godmother who magically got her goddaughter to the ball.

Sons as well as daughters might be unable to marry because of a family's limited treasury. Historian Lawrence Stone has shown that, among the families of sixteenth-century British gentry, male heirs married (and almost all of them did) by an average age of twenty-one or twenty-two, while their younger brothers, who would inherit little or nothing, didn't marry until their early thirties. That's because the younger brothers might take ten years to earn enough to attract a socially acceptable (and acceptably dowried) wife. Depending on the era, from one-fifth to one-fourth of the British gentility's younger sons never married at all; before 1650, three-quarters of the daughters of Milan's aristocracy were sent to convents; and in the eighteenth century—a time of dowry inflation—one-third of the daughters of the Scottish aristocracy stayed single.

Some of these exchanges would strike us as particularly crude. Marriages in the early Germanic clans were distinctly financial transactions: when his family handed over the money, her family handed over the girl. And if your family had money and ambition, you certainly might be married off to a toad. Maybe you'd be allowed to reject one or two suitors suggested by your family or "friends" (those people with a financial or political interest in your family's estate); you might even, if you were male, be able to say no to up to half a dozen brides—but sooner or later you had to say yes. In a famous fifteenth-century letter a British woman, Agnes Paston, writes proudly that, after her daughter obstinately refused to marry on command, the girl was confined with no visitors and "hath since Easter the most part been beaten once in the week or twice, and sometimes twice on a day, and her head broken in two or three places." If you were male, the more traditional method of persuading you to marry was to withhold your inheritance—keeping you a household subject, constantly waiting on your allowance with almost no way to make an extra dollar (or pound or lira). The authority and cohesion of the traditional family, in other words, depended in no small part on the fact that you were dependent—not just for tax purposes but in fact.

The more money involved, the younger (and more tractable) you were likely to be when married. Your Genovese mercantile family might want to go into shipping with a particular prosperous family—and so you'd be engaged by age eight or ten or at most twelve and sent to live with his family (perhaps as his sexual playmate), so that by the time you were officially married you'd have been raised in, and accustomed to, his household's habits. Or your sixteenth-century Corsican clan might decide that engaging you to your father's murderer (and sending you to his house as security, even before the official marriage and payment) was the only way to stop the *vendetta*. Or your eighteenth-century British merchant father might want his grandchildren to be nobility and therefore marry you to the son of an impoverished earl who needed to pay off his mortgage or cancel his gambling debts without cutting back on his lavish parties. (To marry up the social scale, you had to fork over a sharply higher dowry: as Gatsby knew, social climbing costs extra.) Money, in other words, could be a proxy for status and power—and the more your family had, the less voice you had in your marriage.

Today, money management is the number one source of tension between spouses. Imagine how much more tension there could be when not just you and your husband but both families were involved. A Roman father-in-law could peremptorily take back his daughter—and deprive his son-in-law's estate or business of her dowry—if said son-in-law did something he disliked. Even among medieval feudal folks, your family's stake in your dowry could actually protect you from mistreatment: if your husband ran off with some young thing your family could insist he return your dowry, which might ruin his business or estate. (Of course, if *you* were the one who took a lover, you were out on your heels, no cash back.) On the other end of the social scale, a girl married off without a dowry or dower was often no better than a sexual slave, with no say in her new household, no support from her own family, and nowhere to go if the new husband died or tired of her. Billie Holliday was saying nothing new when she sang, "God bless the child that's got her own."

We shouldn't let ourselves feel *too* superior to our predecessors' financial finagling. Think of all the lawyers you know married to other lawyers, doctors to doctors, or others who've married in a comparable strata—an architect to a playwright, a truckdriver to a file clerk, Tom Cruise to Nicole Kidman, Harold Evans to Tina Brown. As free as your choice may feel, your education really has worked much like a traditional dowry. What else, after all, do dating services do but (like traditional marriage brokers) match age, class, income, and ethnic background—via such proxies as whether you listen to Nirvana or Serena or Amy Grant, eat mesclun or cream-of-mushroom-based casseroles or *kimchi*? Love *isn't* blind: it's easiest to get along with people who have similar backgrounds and interests. (Which is not to say mixed marriages—whether mixed by religion, class, race, gender, or some other variable—can't work; it's just that besides bridging ordinary family and personality differences, couples also have to leap the extra cultural gap.) This might be why Samuel Johnson insisted that "marriages would in general be as happy, and often more so, if they were all made by the Lord Chancellor, upon a due consideration of the characters and circumstances, without the parties having any choice in the matter." Reverend Moon would approve. "The arranged marriage works far less badly than those educated in a romantic culture would suppose . . . partly because it is a fact that sentiment can fairly easily adapt to social command," writes historian Lawrence Stone—at least so long as everyone expects companionship instead of intimacy and passion. Since you could not marry without others' financial contributions (not to mention the haggling and string-pulling to get into the presence of, and to get a favorable contract with, a family worth marrying); since your marriage had to be concluded in a way that wouldn't deprive others of their inheritances; since the entire town was involved in enforcing the exchange—how could anyone possibly consider your marriage an entirely private romance?

Making It: The Working Marriage

All that inherited wealth may nevertheless seem exotically foreign, impossibly luxurious. The difference between those well-endowed (financially, that is) characters in Beaumont and Fletcher, Edith Wharton, and most of us today is that I—and probably you—have to earn a living, before or after marriage. So did most of our ancestors—who saw marriage primarily as a complete plan of labor, the way you selected your most important workmate.

For most cultures through most of history, husband and wife have been interlocking jobs. "For the shoemaker, the cooper, the fishmonger ... the wife was business partner, working by his side." Whether Roman or medieval or premodern, a tradesman's wife kept the business's books, sold goods in market, and handled a range of essential tasks that differed depending on her husband's job. "The farmer's wife generally tended livestock, particularly chickens and pigs . . . , grew vegetables, did dairy work, kept bees, preserved and pickled, helped prepare goods for sale and perhaps took them to market, lent a hand at harvest and during haymaking, and exploited gleaning rights or the use of commons where such existed." In parts of Europe—the Alps or Pyrenees, say, or Ireland—the husband might be gone for up to nine months a year to bring in cash, leaving the wife to run the farm. In England a jail was essentially a private business run by a husband and wife; if he died and she wanted to keep the franchise, she had to promise to marry within the year (and maybe even let the civil authorities know who she had in mind). Or if his business didn't assign her specific tasks, the money she brought in by spinning, brewing, making sausages, weaving, preserving and selling fruit, or feeding and keeping house for lodgers and travelers, was essential capital and income. The family business simply couldn't run without both him and her.

"Whatever sadness a man experienced at the death of a young spouse, a farmer or an artisan simply had to find a replacement. He could not run a farm or a business alone. . . . in seventeenth-century Germany 80 percent of all widowed men found new wives within a year." Which meant the wife was too important to spend her time doing menial housework: unless she was the poorest of the poor, for most of history she had at least a housemaid, and maybe (if the family was moderately prosperous) also a kitchen-maid, nursemaid, dairymaid, laundrymaid. The babies were swaddled tightly and hung by the fire, or left in the care of the five-year-old, or sent out to nurse to free up the household's mistress. It's simply ridiculous to call the mom-at-home system more "traditional" than the dad-at-home system: only in the nineteenth century was Mother demoted to housemaid, while Father was banished from the house.

Where did all those maids come from? They were saving up for their dowries, so that someday *they* could graduate to wife. The good news is that the less property you got from your family, the more choice you had in who you married; the bad news is that you had to spend ten or fifteen years in hard labor earning that before you "graduated" into being a wife (i.e., mistress) or husband (i.e., master) yourself. Just as boys headed out to find a trade, girls often set out at age ten or twelve or fourteen to earn a dowry—going out to be a housemaid, nursemaid, laundrymaid, dairymaid, cook, textile worker in a silk or lace workshop, or some other insecure and low-paying job that allowed them, fifteen years later, to come home with enough capital to make a "good" (i.e., remunerative) marriage. Which is why Europeans traditionally married somewhere between twenty-five and thirty, for women, or twenty-eight and thirty-five, for men. Just as today's middle class spends a long adolescence getting educated for a profession or trade—education being the personal capital of our time—so our ancestors spent that time saving enough to stock the farm or fund the shop or tavern. So long as the pair launched their marriage/business with their own money, their parents (if still alive) let them choose a spouse for themselves.

But exactly what would "choice" mean in a village with somewhere between thirty and two hundred families, giving you maybe a handful or a score of eligible women or men in your class and age range? "In English villages," writes historian Olwen Hufton, "up to 80 per cent found a spouse from within a ten-mile radius, and the same seems to have been true in most of rural Europe." How many could possibly have been born in your age and class range— *and* survived to adulthood—*and* have enough money to marry— within those ten miles? Unmarried young men used cudgels to warn off outsiders who began courting "their" girls, or threw what historians call "barrier *charivaris*" that sound like small and barely contained riots—for instance, crowds of screeching, jeering, drum-banging young men might force the just-marrieds onto donkeys, flinging mudballs or ripping their clothes and chasing them through town until they paid a "fine." A *charivari* might be held if a widow or widower married one of the few eligible twenty-somethings, or if a girl married outside the village, thus reducing the potential spouse pool by a hefty percentage—and making it probable that, just for lack of possibilities, some guy in town would never marry. (And you thought *your* odds were bad.) In the extremely poor French parish of Sennely en Sologne, the pastor complained, "They get married out of financial interest rather than any other inclination. Most of them when looking for a bride only ask how many sheep she can bring in marriage. . . . It is a daily occurrence to see a man take a wretched bride, pregnant by someone else and adopt the child for a modest sum." Even outside the villages, how much choice would you have if you were a housemaid who rarely had a half-day off—and therefore met mainly the tradesmen who came to the house?

In reality, people often knew in advance who could marry whom. In the classes that worked for a living, dowry was a kind of "premortem inheritance," the money and property that made it possible for the new couple to start their farm or shop (just as today's middle-class young people get their early inheritance as college education and house down payments, and poorer people through in-kind service when relatives renovate the house or help raise the kids). You were pegged to the land because, as one eighteenth-century parishioner declared, "One cannot take one's vineyard with one." One historian explains that double marriages—siblings or cousins from one family marrying siblings or cousins from another—were common because "A son who inherited a third of a house, a quarter of a parcel of land, could only hope to acquire a home of his own by marrying a girl from his village who had inherited fragments of the same kind of immovable property." One couple gets *his* family's house and farm, the other gets *hers*—and everybody's ready to start work.

The skills you brought to the marriage could be just as important. For instance, vineyards and *vigneronnes* (women professionally designated as grape-growers and winemakers) were simply too valuable to let escape from the familiar circle—and so up to 50 percent of marriages were between cousins or even uncles and nieces. Meanwhile, having watched your cousins and neighbors grow up, you knew for yourself how reliable and well-honed were their work habits. Who'd want to lose half a year's crop by training some unknown from beyond the horizon? As another pair of vineyard petitioners declared when petitioning the Church for a dispensation so that their children could marry inside the forbidden incest limits, "We are neighbors and we know all about one another." That's not so far from the Maryland planter who married his best indentured servant rather than relinquish (or pay for) her labor, as his 1681 marriage contract made explicit: Nicholas Maniere's wife was to "Dresse the Victualls milk the Cowes wash for the servants and Doe allthings necessary for a woman to doe upon the sd plantation." Was that a marriage or an employment contract? Dower—her share of the estate if he died or deserted—recognized that without her contributions there *was* no estate. When our predecessors said marriage was hard work, they weren't talking about feelings.

Of course such marriages included affection. But if your life's income was based on your marriage, you wouldn't be so foolish as to marry only because you "fell in love," any more than you'd hire a business partner based only on sexual infatuation (and if you would, remind me never to buy your company's initial public stock offering). Rather, you'd look more for a stable, reliable, companionable workmate, someone you could get along with, someone you might well grow to care for by sharing your work in the day and your bodies at night. Which is why ordinary individuals, like small business owners, didn't have boards of directors overseeing their marriages, but might still, before deciding on a marriage, consult others who had their interests at heart. As a historian of medieval peasant families writes, "Medieval literature does not contain the same intensity of sentimentalization of family that modern literature does. . . . Affection certainly existed among family members—that shows up clearly in wills—but not sentimentalization."

No wonder divorce rates were low before capitalism transformed marriage's meaning. You'd have to be a terrible worker for your spouse to want to break up the entire household economy and search for someone new. Can you imagine Bill Gates firing 50 percent of his employees because he disliked them personally—making his business vulnerable to Sun and Oracle and Netscape? And no wonder societies discouraged divorce: what economy could survive if estates and businesses were constantly being ripped apart and refigured based on nothing more solid than emotions? Someone had to be relied on to bring in the crops, to spin cloth, to make wine, to hold power—and that someone was the married couple. Mass divorce could too easily lead to an unthinkable mass deprivation, not just for the couple but for everyone.

We might think that contemporary professor/professor or actor/actor pairs are not so different from that traditional working marriage. A shared investment in and knowledge of each other's daily work lives, the ability to rely on each other for feedback, sympathy, and advice—all that's a powerful bond. Madeline and I are each other's number-one career consultants and sounding boards—strategizing how to talk to our editors, ruthlessly criticizing and cheering on each other's manuscripts. Our private joke is that we're not just a couple, but the executive vice presidents of our own editorial corporation. But despite our shared passion for language and understanding, we're quite different from the traditional work-unit marriage. Like my brother the biologist and his wife the physician, or my friend the marketing manager and her husband the management consultant, we may love and rely on each other, we may buy things together, we may build a family together—but our work lives are elsewhere, interwoven with familial strangers. Very rare in the first world is the "traditional" small business that requires every family member's work for the whole to succeed—the farm family, the Korean grocery store, the Thai restaurant. Your work and your spouse's could probably be disentangled without either hurting your employers or slowing the economy. For better or for worse, money has evaporated as the cement of the "traditional" marriage, leaving us radically free.

Being It or Being Without It: Slaves and Paupers

Throughout history a hefty percentage of people have lived neither in the inheriting nor in the earning classes, people who had neither "expectations" nor means to bring in property: slaves and paupers. How did money affect their marriages? Were they exceptions to my generalization that for millennia nobody married without a contract? Not if you remember that such people *were* nobody in the eyes of the law. If you either had no property, or worse, *were* property, it might not even be clear whether or not yours would count as a marriage.

If marriage is something that imposes rights, obligations, and expectations that are enforced by the rulers' formal system of law, then no, slaves usually could not and did not marry. People without property might be refused marriage as well, or might simply ignore the legal requirements; if marriage was about protecting your property, why should paupers bother? The disorienting little insight, for people living in a democratic system that presumes we are all political equals, is that most people throughout history were *not* political adults, but were subject to some other man's authority. Marriage—becoming head of household—was what usually gave men full legal adulthood. Roman men, for instance, might well stay under their father's legal thumb—unmarried—into their thirties. Irish farm heirs were not considered fully adult until their fathers "made over" the farm, their first legal property, and allowed them to marry—in their thirties or even forties. How could a slave or even a pauper be allowed to marry, that sign of legal authority, precursor to such public responsibilities as voting or being justice of the peace or holding public office?

Some slave systems did allow the people counted as property to marry. Slave marriages in medieval Europe, seventeenth-century New England, and most Latin American countries were legally recorded—even though usually the slaveholder could take the slave away as needed. But the most enduring slave systems have denied recognition to slave marriages. How could any system of property law possibly allow property itself to make contracts, to promise to honor and support someone else, to give away rights to their bodies (especially to someone other than the owner), to take charge of children the law considered someone else's chattel? "As one judge put it," writes legal historian Michael Grossberg, "slaves could not discharge [marriage's] domestic obligations without 'doing violence to the rights of the owner.'" Recognizing slave marriage would make a mockery of the very concept of people as property— precisely why we find the bar on slave marriage so galling. From the owners' points of view, that bar was eased by the convenient ideology that slaves were subhuman, childish, lacking a full emotional or moral life. "A Roman would have found it . . . humorous to imagine a slave passionately in love. . . . [R]eligious fanaticism, excessive lust, and immoderate passion . . . were all defects that slave traders were required to make known to prospective buyers." Property must not have its own desires.

But just because they couldn't marry in law, did that mean that slaves never considered themselves married? Of course not. Over and over, when talking about how the history of the family intersects with people who were considered property—Greeks' slaves, Romans' slaves, Hebrews' slaves, medieval Germans' slaves, and of course, American and British slaves—historians write some variant of: "Slave marriage was not recognized by law, which did not prevent slaves from marrying and treating their marriages as serious." The owners' law might define the slaves' rights—but not their hearts.

It's frustratingly difficult to discover what the bar on slave marriages meant to slaves themselves, since those at any social pyramid's bottom leave the fewest records. Some Roman slaves, freed by their owners' wills, left gravestone inscriptions commemorating lifetimes of affection and fidelity—which presumably overlooked rape, separation, or sale as being beyond the spouse's control. There's little else left to know how they felt.

Better documented than ancient slave communities are those of diaspora Africans and their descendants. American slave marriages lasted for decades, and, as various historians have extensively documented, were ruled by their own community norms (apparently inherited from Africa) rather than those of their owners. For instance, since they considered it incestuous to marry first or sometimes even second cousins, enslaved men and women might consider themselves barred from marrying anyone on the same plantation. Slaveowners wanted their property to breed and increase (as appalling as the formulation sounds, they wrote about it in exactly this way), and so they often did give men permission to go court on other plantations—with the understanding that other owners would allow the same. Historian Herbert Gutman quotes a contemporary white commentator as writing, "Saturday night the roads were, in consequence, filled with men on their way to the 'wife house,' each pedestrian or horseman bearing . . . all the good things he could collect during the week for the delectation of the household." Marriage was celebrated in a variety of ways, from the famous ritual of jumping over the broomstick to laying one's blanket next to the other's ("married by the blanket") to going to a preacher who pronounced the couple married "until death or distance do you part"—a heartbreaking recognition that sale was as final as death. Because Virginia law required an ex-slave to leave the state once freed, one woman petitioned the legislature in 1815 to *become* a slave again in order to be able to stay with her husband; her petition read in part: "To guard against such a heart rending circumstance, she would prefer, and hereby gives her consent, to become a slave to the owner of her husband."

Strong as they were, these bonds were not enforceable in the owners' courts. For instance, in Western law, husbands and wives are excused from testifying against each other. One American court decided that one woman—whose *de facto* husband was accused of killing the white overseer who raped her—had to testify against her husband, since the relationship was not legally a marriage. Or as another judge wrote, "The relation between slaves is essentially different from that of man and wife joined in wedlock. The latter is indissoluble during the life of the parties, and its violation is a high crime; but with slaves it may be dissolved at the pleasure of either party, or by a master of one or both, depending on the caprice or necessity of the owners. . . . [Even emancipation cannot] by a sort of magic, convert it" into a "real" marriage. Such circular reasoning—slaves' frivolous sexual bonds can't be counted as marriage because they were formed and can dissolve outside the law, a law that will not let them marry—is quite breathtaking, although certainly familiar enough to same-sex couples today (which is not to imply, by any stretch, that my life is comparable to that of a slave's). Just as familiar is the condescension from a kinder observer in 1866: "What surprises one . . . is that families having no legal bond hang together as well as they do." How little trust these upper-class whites had in their own marriages, apparently believing them to be enforced only by the whip of law, not by the moral guidance of the heart—and how difficult it is for most people to see another group's affections as equivalent to our own.

So did slaves marry? If marriage is a bond recognized by the rulers' law, then no, they did not; but if marriage is a bond that two people and their community count as binding, then yes, they certainly did. Slaves were thus married and unmarried at the same time and on the same land, depending on whose social map was superimposed.

Just one step up from *being* property was being *without* property—people so penurious they couldn't even bring to their marriages a cow and a cooking pot. Could such paupers marry? Not always. Christian Roman law held that "a serf could not contract a fully valid marriage, and servile unions were treated as little more than liaisons that could be broken by the spouses' master"—an idea that stayed in canon law as late as the twelfth century. Meanwhile, as a trade and merchant class slowly grew in Europe, some societies made you pass a "means test"—for instance, requiring a dowry—before the good burghers let you marry officially. Even fundamentalist libertarian John Stuart Mill thought it quite fair to stop someone from marrying "unless the being on whom [life] is to be bestowed will have at least the ordinary chances of a desirable existence."

For some with ambition, means tests or a dowry requirement just pushed back the age at which they could marry, requiring them to spend an extra five or eight years in wage labor. Below those folks on the socioeconomic scale were itinerants and paupers. Comparative legal scholar Mary Ann Glendon mentions John Synge's play *The Tinker's Wedding,* in which Sarah, who's been traveling with Michael long enough to raise several children with him, suddenly and unaccountably wants a wedding. The local priest "rejects as preposterous Sarah's request that he perform a wedding ceremony for them for no fee," a fee they cannot afford, and is a little disgruntled that rabble like Sarah—probably unbaptised at that—wants a church marriage at all. Writes Glendon, "but are not Michael and Sarah already married? . . . Historically, family law paid little attention to the concerns of the poor, or of such ethnic minority groups as the Indians of North and South America or the Afro-Americans of the United States. Prior to the twentieth century, propertyless individuals came to the attention of the legal system chiefly as subjects of the criminal law."

Were Sarah and Michael married? Certainly they were in their own eyes and in the eyes of family and friends—although church and state might well tot them up as social problems. Like slaves, paupers could also be both married and unmarried at the same time and in the same place, depending on who's looking. All that changed in the nineteenth and twentieth centuries, as nation-states started regulating marriage more and more carefully for everyone. How did we travel from a late eighteenth-century world in which those who couldn't pay simply couldn't marry, to a late twentieth-century world in which courts across the postindustrial world have been decreeing marriage a fundamental and universal human right?

Keeping It: Ain't Nobody's Business If I Say "I Do"

The answer is intertwined with the fundamental change that most of us have begun to rule our own *economic* lives—not merely by handling our own wallets, but also by inventing our own futures.

Before examining that, consider how our predecessors would have thought of their economic and marital choices—which were, it's almost unnecessary to say, vastly more limited than our own. Your choices were limited in part by the pyramid of authority in which you lived. People didn't see themselves and each other as political equals: just about everybody lived under a master, not just theoretically but in day to day life. In the upper classes, "everybody" included pages, heirs-in-waiting, unmarried daughters, and genteel female "companions"; among the rest of us, it included all those unmarried dairymaids and servingmaids, apprentices and journeymen. Master and mistress may have been closely allied, but master had—theoretically at least—the final say. Even if you were head of household, you had to obey the lord of the manor; if you were the lord, you obeyed the king.

Your choices were also limited by the fact that your daily life followed closely that of your ancestors. For almost two millennia, most of Europe saw "an almost total lack of change . . . [in] agriculture, diet, the range of commodities available to most people, the imminence of disease and fear and the slow growth of population, with intermittent cutbacks due to famine and pestilence" and war, writes historian Olwen Hufton. Most people "ate from wooden trenchers, sat on hard wooden furniture and wore clothes that were woven at home, roughly constructed and handed down the generations. They ate the same food that their fathers and mothers had eaten." When they went off to work during their long adolescence, they followed exactly the same paths to exactly the same towns and industries (sometimes the very same houses or workshops) where their parents had earned their own marriage portions. They planted potatoes in the same lines, or wove linens in the same patterns, or cooked by the same recipes as their grandparents had. Since your life would probably be much like theirs, it could be quite successfully navigated by tradition. Which is not to say that life was predictable, pocked as it was by disease and death, pogroms and war. Nor is it to say that there was *no* change at all. Rather, the pace of change was glacial compared to our information-panic era which, as we've all heard ad nauseum, requires a once-unimaginable ability to learn and improvise constantly. Before, for most people in most places daily survival was achieved by obedience (and still is for many people worldwide): do as I did and you'll be more likely to live and thrive.

Moral—and marriage—philosophies stayed in that well-worn path, encouraging marital duty and obedience. Since your entire inner life, psychological and religious, followed the path of duty, it wasn't such a stretch to let your parents (or your "betters") choose your outer life for you—your work and your spouse, which were more or less the same thing. Or to put it differently, since you were used to obedience and limited choices in just about every area of your life, obedience—or to think of it from our point of view, very limited choice—in marriage would seem almost "natural," that word tossed around in every marriage battle.

Then we bump into history's big shift: the Protestant Reformation, industrial capitalism, and the republican revolutions, those intertwining phenomena. Let me acknowledge here that I'm about to breeze past a debate that ties historians into knots: which came first, industrialism or individualism? When the early sixteenth-century Protestants showed up and started insisting on each individual's moral responsibilities—on reading the Bible yourself instead of obeying your priest, on developing an inner relationship with God, on revealing your salvation through diligent work habits—did they encourage the initiative needed for the simultaneous boom in industrial investment and colonial exploration that changed the earth's face? Or did things happen the other way around: did the increasing shift of people to merchant-run cities and the new seafaring trades leave a yawning chasm between how the new middle classes lived—thriving by individual and innovative effort—and the old philosophy of obedience, thus setting off the religious and political earthquakes of Reformation and revolution? Did that new frame of mind create—or was it created by—the science and technology that has given us genetic engineering, black holes, antibiotics, and our astonishing confidence that we'll survive childbirth? Or was there some untraceably subtle process by which all those changes amplified each other, expanding the hole in the past and birthing our new—modern and postmodern—worlds?

Fortunately, this book doesn't have to worry about these chicken-and-egg questions. But we do have to notice the clear result—choice, or to put it in our new world's language, freedom. Both choice and personal responsibility became daily financial facts—as well as religious and political ideals. Or to put it even more simplistically, as people began to run their own economic and daily lives, they began to write hymns to "freedom" rather than "duty."

When your financial life stopped being under Dad's control, so did the rest of your life—and your marriage. And that happened once your life was no longer determined by a chances of getting productive land—once Europe and its colonies started shifting, in the eighteenth century, from farming to trade. Land is limited by definition; you have to wait for it to become available through death, whether your father's death at age fifty from ague or your neighbors' deaths from waves of plague. Once land gets replaced by what historians call "more portable forms of capital," the kids are free to make their own mistakes.

They're not immediately free, of course. Such an enormous change in attitude took centuries to really take hold—and to show up in our social rules. Because marriage was such a critical way of arranging the economy, parents with wealth battled for centuries to keep control of their children's marriages. So long as your parents approved, all Europe legally allowed you to be married at twelve (girls) and fourteen (boys). But without your parents' approval? Ah, that was an entirely different story—and depended on money. In France and Holland, where by law you always inherited from your parents—or to put it differently, where your parents could *never* write you out of their will—your parents had veto power over your marriages until you were twenty-five (women) and thirty (men). Things were different in Britain, where after about 1500 your wealthy parents could disinherit you; you were legally free to run off and get married, but what would you live on? When in the eighteenth century the British Parliament did work on a long-needed rejiggering of its incredibly messy marriage laws, Commons and Lords stayed up till dawn in the August heat and almost came to blows arguing over a clause that would allow parents to veto their children's marriages until they were twenty-one. The arguments were economic: Commons argued that the economy would grind to a terrible halt because "the landed elite would marry their sons to all the great heiresses. . . . [T]he tying up of property and liquid capital in a few hands was a threat to a commercial society based on the free market and the circulation of capital." In other words, those in the House of Commons wanted to be able to run off with some of those underage heiresses themselves. "As late as 1823 it was said that the act was passed 'for purpose of protecting patrimony against matrimony.' "

That argument sounds more like American arguments about PACs than about the Defense of Marriage Act. When money and power are at stake, there are consequences far more practical than God's wrath and the death of civilization.

But children were slipping free from their parents' control—as more and more of us were becoming free to earn and therefore to travel, love, marry, and eventually think. And I *do* mean think. New ideas stopped being officially suspect or threatening; two centuries later, they have become our economic engine. No longer do you assume you'll wear your parents' linens and plant your potatoes in the same terraced lines; now you better be open to new fashions, pesticides, techniques, and antibiotics or you'll be wiped out by your competitors (human, technological, or bacterial). As John Stuart Mill understood in making his case for women's equality: "What is the peculiar character of the modern world—the difference which chiefly distinguishes modern institutions, modern social ideas, modern life itself, from those of times long past? It is, that human beings are no longer born to their place in life, and chained down by an inexorable bond to the place they are born to, but are free to employ their faculties, and such favourable chances as offer, to achieve the lot which may appear to them most desirable."

That business of being encouraged to think—or in Mill's phrase, to "employ their faculties"—is a funny one, one that has taken a couple of centuries to work its way thoroughly into Western consciousness. Choosing to invent a better way to make a better life for your family, if that better life is earned by your own efforts, has an unexpected consequence: *your* children are also set free to invent their own lives. Not only can't you control them with the threat of withholding property; you also can't offer them any real guidance about the world or work in which they must make their way. Did you go to work with your father or mother to learn what he or she did? If so, you're an exception in the prosperous classes of the Western world. My mother did go to work and help her immigrant parents run their restaurant—but (except for borrowing the restaurant's cheesecake recipe) she never used what she learned in her various occupations, whether as full-time suburban mom, college math teacher, or mayor. My mother is no exception: what our economy wants from most of us is that we learn how to learn.

The change from the old "traditional" economy to the new "freedom" economy has progressively shuddered more and more deeply into our psyches, philosophies, and legal codes. The traditional ideal was well put by the eighteenth-century advice manual that counseled, "Children are so much the goods, the possessions of their parents, that they cannot, without a kind of theft, give themselves away without the allowance of those that have the right in them." But that traditional ideal was soon losing the battle to one that better fit the new economy. At about the same time, Daniel Defoe could write, however hesitantly, "the limit of a parent's authority in this case of matrimony either with son or daughter, I think, stands thus: the negative, I think, is theirs . . . [but] the positive is in the children's." Not the *children* but the *parents* should take second place. Now *you* suggested your possible spouses while your *parents* had only the right to say no: horrors!

As it began to fit the economic ideas of its day, marriage for love—long the dubious privilege of the poor, nearly a guarantee of penury, a weird refusal to see that one could love wherever duty lay—started to become its own holy ideal all across the West. In Britain, for instance, there was an explosion of novels, from *Tom Jones* to *Pride and Prejudice,* that proposed the new middle-class belief that love should come *before* marriage, that sex merely in exchange for a good estate was venal. The new marriage philosophy was struggling to stay in line with the new economic and political philosophy, as articulated by John Stuart Mill in the 1860s: "There is always need of persons not only to discover new truths, and point out when what were once truths are true no longer, but also to commence new practices, and set the example of more enlightened conduct"—in work, in politics, in marriage.

When the world is getting reinvented constantly, when every change you make leaves behind eddies you can't navigate, how can you require your offspring to trust and obey? The Amish and the Hassidim have it right: you really *can't* dive into the modern economy, with its constant tug away from the small group and into the mass, and keep the same moral conformity, the same obedience to tradition, the same simplicity of true and revealed belief. Once you discover your own way to earn your living, you also discover your own way to make your bed.

Keeping It: What's His Is His and What's Hers Is . . . Whose?

Just about the same time that young people stopped being their parents' property, women noticed that when they married they *be-*

came property. Both ends of that equation had changed. By the nineteenth century, young and/or unmarried men and women had *gained* authority over their own property and lives; and second, married women had *lost* exactly that. And so married women started to rebel.

Historically, married women had usually had some power in the household finances. The Mr. might be the master and the one who managed any ventures into the wider world, but the Mrs. kept the books, handled the selling, and ran the farm or shop when neces-sary—haggling, buying, selling, promising, and refusing in the family name. Home might be her place, but home and work were so intertwined that she had plenty to do and—unless she was in that bottom quintile that barely survived—at least one adolescent servant to help. Censuses recorded the occupations not of individ-uals but of families.

And so a married woman traditionally had some financial pro-tections. Where a wife was full (if subordinate) partner in the fam-ily business, her work was her property; her husband could scarcely edge her out without hurting himself. Yes, she was barred from the more remunerative work—the craft guilds, the profes-sions—but he needed her or his business collapsed. Second, what she did own—whether she was of the wealthy, merchant, or peas-ant class—was probably "real" estate, that vestigial phrase that re-minds us that once upon a time, wealth equalled land and land equalled wealth. And that "real estate" was protected by all sorts of laws. Her husband was in charge of her land, but he couldn't sell it or will it away without her written permission *and* her personal court testimony. If he died she got all her real property back *and* had a right to from one-third to one-half of his land.

But as the world separated work and home, she lost her financial leverage, in two separate ways. It's no mistake that it was in 1765 that Lord Blackstone, who consolidated and passed on British com-mon law, famously extended the biblical idea that a husband and wife become "one flesh" into the precept that "In law husband and wife are one person, and the husband is that person"—meaning that a wife could own no personal property, make no personal contracts, bring no lawsuits. He took over her legal identity—a con-cept called "coverture," because his identity "covered" hers. Real estate and personal contacts in the village market were giving way to the new world of coin and distant, impersonal contracts.

Meanwhile, in the industrializing nineteenth century, work left home. Married men kept heading on out into the ferocious world, whether in trading or travel, factories or finance—while married women stayed home, a place now cut off from the sullying and in-vigorating influence of work and money. The new market world "still depended on mutual trust and personal associations at the lowest levels, but . . . was becoming depersonalized and bureau-cratic. Credit was more and more a matter of assets and liabilities" rather than personal understandings between fellow villagers or aristocrats. This meant a wife couldn't go to market with the vil-lage's understanding that she was doing so as part of the family business. As selling in the market became something that re-quired retail space, bank credit, contracts, and so on, it stopped being women's work. One historian illustrates this shift in the lives of the Cadbury family. "In 1800 Richard, together with his wife, Elizabeth, and his rapidly growing family moved in above the shop he had acquired on Bull Street, one of Birmingham's main thoroughfares." Like most middle-class families, they lived above or near the business. While Richard traveled, Elizabeth bought things on credit and managed the shop. But thirty years later, when their son John opened his own shop next door, he moved his wife and family out to one of the new suburban developments, Edgbaston. Ensconced there in the nursery and garden, John's wife Candia could scarcely oversee anything having to do with the business—not the shop, not the new factory, not the bank loans and more elaborate books. Even the way the house was laid out showed the entirely new world of separate spheres for women and men: "the novel idea of separate rooms for children and of a demar-cation between eating and cooking was associated with the idea of a different space for men to work in." By the 1850s, the British cen-sus not only named the different occupations of each family mem-

ber, but also introduced a brand new occupational category: housewife.

Home was drifting away from work like an ice floe cracked off
from shore. By the nineteenth century's end, the married Victorian woman could scarcely see the family's work and finances at all.
Young women, who would once have taken care of someone else's
dusting and children and been paid after ten years, now went out to
work for weekly wages; meanwhile, married women were doing
things young servants once did, but not bringing in money. When
nineteenth-century builders invented the "servantless" kitchen, it
meant *she* was now the servant. The middle-class Mistress was
downgraded to Mother, spending not her adolescence but her
adulthood as nursemaid, housemaid, laundrymaid. Or if she did
work it was in one of the new Dickensian factories, under an owner
instead of alongside her husband—while her wages still legally
stayed in her husband's name.

Meanwhile, property was becoming increasingly *sur*real—no
longer land and linens and cattle, but coin and paper and stock
shares, wages and savings accounts and life insurance. And since
the law hadn't caught up—since only her "real" estate was protected—what a wife owned or earned was far less protected from
her husband than the family farm had once been. Now that "property" began slithering through the quicksilver world of the new
nineteenth-century corporations, her family no longer had control
over what her husband did with it.

And so, in a peculiar historical twist, a nineteenth-century *un*-
married woman had *more* financial rights—the ability to earn, buy,
sell, own, contract, sue and be sued—than did a married woman.
The husband controlled all the family earnings and all of his wife's
property—in exchange for nothing firmer than the general social
expectation (not legally enforced) that he'd support his wife and
kids.

Wealthy families did not always wait on the legislatures to protect their daughters' property. For instance, through the British
courts (in one of its four nightmarishly conflicting systems of law)

they started to invent safeguards for their daughters' estates. More and more "marriage settlements" and wills assigned property directly to her, or into a trust that either he could not touch or that they owned and managed together. Unfortunately, these newfangled devices protected only those who were familiar enough with the law (or well-off enough to afford lawyers) to arrange their own special marriage rules, protecting a particular daughter or sister or niece against a particularly untrustworthy husband. What if you and your family trusted your husband and yet he still managed your money appallingly, or married your money and disappeared, or drank up all your factory wages, or gambled away your hat shop's profits? Tough.

The very first attempts to protect married women's property were justified *not* by feminism but by the need to protect women, those virtuous angels, from inept, venal, or deserting husbands. The first wave of the nineteenth-century Married Women's Property Acts helped shield *her* property from *his* creditors, so that if his business failed the bank couldn't take everything—and leave the family nothing. Then some American, Canadian, Australian, and British legislators wanted women who had been deserted or separated to be free to manage and own their own property, so that a husband who was a drunk or a gambler couldn't come home every five years, take her money, and go off on another five-year binge. Then a few states allowed a married woman to make her own will, or keep control of whatever she'd had before marrying, or even— this was a breathtaking step—own property without being overseen by a trustee.

That last wave of Married Women's Property Acts set off the death-of-the-family alarums. Protecting women in distress was one thing; giving up economic power to regular old married women—living right there under their husbands' control—would surely break up the family. One 1844 New York legislative committee insisted that allowing married women to control their own property would lead "to infidelity in the marriage bed, a high rate of divorce, and increased female criminality," while turning mar-

riage from "its high and holy purposes" into something arranged
for "convenience and sensuality." A British member of Commons
declared that nothing could be "more frightful than to teach wives
that their interests were on one side, and those of their husbands
on the other." Another said that the new laws "would so free a
woman from restraint in any quarrel she might have with her
husband" that she could say, " 'I have my own property, and if
you don't like me I can go and live with somebody who does.' "
The Times of London harrumphed that reform would "abolish
families in the old sense" and "break up society again into men
and women" while creating "discomfort, ill-feeling, and distrust
where hitherto harmony and concord prevailed."

Whose harmony and concord did *The Times* mean? His. And
that jarred too much with the new reality and ideology of choice
and affection rather than duty and obedience. One 1868 British
magazine article—referring to the statutes that grouped women
with others incompetent to manage property—was entitled
"Criminals, Idiots, Women and Minors: Is the Classification
Sound?" In the 1870s, "Millicent Garrett Fawcett had her purse
snatched by a young thief in London. When she appeared in court
to testify against him, she heard the youth charged with 'stealing
from the person of Millicent Fawcett a purse containing £1 18s.
6d., the property of Henry Fawcett.' Long afterward she recalled, 'I
felt as if I had been charged with theft myself.' " In the new economy, how could such visible tyranny compete with Locke's ideal of
one's right to life, liberty—and property?

You can tell that the anti-reformers were losing when they
started insisting that any change would bring down God, Nature,
and civilization. A New York legislator pleaded with his fellows to
remember "the complexity and fragility of marriage as a social institution ... If any single thing should remain untouched by the
hand of the reformer, it was the sacred institution of marriage ...
[which] was about to be destroyed in one thoughtless blow that
might produce change in all phases of domestic life." A British
Parliamentarian announced that the proposed law was "contrary

not only to the law of England, but to the law of God." The British *Saturday Review* wrote that such proposals "set at defiance the experience of every country in Christendom and the common sense of mankind" and that "there is besides a smack of selfish independence about it which rather jars with poetical notions of wedlock"; apparently letting *him* control *her* property involved no such "selfish independence."

All these arguments are being used against same-sex marriage. Those who fear change are not particularly inventive from one age to the next: they're always predicting an uprush of infidelity, vice, divorce; the breakup of families and society; a change in marriage from something holy to something merely sensual; and of course the death of marriage and civilization itself. But once common sense, or poetical notions, or God's Will, or Nature—and not economic reality—are what's at stake, change is on the way. All the American states, Canadian provinces, and even Britain had passed a Married Women's Property Act by the nineteenth century's end. Eventually these statutes allowed married women to keep their wages, profits, and businesses—so women didn't entirely disappear as they stepped down into the tiny, confining economic room that was marriage.

At least that was the theory. What did those statutory changes mean in practice? Not much, courts kept insisting—using pretty much the same language as had pundits and legislators. Judges were, after all, men of their time, and they tended to believe profoundly that it was immoral to allow women to manage their own lives without being overseen by husbands. One Canadian judge almost visibly washed his hands when he wrote, "It may startle a good many lawyers to be told that . . . the Act [of 1872] enables a woman, living with her husband, to claim her daily or other earnings as her separate property. . . . We are not responsible for the consequences of an Act of the Legislature." A Maryland judge refused to recognize the clear instructions of his state's Act, writing that it was "of doubtful propriety. . . . virtually destroying the moral and social efficacy of the marriage institution. . . . What incentive would there be for such a wife ever to reconcile differences with her husband, to act in submission to his wishes, and perform the many onerous duties pertaining to her sphere? Would not every wife ... abandon her husband and her home?" Clearly, women's "natural" sphere was not so natural after all; keeping wives home required not just vows of obedience but also of poverty.

The funny thing, of course, is that those jeremiads were right. If women can make their own livings separate from the family economy, they *are* more able and willing to leave when they're unhappy. Today's social commentators, on the left and on the right, straightforwardly agree that society could cut divorce if it would "require women to leave the work force." But no one today would dare suggest shoving women back into involuntary servitude (except backhandedly, by insisting that children need mothers at home). It would be wrong under today's philosophies—and besides, rhetoric can't do a job once enforced by worklife. Today's postindustrial economy values brains more than brawn—and so the old gendered division of labor is falling. In their massive and influential study *American Couples,* sociologists Blumstein and Schwartz write about "the intrusion of work into the lives of the couple"—a testament to how far we are from even the memory of family as a cohesive labor unit, from the six-year-old minding the fire to the adolescent apprentice mixing the dough to the mistress taking the bread to market.

The right for married women to return to work, and then the right for *all* women to work for equal pay, has been fought over yet another century of feminism. The fact that we now take women's work for granted shows up in a very weird phrase: the "marriage penalty," or the fact that two people in the same tax bracket are taxed more if they marry. Since married couples in which only *one* partner works get *more* favorable tax treatment, we believe that a wife and mother should work *without* being penalized by taxes —something that might have shocked our nineteenth-century judicial commentators. But the return of women into the market could not be halted—because capitalism has kept spinning each of us outward into individual units. Husband and wife are no longer interlocking parts required to make the economy's wheels turn.

Ignoring It: Can't Buy Me Love

Backed by the coin and plastic and cyberbytes of the new economy, marriage for love has beaten marriage for property—in our wallets and our hearts. Today Americans are work-units as mobile as cellular phones, making a living (or failing to) by making their own decisions about which talents or inclinations to trust. No longer does everyone have to live in a "family"—whether that's one's bio-family or one's employer's—in order to survive.

The new ideology has come so far that—in an almost complete overturning of tradition—"courting couples may discuss their prior sex lives while never raising the question of their economic histories." The meaning of marriage has turned topsy-turvy when you find letters like this in the *New York Times Magazine:* "It is unacceptable . . . [for] anyone's wife to sit at home expecting to be supported financially. Women have to learn to earn, save and invest their *own* money and not have more children than they can realistically afford to support on *their own*." That concept stands in shocking opposition to the old concept of family as corporate holding pen, family as joint labor endeavor. The letter-writer's sentiments are easy enough to understand for those of us who've seen our divorced mothers, aunts, or friends dropped on their butts with a houseful of children, surviving on bulk peanut butter and generic shampoo while they desperately juggle the rent and car repair and utility bills (and beg for help with the kids' college expenses). The new world's economic bargain—the triumph of the idea that each of us rules our own economic destiny—has brought its own conflicts and penalties.

But along with the ideology of freedom and the de-gendering of work, any link between marriage and money now strikes us as a kind of prostitution. A 1968 French high court wrote that an employer's no-marriage clause was an unreasonable restriction of "the right to marry and the right to work"—rights that would have been shocking to those authorities that demanded a jailer's widow prove she had a serious marriage prospect before they renewed her contract. This freedom to marry has been invented even for those once-maligned paupers as well. In 1978's *Zablocki v. Redhail*, the U.S. Supreme Court ruled that the state of Wisconsin could not bar a man from marrying because he was a "deadbeat dad," behind in paying child support for his illegitimate child, announcing that such a rule was "a serious intrusion into . . . freedom of choice in an area in which we have held such freedom to be fundamental." Entertainingly, the Court didn't even manage to notice that its "fundamental" freedom was entirely a twentieth-century invention. Even more dramatically, in 1987 the U.S. Supreme Court struck down a Missouri prison's refusal to allow its inmates—convicted felons, people who couldn't *vote*, much less support their wives or future children—to marry, since "inmate marriages, like others, are expressions of emotional support and public commitment . . . having spiritual significance."

Emotional support? Public commitment? Spiritual significance? It's the kind of rhetoric you get when you drain marriage so that it's no longer financially central, freeing people to examine their own hearts. Law tends to follow social reality—and so has begun to acknowledge that while losing one's family may be painful, losing one's job may be deadly. You're much more likely to sue an employer for breach of contract than an abandoning fiancé. Since losing your marriage won't necessarily throw either of you on the streets, since—theoretically—you can each make it on your own, marriage is now up to you two. Once the "family" is no longer the only way to make the economy turn, once each individual can be a lawyer or locksmith or landlord, more variety is possible in how each person can live.

And, not coincidentally, in how each person can *feel*. Trained from birth to ask ourselves what we want to be when we grow up, how can Americans be expected to guide our marital—and sexual—hopes and lives by anything but that same inner voice? As Max Weber put it in *The Protestant Ethic and the Spirit of Capital-*

ism, "Labour must . . . be performed as if it were an absolute end in itself, a calling. Hence the scrutinizing of one's self, the tremendous habit of it." That tremendous habit of self-scrutiny spills over into affection, love, and marriage—which now come in that order. It's quite entertaining to imagine Jane Austen discovering that, in 1996, a book called *The Good Marriage* doesn't talk about money at all; its subtitle is *How & Why Love Lasts*, with a celebratory conclusion about marriage as a psychological experience replete with developmental "tasks." But these are not to be sneezed at, even economically: if we want a successful capitalism, pursuing the inner life matters. Adam Smith's economy could not run by the obedience demanded by feudal marriage codes.

In the 1970s, Western legislators followed their high courts and their citizens' understanding, and changed family law to fit new realities. No longer did codes explicitly require "husbands" to support "wives"; rather, two equal "spouses" shared equal responsibility. The West German Civil Code, for instance, was revised in 1976 to get rid of the words "husband" and "wife" and now reads, "The spouses are mutually obliged to adequately maintain the family by their work and property. If the running of the household is left to one spouse, that spouse as a rule fulfills his duty to contribute to the support of the family through work by managing the household." Once women and men can earn and live alone; once husbands and wives are theoretically equal at work, in bed, and in chores; once marriage is for love and not for money—how can society fairly bar the marriage of two people of one sex?

Sharing It: So Who Needs Marriage?

Okay, so the economy can run without marriage. And theoretically, each of us can make our living on our own. So why not live alone—or live with someone without any formal ties? Why—straight or gay—marry at all? My young friend Mitch, now making his way through law school, tells me he's waiting to read this book to find out why in the world he and his girlfriend should marry. Isn't legal marriage just an atavistic throwback to a feudal world of family property, of men's desire to control and patrol women's reproductive organs—or, to look at it from a swinging-bachelor point of view, of a woman's desire to tie down some man while her attractions are still fresh? Does today's legal marriage deserve Gertrude Stein's comment about Oakland: there's no there there?

We all know the social trends. Children leave home and live alone before marrying. Husbands or wives leave when the marriage becomes intolerable. More and more people choose to live alone rather than settle for a less-than-good marriage—a "good" marriage in psychological terms, that is. Meanwhile, others who live happily together wonder why they should bother with the law. The U.S. census found that unmarried couples—defined as two unrelated adults of different sexes sharing the same household—increased almost five times between 1970 and 1988, from 523,000 to 2,588,000. The U.S. census category of "unrelated individuals" living together jumped 76 percent from 1970 to 1980, another 34 percent between 1980 and 1990, and then another 10 percent by 1997: although some of these are roommates, many are life partners. What's the just way, in legal terms, to treat those unmarried couples? Sooner or later, any two human beings will disagree over whose interests count. How does society decide when and whether those unmarried couples are equivalent to married ones in the many financial questions that regularly come before family law courts?

Sure, postindustrial capitalism has set us free to exchange our hearts rather than our wallets when we marry. But society cannot fully cut the link between marriage and money. As sociologist William Goode writes, in a family "people are actually producing goods and services for one another. They are buying objects in one place, and transporting them to the household. They are transforming food into meals. They are engaged in cleaning, mowing lawns, repairing, transporting, counseling—a wide array of services that would have to be paid for in money if some member of the family does not do them." Gardening, decorating, doing the wash, patching the basement when it leaks—it's a lot easier to divide tasks than to handle everything yourself. And if your spouse gets rich—unless he or she is a miser or a brute—chances are you also will be eating better, or driving a nicer car, or taking a fancier vacation. Marriage is a shared legal mailbox, a convenient way to tell all society's institutions that you two have chosen to mingle your fortunes both emotionally and financially—while allowing those institutions to hold you responsible for each other in return.

Of course, neither the word "married" or "unmarried" can possibly encompass whatever the two of you are to each other—best pals or intimate enemies; passionate lovers or exhausted parents who can't remember the last time you had sex; a pair who's shared bed and breakfast every day for fifty years or commuter academics who see each other on alternate weekends; a harried homemaker and a wage-earner with half a dozen kids; a childless pair of D.C. power brokers who take for granted each other's dalliances. All that variety—quite rightly—gets collapsed in the eyes of the law. While marriage may be many things—sacred, personal, sexual—its *civil* incarnation is an unbelievably comprehensive system for sorting out disputes over who's entitled to what, especially at life's extremes.

Marriage laws and rules weave a much more delicate and invisible web than most of us know. "Married" is a shorthand taken seriously by banks, insurers, courts, employers, schools, hospitals, cemeteries, rental car companies, frequent flyer programs, and more—a word understood to mean that you two share not just your bedroom but the rest of your house as well. In the United States, the General Accounting Office issued a January 31, 1997 report listing 1,049 "federal laws in which benefits, rights, and privileges are contingent on marital status." Each state also has several hundred of its own. We can grasp the scope of those rules by glancing at some that fit each part of the marriage vows: for richer and poorer; in sickness and in health; and till death do us part.

For richer, for poorer . . .   Civil marriage is a kind of legal membrane that allows two people to share their vital financial blood, to help care for each other and their children, if any. The wedding itself is no longer an occasion for receiving your life's biggest one-time infusion of property, no matter where you registered for gifts: in fact, if you have the kind of wedding many people have—spending $10k or more—it might be a net cash loss.

But while the wedding may not suddenly improve your bank balance, civil marriage still does dramatically alter the pair's financial relationship in the eyes of the state. A legally recognized marriage allows spouses to pass property back and forth without counting it as a tax gain or loss on either side. The law gets excrutiatingly detailed about what exactly can pass within that legal membrane. Copyright ownership, farmlands, cars, trailers, boats, planes, Puget Sound sea urchin licenses, Cape Cod clamming licenses—all can pass (or be sold!) between spouses without taxes. When the federal government acquires certain lands for national parks, either spouse—no matter who had title at the time—gets to use those lands until death. If you win the Massachusetts lottery, you can assign your winnings to your spouse (but no one else). On the flip side, you and your spouse are both restricted by limits on either's authority. If she's a member of the Massachussetts Horse Racing Authority, say, or an auto-dealer inspector, or on the Board of Land Surveyors, you better not have any big racing winnings, or take any free cars from those dealers, or have any financial boon from land surveying.

Does all that financial and regulatory unity sound commonsensical, even . . . natural? Natural it's not—except in the sense that human societies "naturally" try to thrash out arrangements that seem just. All these details have been argued out painstakingly over the years, in geologic layers of statutes and debates. In most of the West, none of it applies to Mitch and his girlfriend, or to Madeline and myself.

The same is true not just if you're richer but if you're poorer. The state counts you as responsible for your spouse when deciding who's eligible for state benefits—Medicaid, AFDC, food stamps, public drug rehab or psychiatric hospitalization, first-time homebuyers' programs, student loans. Massaschusetts's hot lunch program for the elderly is for people over sixty—and their spouses. If your spouse is a work-release prisoner, your alimony or child support money is automatically deducted from his salary.

Not just the state but other institutions also treat you differently depending on whether or not you're married. When Madeline and I bought a house, for instance, the bank required us to buy life insurance, naming each other as beneficiaries, because neither makes enough to pay the mortgage on her own. But insurers refused to issue a policy, since we have no legal relationship. Our determined insurance agent finally put us down as "business partners"—co-owning a house—and snagged us a policy. In 1997, the Canadian Parliament extended the free travel allowances for M.P.s' spouses to M.P.s' same-sex partners as well. Shared frequent flyer miles; waiving the "extra driver" cost if a married couple rents a car; joint auto or home insurance policies—the list of financial entanglements continues for quite awhile. Alone, each of these shareable perks is petty (except maybe the M.P.s' spouses' free travel). What's common is that financial interests are always at stake—and that society uses marriage as shorthand to define who gets to share and who does not.

Nations and states, of course, have elaborate laws defining how intertwined a married couple's finances must be. That doesn't mean that married people actually manage their money the way the state thinks they should. Contemporary professional couples without children, or partners in second marriages, often keep "separate purses." Working-class couples or couples with children usually pool their money. And most studies find that, so long as at least one spouse is male, whoever earns or has more money has more power at home—except among lesbians, who work hard to keep money irrelevant. None of that is the state's concern—unless you split.

But even while you're together, the marriage rules do help decide who has a right to what if you disagree. Say you're a stay-at-home mom whose husband doesn't hand over any money to buy groceries or pay the utility bills. Can you take funds from a bank account that's just in his name? Can you take him to court and insist he pay up? Can you get a court order blocking him from taking all the money to Vegas? Before the Anglo-American Married Women's Property Acts, the answer was a resounding *no*. Or say you're a man who has just been downsized from your middle-management job: does your physician-wife have a legal right to stop you from using your buy-out package to invest in a Friendly's franchise? Ask what your state's marriage laws are (and get a good lawyer).

The point here is not to decide the fairest answer to those specific questions. The point is that such questions regularly arise—and marriage law is the mechanism society uses to decide what's fair.

Few people have to pay any attention to marriage's property laws—unless they want out. That's when they discover marriage has a steep exit penalty: that the state helps decide who gets what. The easy part (which, of course, is hideously difficult) is dividing up what you own, actual property in hand—cash, land, houses, cars. The hard part is deciding whether both of you have a right to today's more important property—education, experience, and career, those intangible valuables that live in individual heads. If she stayed home taking care of the kids while you became a more and more skilled machinist, how much should she be compensated for "opportunities lost"? If she chose not to go to law school and became your hostess, ran your household, handled your drycleaning, and in other ways became your silent partner while you climbed to CEO—and since her "opportunity cost" was astronomical, or to use non-economist-speak, since she can never get back the years invested in your joint career—does she have a lifetime stake in your intellectual property, the skills in your mind? Again, marriage law is how society helps the two of you resolve that dispute.

Some people object that marriage is one of the few contracts—and certainly the most complicated—that we enter with no advanced disclosure. But breaking up without the state's involvement can also be nasty. If you have legal title to something, it's yours—even if your partner did pay into the mortgage for many years, or did stay home and take care of your children while you were putting your name on that bank account. As one observer writes, going only by what's on a given piece of paper may ignore "the moral implications of a long-shared life."

Someone has to decide who's right—however difficult that may be. Those without law are at the mercy of whoever's stronger; those with law are at the mercy of the reigning ideology. The rich have always written contracts that could be fought over endlessly in courts; the rest of us have lived by common consensus—whether an ecumenical decree, a village's set of beliefs, or national legislation. The rules have sometimes been based on one social ideal (an adulterous wife should be kicked out of the house with nothing, not even her dowry), and sometimes another (each spouse has a theoretically equal ability to make a living after the marriage). But anyone who wants to benefit from the social consensus on what's fairly shared while you're together—those lobstering licenses, say, or her years spent cooking and diapering, or his military pension—has to swallow hard and live by the social consensus on what's fair if you break up. Perhaps letting same-sex partners marry would help force these decisions to become gender-blind—and therefore more fair, in that legislators and judges would have to consider who is caring for whom, and who has sacrificed what, rather than who is female and who male.

In sickness and in health . . .   Perhaps even harder to measure is the unpaid economy of marriage. Who gets to care for whom at life's extremes? Since we're all mortal, we can all expect to face that question. Civil marriage is the marker that allows you to visit your spouse in the hospital, or to assume control—you, not his brother or child by an earlier marriage—if, say, he goes into seizures and needs intubation, or heads into a bipolar mania, or descends into drug addiction and needs to be committed. Most people think these abilities can be acquired by signing certain pieces of paper. It's not so simple. The difference between powers of attorney—or domestic partnership, for that matter—and marriage is the difference between a skateboard and a jet. An unmarried couple might sign a notarized healthcare proxy, but it will take effect only if one of you becomes incapacitated. For instance, the documents that Madeline and I have signed allow me to care for her if she's in a coma—but so long as she's conscious, no nurse or physician has any obligation to tell me anything about her condition or care. And those notarized pieces of paper can be overridden by disapproving hospitals or family members who insist they are outdated or were signed under duress—and rare is the distressed spouse who has the savvy and energy to fight during such terrifying moments.

All of which adds an extra layer of fear, for many same-sex couples, to the prospect of illness. If we got hit by a Range Rover while vacationing in, say, Utah's Canyonlands or Wales—and we'd forgotten to pack our envelope of notarized papers (or if they'd burned when the car exploded)—how could I persuade the hospital that she belongs to me? I wouldn't even be able to lie and say we were married, as unmarried different-sex couples can. Every administrator, nurse, or physician could decide for themselves—based on their own ideologies—whether I had the right to know whether she was in the ICU, or surgery, or alive, or whether I could stay in her room overnight.

These are not idle speculations: every same-sex couple I know has a personal horror story, whether their own or a close friend's. My friend John's spouse Martin was robbed and shot on a business trip—and for four hours John was on the phone from Boston, desperately trying to get anyone in the Dallas hospital to tell him whether Martin had survived. Many people know of the Sharon Kowalski and Karen Thompson case. After the two schoolteachers had shared their life and home for ten years, a terrible car accident left Kowalski almost paralyzed and unable to speak. Kowalski's parents insisted they, not Thompson, had the legal right to control their daughter's care. They parked Kowalski in a nursing home, and Thompson fought for seven years before she was able to bring her spouse home.

Sometimes the hospitals or families are friendly. But the history of humanity is a history of disagreement. The law is too blunt and gross an instrument to make fine-tuned decisions about individuals' wishes. Marriage is one of the most convenient ways we have to tell the law—and thus those who may disagree with how we live our lives—who we've chosen besides our blood family to care for us in sickness and in health.

Under "sickness and health," I'd include heart-sickness as well: marriage is a way the law recognizes and respects a committed emotional bond. If a Canadian man falls in love with an American woman, simply by marrying they can stay together in one country. All the Scandinavian countries, the Netherlands, Britain, Australia, and Canada offer that to same-sex couples as well. But most of these countries have excruciating procedures for sorting out which same-sex bonds count; why come up with an entirely new set of procedures when societies already have the shorthand of marriage? Only a civilly married spouse is exempt from testifying against the other in court. Only a legal spouse need be notified if a state facility transfers a psychiatric patient or mentally retarded person. What's more, marriage recognizes as well the delicate web of ties you have with your spouse's family—so that most employers offer, for instance, bereavement leave if your father-in-law dies. None of those recognitions of shared responsibility exists for couples who are not married under civil law.

Why should society care? Simply because it's right to help spouses fulfill their vows in life-or-death moments? Or is there some social benefit when married people find it easier to take care of each other? The answer is: Both.

In a working marriage, the two of you care for each other both emotionally and physically. You are, to use HMO-speak, each other's primary healthcare provider. In part that means it's often a spouse who'll bring an icepack (and open the aspirin container) for her arthritis . . . or go to the all-night drugstore to get Robitussin if he's coughing so hard he's bruising his ribs . . . or hold her hand while she's getting chemo . . . or talk him through his nightmares after he loses his job. But of course it's sometimes friends or family who offer that personal care, and besides, the law is not interested in enforcing such details. And so what I mean is something measurable: Married people live longer, healthier, more productive lives.

In 1858, British public health statistician William Farr noted that, on average, married people outlive singles: "Marriage is a healthy state. The single individual is much more likely to be wrecked on his voyage than the lives joined together in matrimony." The data have been eerily consistent ever since: whether measuring by death rate, morbidity (health problems such as diabetes, kidney disease, or ischemic heart disease), subjective or stress-related complaints (dizziness, shortness of breath, achiness, days in bed during past year, asthma, headaches), or psychiatric problems (clinical depression or debilitating anxiety after a cancer diagnosis), married people do better than unmarried—single, widowed, divorced.

Why? For the past twenty years, researchers—epidemiologists, sociologists, biologists, and psychologists have been trying to find an answer. You have to actually hold this hefty pile of studies to grasp how many theories they've been testing. Can it be explained by a "marriage selection effect"—that healthier people are more likely to get married? Perhaps: you may (fairly or not) have fewer chances of marrying if you're severely obese, say, or trembling with MS. But it doesn't fully explain the gap. When researchers match married and unmarried people with the same health status—with cancer, say, or cardiovascular disease—the unmarried die earlier than the married. And when they followed otherwise matched sets of women over time, the unmarried women's health went downhill faster than the married.

Can it be explained by the theory that spouses force each other to live in healthier ways—that women make men moderate their drinking and smoking, snowboarding and carousing? Maybe—but even badly behaved married men live longer. In studies of from 1,000 to 7,735 subjects, when researchers matched men for such factors as age, smoking, past heart disease or diabetes, obesity, exercise, drinking, blood pressure, and cholesterol levels, the unmarried ones got sicker and died earlier.

Can it be explained by the fact that married people have more resources, including the built-in financial safety net of someone else's help (whether your wife's or your wife's family's)? Sure, that helps: poor people get sicker and die younger, for reasons that only start with such obvious things as food, housing, and health care. A rich single man has, statistically, a better shot at a long healthy life than a very poor married couple. But that explanation doesn't cover everything. When researchers match people's resources—adjusting for such things as total household income, home or car ownership, or (in the U.S.) having health insurance—unmarried people still get sicker and die earlier.

Some opponents of same-sex marriage argue that none of marriage's health protections would work for same-sex couples. Husbands do *so* much better than wives that they obviously benefit from having a woman around, someone trained in listening and caretaking—so why would it help a man to marry another man? Meanwhile, women are widely known to have stronger social networks, more friends to talk to in hard times, mothers or daughters or friends who might massage their feet during a frightening MRI—so why would marrying another woman make a difference? But those arguments fall apart once you notice that even women live longer when married—which suggests that even being married to a man is good for your health. Why wouldn't that work for a man as well—especially a man who'd be unhappy, and therefore no better off than single, with a woman? And since living with another adult (a widow with her daughter, for instance, or a divorced man with his parents) works just as well as marriage, why shouldn't two women who are happily married do better as well—especially women who would be unhappy with men?

There are more theories than you could guess—but the figures hold stubbornly true. Variations do show up in these hundreds of pages of data. So long as young women work, for instance, they do about equally well whether they're married or unmarried. In fact, the health difference between single and married is *much* greater for men than for women: Men who want to live should get married, pronto. And the never-married, separated, recently divorced, long-divorced, and widowed have different prospects, which vary from study to study. Finally, of course, predicting individual lives from such aggregates and averages is foolish: despite my offhand comments, these numbers don't really predict anything about the health or mortality of your single friend Janet or your married brother Carl.

But if our question here is a large social question—why should society reward marriage?— it's important to ask what researchers *mean* here by marriage. Does the health boost of marriage happen when your marriage is *de facto*—unmarried but committed couples, straight or gay—or only when your marriage is *de jure,* recognized by law? Does it matter whether you're just tolerating each other or whether you're in love?

The answer: living with another adult (whether your lover or your widowed mother) apparently helps your health just as much as marriage—but only if you get along. The first half of that sentence comes from a Dutch study of 18,973 people, ages fifteen to seventy-four. The second half comes from a few studies that have tried to peel apart happy from unhappy couples and found that the unhappily married do just as *badly* as most single people (although not *quite* as badly as the just-divorced).

Although researchers seem baffled about why, the rest of us needn't be. Most of us know how we relax in the daily hum of someone else's physical and conversational company, the simple animal comfort of being heard or held when you're tired or scared, the exhausting arguments followed by that incredible gratitude of knowing you've been seen at your worst and are still loved. TV just doesn't cut it as a substitute. Most of us know that we can concentrate more productively when we belong somewhere. Why bother even trying to link loneliness or late-night fear or higher anxiety to distressed functioning? Happiness—or even the simple security of being near someone who cares about you, of being responsible not just to yourself but to and for another—is good for you.

I hope my conclusion is obvious. Because being contentedly paired is good for each citizen's health and productivity, society should open civil marriage to same-sex pairs, making it easier for them to care for one another. We needn't worry about recognizing those widowed mothers who live with their daughters, or young adults who live with their parents, or siblings who room together, since the law already puts blood relations first unless overridden by marriage. Nor need we worry about best friends or roommates, who—if same-sex marriage were legal—could marry if they chose, with no more inquiry into their sex lives than is currently put to a different-sex pair who've decided that being best friends is a good enough reason to marry. The unpaid economy of coupled life—which shores up our interdependence, so full of sacrifices and joys, so tremendously valuable in an isolating society like our own—*should* gain all marriage's recognitions, in sickness and in health, even when those couples are the same sex.

Till death do you part   Civil marriage recognizes the couple after one dies—in an inordinate number of ways that unmarried pairs cannot hope to replicate. Marriage laws let the widowed claim her remains or decide whether or not to donate her organs, or permit you two to share a burial plot. Such things cannot be taken for granted if you two are not legally married. In one recent American legal case, Sherry Barone and Cynthia Friedman had been together for thirteen years when Friedman got cancer. They signed as many legal documents—wills, powers of attorney, health proxies, written instructions to the survivor to carry out any wishes—as they could to ensure Barone would be in charge. But after Friedman died, the cemetery refused to follow Barone's instructions to inscribe the epitaph Friedman had requested—"Beloved life partner, daughter, granddaughter, sister, and aunt." The bereaved Barone took the cemetery to court—and after a year of legal wrangling, was allowed to honor her dead beloved's wishes. If that's *after* the pair took every available legal precaution, what happens to couples who haven't so carefully planned?

And that was just a fight over someone's memory. Disputes get *really* nasty over money. Wouldn't you—at least, if you're an American—think that everyone would be able to pass along property in just the way he or she wants? It ain't necessarily so. For a society that does *not* survive by passing on property from one generation to the next, the subject of who can and should and will inherit occupies an unbelievable amount of legal airtime. While legislation does its best to define who gets what, there are inevitably court skirmishes over who gets what, on what grounds—and, of course, whether it's taxable. If you can't recall any family fights over inheritance rights, your family stands with the angels. Once you get to court, marriage is the marker that lets courts assume that you two wanted your relationship to be respected after death.

All Western countries, states, and provinces assume that your spouse gets something if you die without making a will. If you want to make a will that leaves your property to your spouse, you don't even need a witness. And even if you *want* to disinherit your spouse, you can't: society finds that too unfair (and doesn't want your widow on the dole). In fact, the spouse now consistently gets a larger share than in the past, when offspring or other relatives got their portions. And polls show that a larger share for spouses is what most people now want.

Just about everything else in a will is open to challenge. If you left something to your mistress, your widow might try to get that overturned. Your adult children might challenge your will if, at age seventy-eight, you married a twenty-two-year-old a month before you died. There are certainly arguments to be made on either side of those aisles—arguments decided by society's most recent agreement about who deserves what, and what is fair.

If you have *no* legal relationship, your partner's death is especially bad news. Marriage really matters when it comes to property. Your state or nation's probate code has a list of people who automatically inherit—children, parents, siblings, and so on—and if none of those people can be found, the probate judge assigns everything to the state. "Friend" or "roommate" is not on the list. Meanwhile, even if she did write a will that gave everything to you, her parents or children or siblings or cousins can challenge you for any number of reasons: as someone who warped their beloved daughter into sin, or as a legal stranger with no right to the house in which you spent your entire adult life. And we haven't even waded into taxes—where the spouse gets special treatment in things large and small. For instance, a legal widow pays no inheritance taxes on their jointly-owned house or furniture or car. What about Madeline and myself, co-owners of our house? We're legal strangers: if one died, the other would pay a far higher rate of inheritance taxes just to "inherit" her own furniture and house.

Still more complex is the question of who, if anyone, gets the less tangible inheritances that make up so much of our wealth. Who has the right to your social security benefits or your pension? Who has the right to keep running your joint business, if your dead spouse's name was on those lobster or liquor licenses, or leases to Manhattan property that's increased in value? If (god forbid) you're murdered, who gets victim services or compensation? If you're hit by a car, who can sue for wrongful death? The statutes go on for pages, insisting that a spouse should get compensation or scholarships if married to a police officer or firefighter killed in the line of duty; or forbidding the business's suppliers from cutting off merchandise if there's a surviving spouse qualified to take over; or forcing an employer to hand over any unpaid wages to a surviving spouse.

The legal definition of "spouse"—whether it means only the legally married or also includes committed partners—is up for grabs as the world changes. One famous case is *Braschi v. Stahl,* in which a New York court insisted that a gay man's partner be allowed to stay in the rent-controlled apartment they'd shared, even though his name had not been on the lease. In 1997, an Israeli court insisted that the military pay the military pension of Col. Doron Meisel, who in 1991 died of cancer, to his widower Adir Steiner. Canadian courts have recently decided that for *all* practical purposes "spouse" must include a committed same-sex partner. As lesbian and gay men grow more accepted and more confident in their partnerships, an increasing number of such cases will occupy the courts. Why should they be decided one by one, in expensive and exhausting lawsuits? Civil marriage would make such decisions clear: if you stood up and stood by a spouse, you get the goods.

But why does it have to be marriage?   Some people stay away from marriage because they don't want the state to make surgical decisions about their functioning as a couple. People who don't want to live by the general social understanding needn't enter the institution, or should feel free to try to change it. Certainly many of us would like to see healthcare benefits untangled from coupledom. But in any society, pluralist or otherwise, one hardly expects agreement with every social detail. Only totalitarian government is free of compromise, over time and across groups. Others object that marriage is too facile a way to consider the relationship between people. But I feel slightly ill at the idea that a hospital or a state would have to conduct an inquisition into my relationships before deciding who to listen to about my life: what if some hospital administrator listened not to Madeline, or my brothers, or my dear friend Laura, but rather to some obsessed and sociopathic stranger?

Some would like to offer same-sex couples not marriage but rather domestic partner policies. Certainly one can make a case for undoing the either/or of modern marriage, returning to history's more pragmatic approach: having a variety of marriage forms, some looser and some more binding than others. But marriage laws and regulations have accreted over centuries of understanding how two people work together; their comprehensiveness cannot be replaced by piecemeal or sometimes purely ceremonial policies. American domestic partner policies offer very few things and affect *only* the employees of the particular city, company, university, or other organization that adopted them. Yes, its employees—*not* its residents. For instance, if Cambridge, Seattle, or Atlanta offers domestic partner registration, those cities' municipal employees can enroll their partners on the municipal health insurance plan. Or if the DP-giver is Lotus or Harvard, maybe those employees can use the corporate childcare center (if it exists) even if the co-mom, not the bio-mom, is the one who's employed. There's not much else to gain—and even that little gets taxed. Even if I lived in DP-granting Atlanta but my employer did *not* offer DP policies, the city's DP registration would affect Madeline and me not a whit. We'd remain legal strangers when it comes to such things as inheriting our own house and all the rest.

Surely some couples might, given the choice, decide to enter what one French magazine calls "mariage light." But two questions arise about domestic partnership or "pactes de civil solidarité." Won't DP inevitably drift toward all the long-argued rules of marriage, as one couple after another winds up in court over the same questions that wrench apart post-marrieds? And why should only same-sex couples have *no* choice, be relegated only to the second-class option, for which you pay more and get less?

While current domestic partnership policies are miniscule in scope, they are actually harder to get than marriage. In most American states marriage itself requires only a blood test, a $50 fee, and a few minutes in front of some municipal official. Signing up for DP benefits usually requires, for instance, affidavits of shared residence (for a proven length of time) and bank statements proving financial interdependence—making DP seem much more like "traditional" marriage than like contemporary marriage. So why do people fight so hard for domestic partnership when marriage has the real goods?

In the Netherlands, Denmark, Norway, Sweden, Finland, Greenland, and Iceland, same-sex couples can already enter legal partnerships that are "all-but" marriages—gaining all marriage protections except the ability to marry in the state church, to adopt, or to use assisted fertility services. And those last two bars are coming down: the Scandinavian countries are all considering extending adoption and fertility services to same-sex pairs, and the Netherlands—where at this writing 78 percent of the population favors same-sex marriage—already has. And the world has not come to an end. Society need not reinvent the wheel—or in this case, a parallel institution that attempts to replicate years of accreted decisions about what's fair—simply to keep the word "marriage" pure from the taint of homosexuality. It need only ask itself: what is marriage for? If it's to let equal partners willingly share responsibility for each other's lives and fortunes, then same-sex couples belong.

TWO:

Sex

Item: For many centuries, the "crime against nature" included any sex that attempted to prevent conception—coitus interruptus, sex *con bouche,* sex *con mano.* According to one key theologian, if a married couple tried to prevent making babies while making love, the wife was no better than "a harlot and the husband an adulterer with his own wife"; if they used contraceptive techniques, "I do not see how we can call it a marriage." For many centuries the Church refused to bless remarrying widows and widowers, especially if the woman was too old to bear children. When in the nineteenth century the Western world's birth rate began to drop dramatically, pundits, priests, and politicians cried out against a world of "harlots and adulterers." But by the mid-twentieth century, that older rhetoric had faded away: the Western economy had come to favor individuals who ran their lives by their own consciences rather than couples who constantly churned out babies. In 1965, the United States Supreme Court decided that married adults had a right to regulate their own sexual behavior. The crime against nature had become a Constitutional right—except for one last nonreproductive group.

TO MANY PEOPLE THROUGHOUT HISTORY, THE ANSWER to my question—"what is marriage for?"—is so obvious that the question defies common sense. Marriage has long been seen as what makes sex legitimate—literally making it legal, roping it off from all those other kinds of sex for which an appalled neighbor might haul you in front of the local ecclesiastical or county court. Sex outside marriage's white picket fence was long considered adultery or fornication—"th'expense of spirit in a waste of shame," as Shakespeare once sonnetized. It's an interpretation that's disappearing in our era, when living together is no longer remarkable, when consumer culture sells sex with every pair of jeans, when pop magazines explain how to wow your boyfriend in bed, when the latest political scandal seems nothing more than an excuse for voyeurism.

But even in our jaded era, sex brings up profound moral questions. That's true partly because sex involves our own bodies, spirits, and hopes—and partly because, to have sex, we must either arouse or overpower not just ourselves but other human beings. Most of us know that sex can be a powerful force for joy or for chaos, either strengthening or destroying us with sensations and desires that threaten to erase the rest of our own (or others') lives. And so many of us conclude that there should be *some* rules about sex. Every human society obliges, offering a wonderful variety of systems. The system might include just a few laws against rape and molestation, or it might be a comprehensive code punishing sex outside marriage. Whatever the system, it means we've agreed that somehow the traffic among us must have stoplights so we don't all crash. And whatever the system, it involves the marriage rules.

In other words, one of the questions hiding inside this book's main question is: What justifies sex? In the West, that question has found many expressions over the millennia. Is sex justified by power, so that people captured into slavery (or drafted by the Roman army, or handed over to a husband) can abandon all hope of owning their bodies? Should marriage confine sex entirely—or confine it only for women, while men still range freely—or confine it not at all? Are there limits even between spouses? Is sexual pleasure a sin and a rebellion against God, or a sign of God's joy in creation?

In the hopes of illuminating today's marriage debates, this chapter examines a few pivotal times and places in the ongoing battle over the West's sexual philosophies. Three philosophies have dominated the West's answers about sex: Refraining, Reproducing, and Refreshing. Depending on what your world currently counts as *right* thinking about sex, what's demonized as *wrong* shifts from one act to another. If refraining is the right thing, then any sexual pleasure is evil. If reproducing is the right thing, then the "crime against nature" is any act that prevents babies—whether *coitus interruptus* or drinking pennywort tea as a contraceptive. If sex is for refreshing each other's spirits, then someone besides contracepting pairs must become society's sexual scapegoat—and lately that scapegoat has been Madeline and me. Are we necessary scapegoats, or is the debate over same-sex marriage actually rehashing a debate settled half a century ago?

Refraining, 1: Christians Reject Marriage

Our first battle lies between the radical sect of early Christians and its philosophical forebears: Rome, Christianity's father, and Judaism, Christianity's mother. Asked what justifies sex, Rome would answer *procreation* and *power;* Judaism would answer *procreation* and *praise.*

It's easy to recoil from the Roman Empire's official sexual attitudes and habits. Remember the grade-school joke, "Where does a 400-pound gorilla sleep?" Like the gorilla, the upper-class Roman male patriarch slept anywhere he wanted to. His wedding night, declares one historian, was an officially sanctioned rape. Both before and after marrying he was free to entertain himself sexually not just with his official wife but also with any of his slaves, servants, and hangers-on, all of whose bodies belonged to him—female and male, adult and child. Their unwanted offspring he could choose to raise or to abandon in public to die if no one else picked them up. If his slaves' babies were beautiful—whether or not they were his own bastards—he could sell them to be reared as specialists in particular sexual practices, for which he (or some other patriarch) could later buy them.

Which is not to say that every Roman male was an unrestrained satyr: there *were* moral and social limits. Some philosophies urged him to practice sexual restraint—for the sake of his own power and respect, not because he owed fidelity to his wife. He wasn't ever to touch some other citizen's daughter or wife, unless he got the father's or husband's permission and turned her into his own wife or concubine. He wasn't to touch a young male Roman citizen; the law got very nasty about that. But if you were born into the wrong nationality or class—taken as or born a slave or freed but still living gratefully under your ex-owner's protection—tough. Declared one senator: "Unchastity in a freeborn person is ground for prosecution, in a slave necessity, in a freed person duty." What the Roman patriarch wants, he gets: to the victor goes the spoils, and it's you. You expected, maybe, some kinder sexual morality from empire-building conquerers?

The male Roman aristocrat did face a few other limits on his penile behavior. He was vehemently urged, even coerced (either by his father or by Augustinian law), into a legal marriage by the end of his teens, since someone had to produce more ruling-class Roman citizens. And he couldn't—at least, not if he wanted his fellow citizens' respect—let some other man use *him* the way he could use women, prepubescent boys, and slaves. If he voluntarily bent over, "he invited scorn in metaphorically abdicating the power and responsibility of citizenhood." A man wanting a man was not seen as a problem, since he was still displaying his own desire and power. For a man to refrain from sex (after, of course, he'd produced his three official offspring) was an impressive display of personal power, this time over himself. But a man choosing to be passive was disgusting. Power—using it, proving it, hanging onto it—was what mattered.

The Jews, on the other hand, wanted to mark themselves off from every other tribe—marking every daily act as sacred and uniquely Jewish through special codes, disciplines, and requirements. Just as Jews could eat only food that was kosher (and therefore could not accept the hospitality of non-Jews), so Jews could have sex only within marriage—which therefore meant only with other Jews. But within marriage, that holy obligation, sex was a *mitzvah*—an obligation and blessing so important that the truly holy performed their marital duties on the Sabbath. As the rabbis commented, " 'The holy person performs an act of holiness at a time of holiness." A good part of the mitzvah was in making more little *mitzvahs* who would, in their turn, praise God with their own hearts and bodies—and not coincidentally help make Abraham's tribe as numerous as the stars in the sky. Procreation was so strong an obligation that for many centuries Jewish men *had* to marry again, with or without divorcing, if Wife Number One did not deliver offspring within ten years—an injunction that was a bit shocking to their officially monogamous contemporaries, such as the Romans (whose polygamy was more tacit). Being a small merchant rather than a powerful patriarch, the Jewish husband had to take his wife into account far more than did the Roman. Even though the rabbis discussed the man's purchase of his wife's virginity, or rather, of her untouched womb, as if he were buying a head of cattle; even though he could divorce her for any reason at all; even though *her* adultery was a permanent blot and punished in the extreme while *his* was bad only if it marred another man's sexual property—despite all this, rabbinical tracts went into great detail about his obligation to put her pleasure before his. Her womb might be some man's property, but as a sexual being she was her own person.

What the Romans and the Jews had in common was that everyone had to marry. Procreation was a social duty, with personal pleasure as a kind of bonus.

Christianity turned all this on its head. When Jesus's early followers insisted on their right to celibacy—to personal freedom from society's expectations—theirs was a defiant rebellion against marriage. And it was quite definitely understood that way, by both Romans and Jews.

That first insistence on the ideal of refraining from sex was far more radical than we imagine now. Some Roman Stoics and other philosophers advised sexual restraint; a very few Jewish prophets and preachers chose asceticism to show their outrage at how far Israel had fallen from God's expectations. But when Jesus's new followers took celibacy up as a communal ideal, they meant to stop birth and death entirely, bringing on the millennium. As one historian explains, "By refusing to act upon the youthful stirrings of desire ... Christians could bring marriage and childbirth to an end ... organized society would crumble like a sandcastle." So there, Mom and Dad: no grandchildren for you! My body is my own, and anyway, the world is rotten!

To some, especially women, Christian celibacy was appealing as the only way to avoid an arranged marriage, a marriage that would define the rest of your life. Through sexual renunciation you could defy tradition, declare your independence, and choose your inner life over society. The celibacy impulse was not so different, in other words, from the impulse a young lesbian today might feel when declaring herself to her parents—deciding that she'd rather reject traditional society than violate her inner life, her conscience. Comments one historian, "Even today, an adolescent who takes time to think before plunging into ordinary adult society—into marriage, and the double obligations of family and career—may hesitate, for such obligations usually cost nothing less than one's life, the expense of virtually all one's energy." For girls whose marriages had been arranged as early as age six and who were expected to marry as soon as they spotted that first pubescent drop of blood, celibacy could be irresistible. Popular among Christians in the early centuries was the (perhaps true) story of a young Roman woman named Thecla, who—after hearing Paul preach through an open window—chose celibacy and refused an arranged marriage with a fiancé who would have supported both herself and her impoverished mom. The fiancé denounced Paul to the government: "This man has introduced a new teaching, bizarre and disruptive of the human race. He denigrates marriage: yes, marriage, which you might say is the beginning, root and fountainhead of our nature." Precisely the point: smash nature, smash society, and come closer to God.

All this celibacy was considered shockingly antisocial by the Romans and sinful by the Jews, who over the next centuries never tired of noticing how badly the Christians misinterpreted the critical Genesis verse, "It is not good for man to be alone." It's one of those wonderful moments of conflict in history's marriage battles:

three civilizations, three religious traditions in absolutely flagrant disagreement about a central element of marriage: sex.

In this early Christian view, what is marriage for? Promoting the corrupt secular world, which early Christians wanted to reject. Sex and marriage were the big sell-out, the compromising Wall Street job rather than the pure-art garret.

Reproducing: Is It a Marriage . . . Or Is It a Brothel?

But as Christ's return kept getting delayed, and as Christianity morphed from a fringe cult into an imperial religion, Church fathers faced a new question: how could that fever to *just say no* be translated back into daily life—in other words, into marriage?

Peculiarly, figuring out marriage's purpose was the job of monks, men who considered sexuality an affliction. The perfect, and most influential, example lies in the well-known experience of the great, dour theologian Augustine. In the late fourth century, Augustine was an ambitious young man studying to be a Roman rhetorician. For eleven years he lived with a concubine, as was expected for young men of his class; presumably aided by contraception, they had just one son. When he was about to move to Rome to take up his career, he let his mother banish his concubine and bastard, a preparatory step to marrying him to the *right* kind of girl. Ah, but then—in a wrenching and famous religious struggle—Augustine converted. He repented all the time he'd spent turned in any direction other than the Christian God. He recoiled at his memory of "the mists of slimy lust of the flesh" and "the bubbling froth of puberty [that] rose like hot breath beclouding and darkening my heart."

And so Augustine, who won the contemporary theological battle to write Christianity into the Empire's rules, took early Christian celibacy just a bit further and redefined celibacy as normal and natural. No longer was celibacy just a rebellion against nature, a way to mock the social order, to insist that even the meek, the poor, the outsider, the eunuch still mattered in God's eyes. Now *sex*—perhaps our signal "natural" impulse—was the *un*natural act. That attitude made the question "What is marriage for?" a real stumper. How could sex be excused for us ordinary folk who could not, or would not, rise to the celibate perfection Augustine's God demanded? Augustine and his followers came up with three justifications for marriage: *proles* (procreation); *fides* (fidelity, or avoiding fornication); and *sacramentum* (a permanent bond—unlike, say, Augustine's seamy abandonment of his concubine). And they quite definitely put them in that order. "I do not see what other help woman would be to man if the purpose of generating was eliminated," Augustine wrote: otherwise everyone could stay celibate, i.e., good. Was sex a sin if you didn't actively *intend* babies while you did it? Some thought it was, but Augustine let a couple off the hook "if, although they do not have intercourse for the purpose of having children, they at least do not avoid it. . . . [Otherwise] I do not see how we can call this a marriage."

That attitude was very generous, really, since Augustine still believed that even if you were married, sexual pleasure was a venial sin. But then, Augustine believed it was essential to make accommodations for us ordinary folk. To prevent us from falling into the mortal sin of unrestrained fornication was the purpose of *fides*— the idea that each spouse had an obligation to fulfill his or her sexual duties. "Paying the marital debt" meant a spouse had to say yes if her husband asked—otherwise hubby might be forced into adultery or masturbation. She shouldn't worry if she didn't enjoy herself—in fact, that made her a little bit better than he was. As St. Jerome, another church father, wrote in a phrase that echoed down the centuries: "An adulterer is he who is too ardent a lover of his wife."

So for the early Catholic Church, that's what marriage was for: to dutifully make babies and to avoid mortal sin. The monks and theologians offered a little jumpstart toward angelic life by helpfully ruling sex off-bounds just as often as they could—for instance, during menstruation, pregnancy, or nursing (which could be as long as two years), and on holy days—such as Thursdays, in memory of Jesus's betrayal, Fridays, in memory of his death, Saturdays, in honor of the Virgin Mary, on Sundays, of course, on Mondays, in memory of the departed souls, as well as forty days before Easter, Pentecost, Christmas, on feasts, fasts, and even— imagine!—on the wedding night and the few days after, to train you for a lifetime of continence. One medieval Jewish commentator noted dryly that perhaps there would be an occasional Tuesday or Wednesday on which a baby might be made.

Did people really live by these rules? Hardly. As the early Church became a medieval power, those theologians were quite distant from a more practical Church administration. Throughout medieval and premodern Europe, plenty of people outside the monks' aeries lustily enjoyed themselves. Much of medieval European peasant society took it for granted that courting young men and women would go walking all night, so long as the pair kept company only with each other—and so long as the couple married once she was pregnant, which is why roughly a third of brides were pregnant on their wedding day, and why most suits in ecclesiastical courts had to do with "pre-contracts"—one person insisting that the other, now trying to marry another, had already implicitly married her in some midnight rendezvous. (If a girl changed her boyfriend too often, however, on May Day she might find some foul and smelly tree planted priapically in her front yard, a way for the village boys to jeer in judgment on her reputation.) As late as the fourteenth century, European newlyweds might be put to bed with bawdy encouragement by a crowd that burst back in next morning to find out how it had gone—hardly a ritual carried out by people who believed in sexual restraint. The Church licensed prostitutes' guilds and collected regular dispensation fees for their trade, assuming prostitution to be the only way to stop male lust from overwhelming honorable mothers. Priests took concubines so often that by the late Middle Ages there was actually a Church fee schedule for priests' concubines and bastards. Among the Swiss, dispensation prices were one and one-half to two gulden per year per concubine, so long as the priest stayed with the same woman: an additional absolution fee was due if the priest started a new relationship; one gulden was required to legitimate each child.

And so perhaps more realistic than the monks' restraining orders was the Church's absolute ban on contraception. Augustine and all his followers had seen clearly his argument's logical consequence: if procreation was the only way marriage could be justified, then contraception was a terrible sin. If you used anything to block conception, Augustine wrote, "I dare to say that either the wife is in a fashion the harlot of her husband or he is an adulterer with his own wife." Or to put it more clearly, any attempt to prevent pregnancy "makes the bridal chamber a brothel."

Can this have mattered to people who lived before the Pill? Indeed it did. Human beings have been trying to snip the link between sex and babies through all of recorded history. For instance, the Egyptian Petrie Papyrus of 1850 B.C. contains three prescriptions for vaginal pessaries, including various substances that would coagulate over the cervix and block sperm. The Greeks and Romans prescribed an endless variety of contraceptive drinks that included such slightly poisonous ingredients as copper (in liquid form), willow leaves, barrenwort, rue, fern root, aloe, ginger, and poplar root; they also used pessaries, spermicides, coitus interruptus, anal intercourse, and, harsh as it seems to us, infanticide. For the Jews—for whom procreation was one of marriage's two key goals—contraception was a complicated concept, requiring some serious theological attention. So long as the couple weren't trying to keep themselves from *ever* having children, contraception to protect either spouse's pleasure or health was perfectly fine; the rabbis therefore prescribed "the cup of roots," a drink of Alexandrian gum, liquid alum, and garden crocus, as well as coitus interruptus, pessaries, and vaginal sponges.

Effectiveness was another question entirely. Amulets and prayers were often prescribed alongside these other methods, which suggests that contraception often led to rue—the emotion as well as the abortifacient herb.

What the long history of contraception—as well as the call to celibacy—suggests is that if humans do have a "nature," it may well lie in the desire to master the consequences of our sexual lives. Those different approaches aren't necessarily opposed—unless the one side believes the other to be positively sinful, a rebellion against God. Precisely that happened with early Christianity, which turned the refraining ideal into a critical battle line in the marriage wars with an idea that still rocks political conversation today: is sex evil unless it leads to babies?

Medieval theologians thought the answer obvious. And so they started more than a millennium of outcries against the "vice against nature": any attempt to block offspring. Most of us, today, think of the "crime against nature" as any sex between two men or two women, or maybe as the act of a man who forces himself into a woman's anus. But only recently has the "crime against nature" dwindled to something so minimal. For most of theological history, the monks meant any nonbegetting sex. The ninth-century theologian St. Bernardine of Siena wrote, "It is better for a wife to permit herself to copulate with her own father in a natural way than with her husband against nature" and "It is bad for a man to have intercourse with his own mother, but it is much worse for him to have intercourse with his wife against nature." Oedipus, stop agonizing: at least you didn't wear a condom!

And yet, however horrifying he thought it was to have sex while avoiding conception, Bernardine believed everyone was committing this sin: "Of 1000 marriages, I believe 999 are the devil's." Other theologians believed that the "crime against nature" included any kind of "conjugal onanism," such as withdrawal, oral or anal intercourse, or even any variation from "the fit way instituted by nature as to position"—woman on her back, man on top, which according to contemporary medicine was the best way to make babies. At certain points in Catholic theological history, these "sins against nature" were considered homicide, since they killed potential children: priests couldn't give penance and absolution but had to refer such sinners to the bishop. One theologian wrote, "May a person copulate and prevent the fruits of the marriage? I say that this is often a sin which deserves the fire."

Refraining, 2: The Protestants Rebel
Against Celibacy

By the time Martin Luther nailed his ninety-five theses to the Wittenberg Church door on October 31, 1517— hammer blows whose echoes were violent religious battles across Europe for the next several hundred years—a vast number of people saw the Refraining ideal as rotten and hollow. According to one Franciscan who became a Protestant pamphleteer, the Refraining ideal was this fictional priest's chief lament: "Thus am I entangled: on the one hand, I cannot live without a wife; on the other, I am not permitted a wife. Hence I am forced to live a publicly disgraceful life, to the shame of my soul and honor . . . How shall I preach about chasteness and against promiscuity, adultery, and knavish behavior, when my own whore goes to church and about the streets and my own bastards sit before my eyes?" The celibacy ideal wasn't the only marriage problem. Out of the Church's high-minded beliefs about sexual union had grown—as one would expect from any large bureaucracy—a vast and tangled thicket of sometimes contradictory marriage rules, rules to be examined elsewhere in this book. Those marriage rules led to endless ecclesiastical court litigation and expensive dispensations, the scandal and frustration of Europe. One 1875 Protestant reformer believed, "What more natural than when a set of greedy priests found that people were ready to pay a price to be allowed to marry, they should have made marriage yet more difficult, that they should increase the number of meshes in their net, and with it the amount of their revenues?"

Given such a messy state of affairs (and marriages), when Luther decried the Church's sexual hypocrisy, he could preach in outrageous language:

> Pope Gregory wanted celibacy established . . . by chance he wanted to have some fishing done in a pond he had in Rome, and in it more than 6,000 heads of infants were found [presumably monks' drowned bastards]. . . . A similar example happened in our time. The nuns in the Austrian village of Closeter Neumberg

were compelled to move to another place because of their disgraceful life ... twelve jars were discovered in the new cellars. Each jar contained the corpse of an infant. . . . I pass over in silence countless other facts which my mind shrinks from relating.

Of course these are nonsense charges, equivalent to the medieval cry that Jews killed Christian babies for their Passover feast—or, to use similarly ludicrous charges from contemporary anti-gay pamphlets, that most gay men eat feces and prey on young boys, or that lesbians die by age forty-five. Luther could get away with such exaggerations because everyone knew some local sexual irregularity (or, to be contemporary again, because anyone can see on TV some scantily leather-clad man gyrating drunkenly on an urban Pride float)—and so listeners could imagine that, far away, things could be much, much worse.

In other words, the crusading Protestants were outraged that the Refraining ideal had led to rampant sexual irregularities. And so, like any group burning for idealistic reform—like, in other words, the early Christian celibates before them—they wanted one correct rule, to be followed by every correct believer. This time, the rule wasn't celibacy but marriage. The Protestants wanted everyone to marry, in exactly the right way—and they were practically ready to post a shoot-on-sight border patrol to ensure that no one strayed. The Protestants wanted no more impediments, annulments, exemptions, dispensations, concubines, bastards, adulterers, secret promises made in the heat of lust and forever enforced. From now on you were in or out, licit or il-, married or un.

The Protestant campaign to sweep everyone firmly into marriage was a Through-the-Looking-Glass mirror of the early Christians' enthusiastic civil disobedience action against marriage. Now priests, monks, and nuns were urged to come out of their sinful solitude (or sodomy) and marry. Luther shuddered at the fact that most Europeans then didn't marry until their late twenties—too much time to fornicate!—and urged that girls be married off promptly at fifteen and boys at eighteen.

But for this campaign *against* Refraining to succeed, the ideal had to be replaced with a new and improved ideal: Holy matrimony. Protestant sermons repeated the phrase constantly. Holy matrimony! What a shocking oxymoron to contemporary Catholic ears! Holy motherhood, sure—but matrimony, the least of the sacraments, had been just a repository for your concupiscence, a reluctant defense against hell. What in the world could make marriage *holy*, not just a slightly dirty but necessary runner-up to celibacy?

The answer lay back in Augustine's three justifications for marriage: *proles, fides*, and *sacramentum*. The Protestants insisted that marriage was a secular ceremony, and not (as the Catholics had finally decided in 1215) a mystical and irreversible sacrament. *Sacramentum*, in the early Protestant reformers' theologies, meant something much more daily, more human, more—if you'll excuse me—bourgeois. Marriage's purpose, wrote England's Archbishop Cranmer in his 1549 Prayer Book, was "mutual society, help and comfort, that the one ought to have of the other, both in prosperity and in adversity." In this view, human companionship was the sacrament. Marriage was holy not merely because it made legitimate babies and kept you from fornicating, but because being good to each other (that profound daily challenge that many of us know well) was pleasing to God.

This Protestant interpretation flew wildly in the face of one of Catholicism's favorite texts, Paul's words to the Corinthians: "He who is unmarried is concerned about the things of God, how he may please God; but he who is married is concerned about the things of the world, how he may please his wife" (Cor. 7.32–33). These Protestant sermonizers and pamphleteers—many of them ex-priests firmly trained in the Refraining ideal—were justifying their slippage into marriage by repudiating that idea and insisting on the opposite. In this new view, the challenge of respecting and living with a spouse didn't *block* holiness; rather, it *was* holy.

And yet, although the crusading early Protestants found marriage holy, they weren't ready to say the same for sex. Luther knew what marriage was for: it was to show "how the man and the woman should be taught to keep the passion of lust in check."

That's hardly a ringing endorsement of sexual pleasure; rather, it's a pragmatic understanding that sex is a powerful impulse and needs a decent channel to keep from ravaging human lives. The Protestants were outraged that Catholicism had overlooked a host of marriage irregularities, such as taking for granted the custom of sex between betrothal and wedding. Such horrifying and unkosher sex (in Protestant eyes) had to be stopped. Some Protestant jurisdictions levied a ten-pfennig fine on couples who "mingled themselves sexually" before going to church, while others excommunicated couples for "anticipatory" sex. Geneva threatened adulterers with execution. The Church of England, backed by the British Parliament, likewise urged magistrates to levy the death penalty for adultery, three-months' gaol for fornication, and the stocks and branding—"marked in with a hot iron in the forehead with the letter B"—for brothel-keepers. The Protestants, in other words, had banished the Refraining ideal not because they thought sex was good but because they wanted to restrain it properly: inside marriage.

As quaint and distant as this idea seems—death for adultery? wouldn't that wipe out our government?—it makes a little more sense when you realize that these people were living in a chaotic and dangerous world, a world that felt out of control. Wars were raging across Europe (religious, rebellious, civil, territorial); farmers were losing common grazing land; artisans and merchants were losing their trades to abrupt and violent industrialization; plagues, smallpox, pneumonia, typhus, typhoid, measles, diphtheria, scarlet fever, and chicken pox could still ravage a village or city or region within months; a good fifth of the population teetered just above starvation. Meanwhile, an ocean away, the New England Puritans perched on the edge of a vast, dangerous continent—an upright, chosen tribe launching a new and purified moral civilization, a beacon in the wilderness. Theirs too was a precarious world, where anyone's deviance might upset the entire social balance, where "solitary living" was literally against the law, since it was common knowledge that solitude encouraged evil. Any sex outside marriage—adultery, buggery, sodomy, or rape, more or less interchangeable sins—was considered a capital offense, along with other willful threats to the colony's survival, like treason, murder, and witchcraft.

Keeping sex off the extramarital streets also meant requiring sex inside marriage. Yes, requiring sex: the Protestants were just as stern about enforcing marital sex as they were about banning the extramarital. They weren't alone in this: Talmudic rabbis had also required sex within marriage, even laying out a timetable for how often husbands should "rejoice their wives": "for men of independent means . . . every day, for laborers twice a week, for ass-drivers once a week, for camel-drivers once in thirty days, for sailors once in six months." But that rabbinic timetable merely gave a wife grounds for asking for a divorce. The early Protestants actually punished those who were derelict in their marital duties. One seventeenth-century Massachusetts husband was put in the stocks alongside his adulterous wife and her lover—because, the community reasoned, she wouldn't have strayed had her hubby been doing the marital deed. Everyone had to do their part, or these uneasy worlds would fly apart. Sex was not, as we think of it today, an expression of profound personal intimacy: sex was an obligation (albeit one you might enjoy) comparable to churning the butter or going to church, part of your duty in keeping town order.

But because the Protestants' ideas grew from a profound theological history of recoil from sex, they still found sexual pleasure—if unmitigated by duty—to be pretty seamy. If asked what justified marriage, they'd still put *proles*—procreation—pretty high on the list. Luther agreed with Augustine that "even if [women] bear themselves weary or ultimately bear themselves out, this is the purpose for which they exist." In the seventeenth century, the great poet, preacher, and dean of St. Paul's, John Donne—who, like Augustine, converted to serious Christianity only after abandoning the licentiousness of his youth—echoed Augustine when he preached, "To contract before that they will have no children makes it no marriage, but an adultery."

Refreshing, 1: Heart and Soul
v. Womb and Sperm

The Protestants' new belief in holy matrimony wasn't *entirely* new. All along, standing side by side with the Catholic theologians' official recoil from sex, some Jews held a sexual theology that we might call Refreshing. To simplify, the rabbis believed God had created human being *as flesh,* creating and intending both sexual pleasure and procreativity right from *B'rashit,* right from the beginning. Even when a particular rabbi did believe in asceticism, he was still required to have a wife and children or he could not *be* a rabbi. But most of the early rabbis rejected asceticism vigorously, even insisting that a man who kept his clothes on during sex must divorce and pay the *ketubah,* or marriage settlement. Wrote one rabbi, "To rejoice his wife . . . behold how great is this positive *mitzvah.* Even when his wife is pregnant it is a mitzvah to cause her thus to be happy if he feels she is desirous." To them, the husband's most unshakable duty—more important, even, than providing food or clothes, in an era when the husband signed a contract promising to do precisely that—was *onah,* his wife's sexual pleasure. He wasn't allowed to take a celibacy vow that lasted more than a week, lest he neglect her—even if she gave him permission. By the thirteenth century, the Refreshing ideal was in full bloom within Jewish commentary. "Understand that if marital intercourse did not partake of great holiness, it would not be called 'knowing,'" wrote one rebbe, Moses ben Nahman, in a thirteenth-century marriage guide that was reprinted for many centuries. So long as a couple did produce at least a few children in their lifetime, contraception was actually *good*—that is, if making a baby would either endanger the wife's health or (presumably because they had too many children already) affect the couple's happiness. Chiding someone who, influenced by Christian ideas, had called sex "unworthy," Nahman added, "Had he believed that one God created the world he would not have slipped into such error."

In other words, the Jews explicitly rejected the asceticism promoted around them in medieval Europe. Sure, unmarried sex was a seriously evil temptation—just as eating non-kosher food was bad. But *married* sexual joy was a gift from God—just as eating kosher food was good. And just as kosher food was good no matter how you cooked it, so any married sex—whatever the act might be—was still kosher, so long as it was not against the woman's will. What mattered was the pair's intimacy, the affection that could be refreshed by sex. The thirteenth-century sage Maimonides wrote, "One might say: inasmuch as jealousy, passion, love of honor . . . [may] bring about a man's downfall, I will therefore remove myself to the other extreme. I will refrain from meat and wine or marriage or a pleasant home or attractive garments. . . . This is an evil way and forbidden. He who follows these practices is a sinner!"

God abides in sex! Asceticism is sinful! No wonder the Jews were regularly accused of being sex-crazed (or is that just the charge hurled at every despised minority?) when their homes were torched and pillaged by the locals. What we might today consider a sex guide was written by one religion's sage while, in the very same century, on the very same continent, the reigning religion's authorities were warning men not to enjoy *married* sex too much or they'd be no better than adulterers. But the Jewish idea was still very far from our own. For one thing, theologians were talking only to men, men who thanked God every day that they were not created women. One rabbinical school even permitted a man to divorce his wife for no other reason than that some other pretty girl caught his eye (well, maybe that *is* the same as today). Since Jews never influenced the West's marriage laws, what matters to us is that neighbors living side by side, considering each other equally married, could hold diametrically opposed viewpoints about a central fact of marriage: sex.

As the economy in which the Protestants lived transmuted into our own, the idea of holy matrimony began to stress companionship and even—here comes a big jump—intimacy. As marriage stopped being about shared work duties, as we saw in the last chapter, it began to be about a shared *inner* life. And so, necessarily, did sex.

Sex about a shared inner life? That's a long way from sex as marital obligation, something you might or might not enjoy but owed your spouse, something you could have with anyone, with pleasure more or less secondary. But capitalism and Protestantism had a big impact when they started earnestly cultivating parishioners' and entrepreneurs' inner lives. Bible-reading and diary-keeping went up dramatically, perhaps because literacy was expanding—or perhaps literacy expanded dramatically because the Protestants were urging all that Bible-reading and diary-keeping as a way to examine your conscience, your motives, your insides. If salvation was not communal but individual, the inner life had to be carefully scrutinized. How could all this self-scrutiny *not* affect how people thought about marriage—and sex?

Enter the free-lovers. Throughout this book we'll stumble repeatedly across the nineteenth-century free-lovers, a ragtag minority that horrified their contemporaries when they articulated the sex and marriage ideas by which we live today. The Victorian "free-love" movement—if you can call it a movement, this cornucopia of visionaries and idealists, spiritualists and water-cure practitioners—was frequently accused of "libertinism." But most adherents were not libertines at all; rather, they were fierce moralists who took the "holy matrimony" ideal very seriously—and were appalled that it did not match the sometimes brutal realities of married sex, as some wives suffered nightly rapes or endured a seemingly endless series of life-endangering pregnancies. "She is his slave, his victim, his tool. . . . Her body is prostituted to his morbid passions, her mind must bend submissive to his will . . . They are sacrificed to the great Moloch of society," wrote one of the early free-lovers, Mary Nichols, in 1859, who had fled (and lost custody of her children to) her abusive husband and eventually took up a "free" union with Thomas Nichols. Wrote another free-lover, Leo Miller, in 1885, "I presume it would be impossible to find an intelligent supporter of the marriage institution, who would deny the proposition in the abstract, that the only natural basis of sexual union is mutual affection. . . . and that any other kind of union is naturally adulterous and immoral."

Freeze that frame: "The only natural basis of sexual union is mutual affection." That's a big leap from the older idea that you owe your body to your spouse in order to prevent him from sinning elsewhere. That's taking the idea of holy matrimony to its extreme. Miller is pushing his contemporaries to agree (and not all would) that sex and marriage are justified not by preventing sin or by making babies but by *refreshing* the spirit, uplifting it as part of an intimate union.

The free-lovers saw several consequences to this demanding ideal that justified sex by affection, not by duty. They believed that if sex was for intimate union, for refreshing the spirit, then women should no longer be beasts of burden, constantly shoving forth progeny. If sex was for refreshing the spirit—if the union itself was not filthy but sacred—then why should women risk life and health each time they did the holy deed?

The more daring free-lovers actually published contraception tracts. In the mid-nineteenth-century United States, Robert Dale Owens published *Moral Physiology,* instructing people in *coitus interruptus*—saying that sex's influence was "moral, humanizing, polishing, beneficient." By the 1920s, when British physician Marie Stopes published the shocking book *Married Love,* she justified contraception by describing sex (contracepted or not) in spiritual terms: "The complete act of union . . . symbolises, and at the same time actually enhances, the spiritual union . . . it is a *mutual,* not a selfish, pleasure and profit, more calculated than anything else to draw out an unspeakable tenderness and understanding in both partakers of this sacrament."

Sex as intimate sacrament? Sex without babies? These were battle cries. These were flat-out rebellions against the Reframing ideal, appalling both Catholics and Protestants who believed God called us to self-denial rather than mutual exploration. Perhaps the free-lovers and contraceptive activists would have been ignored if they'd been solitary wackos to whom no one paid any attention. But they were articulating a much wider trend. By Augustine's and John Donne's standards, a vast number of Europeans, Americans, Australians, Canadians, and other Westerners became harlots and

adulterers in the nineteenth century—as they steadily, deter-
minedly, and dramatically cut the birth rate. From 1770 to 1860,
the French birth rate per thousand persons dropped from 38.6 to
26.3—by nearly one-third. Between 1800 and 1900, children per
U.S. white women (the race about which ruling- and middle-class
demographers and policymakers cared most) dropped from 7.04
to 3.56—by one-*half*. Numbers kept falling precipitously until the
birth rate threatened to dip below the "replacement rate," horrifying commentators who foresaw disaster (and not the demographic surprise of the 1950s). By 1940, the U.S. average was a terrifying 2.1 children per woman.

Had married couples massively converted to continence? Certainly not. Everyone realized that contraceptive attempts—or to
sample contemporary language, "voluntary control of the maternal function," "methodizing conjugal relations," "marital masturbation," "conjugal frauds," and, of course, the horrible "crime
against nature"—had invaded just about every nuptial bed. Pre-
Pill contraception may have been fallible, but it was still an incredible relief to women and their families: the difference between one
child a year and one child every *two* years was enormous. As people
flooded from rural villages to cities, an uninterrupted flow of children stopped being a labor boon and became a poverty guarantee.
And with improvements in public health and medical care, fewer
children were dying—which meant that even if you gave birth to
no more children than your grandmother did (say, eight) you
might nevertheless have twice as many to raise to adulthood. Why
keep bearing until you starved or dropped dead? Why have twice or
three times as many as you could afford to educate into the middle
or professional classes? As people worked out their relationship
with money and God by turning to their individual consciences
rather than following one unbending set of rules, the answers became clear. The Refraining ideal was up for referendum: people
were voting silently with their bodies.

It wasn't especially hard in the early nineteenth century to get
information about contraception. The sin that "is so foule and
so hidous that [it] scholde not be nampned" was widely adver-

tised. That included, for instance, the rubber condom—although Charles Goodyear, who made his fortune when he vulcanized rubber in 1837 and "rubbers" quickly replaced sheepskin condoms, found the source of his wealth "so notorious in reputation that the inventor never dared take any credit." American women's magazines included advertisements that called attention to Lydia E. Pinkham's Vegetable Compound and Uterine Tonic or announced that "Carter's Relief for Women is safe and reliable; better than ergot, oxide, tansy, or pennyroyal pills"—herbal contraceptives all. The Colgate Company advertised Vaseline with a physician's statement advising that Vaseline "with four or five grains of salicylic acid, will destroy spermatazoa, without injury to the uterus or vagina." Lysol—unbelievably, the very same chemical you use today to clean your toilet—was the biggest-selling contraceptive douche in the early twentieth century. Pamphlets and books like *Married Lady's Private Medical Guide* and *Married Woman's Private Medical Companion* proliferated—until you'd think that all married women ever thought about was contraception.

Those who saw contraception as a disgusting attempt to have your cake and eat it too looked at this demographic evidence of moral decay—and brought forth cannons of outrage. The 1876 book *Conjugal Sins* insisted that contraceptive attempts "degrades to bestiality the true feelings of manhood and the holy state of matrimony." Birth control opponents understood that separating sex from reproduction meant women could behave like men—and men could no longer be pressured into being honorably married dads. Wrote one anti-contraception pamphleteer, "Why should men and women marry? Friendship between man and woman, if possible at all, is as possible outside marriage as inside. [If contraception becomes respectable], comparatively few people will marry . . . because the natural reason for marriage, physical satisfaction, will be obtainable, without loss of respectability, outside marriage."

And so the Refraining ideology staggered back into the marriage battles—in the United States, in the person of Anthony Comstock, a failed dry-goods salesman turned purity crusader. Comstock's

April 10, 1873 diary entry might well have been the keynote for his life's crusade (as for so many purity crusaders since): "It seems as though we were living in an age of lust." And God forbid Comstock should miss even a minute of it. He plunged right in like a life-guard, mucking about until he was up to his ears in vice, determined to save his nation's youth. Frustrated by how little he could do under existing laws, in the late nineteenth century Anthony Comstock brought his bag of pornographic postcards and contraceptive devices—two sides of the same sin—to the halls of Congress and demanded a law protecting the nation's youth. He declaimed against the terrible spread of "rubber articles for masturbation or the professed prevention of conception." In response Congress passed an 1873 law that barred use of the U.S. mails for distribution of "obscene materials or articles for the prevention of conception" and gave Comstock a job as postal inspector.

Comstock eventually became the crusade's public buffoon, so widely caricatured that even today readers might be able to picture his vested belly and muttonchops. But just as the free-lovers gave voice to a vision of our future, so Comstock gave voice to those trying to hold on to marriage's past. He seized hundreds of thousands of pounds of books, pictures, photographs, "rubber articles," playing cards, "pills and powders." He entrapped, arrested, prosecuted, and imprisoned dozens of pornographers; physicians who published pamphlets about sexual physiology and diseases; abortionists; and drugstore owners who mailed out pessaries, condoms, "female syringes" (or contraceptive douches) and "uterine tonics" that could have been sold over the counter without prosecution (although he never went after Colgate or Lysol). And he especially targeted free-lovers like a Boston publisher and bookseller who sold the contraceptive pamphlet *The Fruits of Philosophy*. In Britain, sellers and publishers of the same pamphlets were similarly hounded. In 1877, Britain's pro-contraception crusader Annie Besant lost custody of her daughter when her abusive husband (from whom she was separated) accused her of being ready to expose the child to (gasp) "the physiological facts."

In the United States, Societies for the Suppression of Vice

sprang up around the country and urged individual states to pass local laws like the federal Comstock Act. Connecticut went so far as to prohibit the *use* of contraception—presumably deputizing God to make the necessary arrests, since it's hard to imagine who else would. The statutes outlaw in one sentence any "lascivious book, pamphlet, paper, picture, print, drawing, figure, or image ... [or] any drug, medicine, article, or instrument whatsoever for the purpose of preventing conception, or causing unlawful abortion." Dirty pictures or pennyroyal, racy playing cards or pessaries—they were all the same to those intent on enforcing the Reproducing ideal, since they either aroused lust or prevented its "natural" consequences. (Imagine how those crusaders would feel about Viagra!) And since chest-thumping about "the children" is a specialty of moral panics, such laws tended to specifically penalize anyone who sold such items to "any family, college, academy or school." At the height of this moral panic, more than half the states passed what we might call Defense of Decency laws (or as one state's was titled, "An Act Concerning Offenses against Chastity, Morality, and Decency"). These laws' purpose was precisely the same as today's Defense of Marriage Acts: criminalize and prevent any sex acts that make love without making babies, because otherwise the very meaning of marriage might change—from an institution aimed mainly at procreative duty to an institution that accepted sexual love.

Comstock was not alone in decrying this new view of sex and marriage as perverted. Attacks were widespread and ferocious, far more so than we remember today, with rhetoric heated enough to match anything in today's marriage and family wars. As late as 1926, the *Atlantic Monthly* winced at the political and spiritual consequences of contraception, which "challenge[s] the permanence of the State. . . . Such activity is distinctly antisocial, for it enables selfish people to escape their responsibility, ultimately to their own detriment and to the injury of the State . . . and what is the usual effect on the spiritual life of those who . . . keep their families down to a miserly minimum?" Clearly the *Atlantic Monthly*, like many others, thought the effect was, to put it mildly, vile. That was a high-minded version. The anti-immigrant fever sweeping the U.S. at the time allowed more unsavory arguments against native-born whites' parsimonious childbearing: what would happen as proliferative Germans, Irish, Italians, Jews, Slavs, and emancipated blacks poured into the industrial north while white women abjured their reproductive duties? "Race suicide" was the code phrase hurled from the bully pulpit. Teddy Roosevelt, himself the father of six, announced that any (white) person who didn't pour out children was "a criminal against the race" and "the object of contemptuous abhorrence by healthy people." Thundered Teddy, "Willful sterility inevitably produces and accentuates every hideous form of vice. . . . I rank celibate profligacy as not one whit better than polygamy."

The Catholic Church was, naturally, aboil about how to respond to this religious rebellion, especially in late nineteenth-century Catholic France, which—if you read the demographic data—had to be sinning massively. One radical theologian wrote that priests should advise couples to have sex only during the newly discovered "sterile period." Hardliners immediately attacked this new "rhythm method." Wrote one, "This pernicious sensualism is entirely contrary to the laws of God . . . It constitutes the horrible crime against nature." The rhythm-method book was quickly ordered out of circulation. In 1930, Pope Pius XI issued his encyclical *Casti Conubii (Of Chaste Marriage),* which endorsed the old Refraining/Reproducing ideal by intoning that contraception "violates the law of God and nature," and grew out of women's "false liberty and unnatural equality"—a clear recognition that contraception and female emancipation went hand in hand.

But still the birth rate kept dropping, until one would suspect that more than half the nation—probably including the legislators themselves—were sex criminals. In Stanford researcher Dr. Clelia Mosher's 1890 survey of white middle-class wives, she found that almost every one of them practiced some kind of birth control. Which didn't mean, of course, that they were ready to "come out" publicly. By 1916, a pained Anthony Comstock was asked by a women's magazine reporter what he thought of the birth control movement and efforts to help poor women keep from having more children than they could afford. With pure Augustinian rhetoric, Comstock cried, "Are we to have homes or brothels? Can't everybody, whether rich or poor, learn to control themselves?"

Poor Comstock: the answer was no. The children Comstock had tried to save from depravity were launching the Jazz Age. Women dropped pounds of petticoats, bustles, hats, and ankle-length skirts and ran around looking like prostitutes with their short skirts, short hair, lipstick, cigarettes, and shaved legs. Their petting parties and speakeasies became the scandal of the age. Against his will, Comstock was about to pass the historical baton to Margaret Sanger and the birth controllers.

It was no mistake that Margaret Sanger came out of feminist and socialist organizing. Perhaps *the* central issue at stake in the contraceptive wars was a woman's freedom to choose the course of her life. Should she be the angel in the house, belonging to her husband—or should she be an independent person, free to vote, work, own property, and marry for companionship and shared sexual pleasure? From 1890 to 1910, female college enrollment tripled. The number of women doing paid work doubled from 1880 to 1900 and then went up another 50 percent between 1900 and 1919. More and more, the new middle classes believed that it was only fair for women to take an equal place in the world. But all this female emancipation quite definitely depended on freedom from children by accident—without sacrificing pleasure. Not just impurity in the marriage bed, but this firehose of social change was what birth control opponents were battling. And since economic and social change is difficult to fight, it's much easier to launch a social panic about sex—since changes in sexual order can feel intuitively, viscerally disturbing, especially if you've been taught that sexual restraint equals morality. In the 1890s, physicians were warning parents against letting their daughters ride bicycles, lest they deflower themselves, have orgasms from the bicycle seat, and be picked up by men in strange parts of town. That same sexualized fear of female freedom fueled the campaign against contraception. Was sex—and therefore marriage—about duty, subordination, and respect, or was it about shared interests, equality, and love?

Feminists understood that battle line. After fifty years of pamphlet wars on contraception, the free-love ideals were no longer quite so marginal. And so Margaret Sanger opened her first—illegal—birth control clinic in Brooklyn's Brownsville district in October 1916. Her goal was to keep women from suffering the unnecessary poverty of rearing a large brood, and to keep them from an early grave after being exhausted by ceaseless childbearing—which she believed had happened to her Catholic mother Anne, dead of consumption at fifty. Sanger advertised in English, Yiddish, and Italian—and patients lined up so immediately that the clinic recorded 464 visits in only a few weeks. The New York vice squad shut down the "obscene" clinic within three weeks—much as, forty years later, two women seen kissing could count on being arrested. Sex without babies? Call the vice squad!

The Sanger trial became a cause célèbre, trumpeted daily on tabloids' front pages. In the courtroom, wealthy suffragettes in furs and Brownsville mothers with paper bags of bread and cheese sat side by side, united in their desire to shake off household slavery, to choose sex while still controlling their family lives—to be "unnatural" wives and change the very meaning of marriage. Or to quote the credo issued by Margaret Sanger's supporters: "Whether or not, and when, a woman should have a child, is not a question for the doctors to decide, except in cases where the woman's life is endangered, or for the state legislators to decide, but a question for the woman herself to decide." Indeed! Can we be surprised that Comstock—his era over—caught a cold and dropped dead of pneumonia within a few weeks of the trial?

In those first decades of the twentieth century, as the Refraining ideal began to fall, its adherents' rhetoric got even more extreme. One pundit sputtered that by using contraception, "sexual congress is thus rendered but a species of self-abuse." A Lutheran synod accused the American Birth Control League of "spattering the country with its slime." And a New York archbishop's 1930s fundraising letter leaned on the demon of the birth control campaign: "The downright perversion of human cooperation with the Creator in the propagation of the human family is openly advocated and defended. It is not what the God of nature and grace, in His Divine wisdom, ordained marriage to be; but the lustful indulgence of man and woman. . . . Religion shudders at the wild orgy of atheism and immorality the situation forebodes."

Interestingly, those who feared that the birth controllers were in vice's vanguard (at least in the terms of the day) were correct—and even more interestingly, we no longer much care. Despite their respectable public rhetoric about freeing married women to have children by choice instead of accident, privately Sanger and many of her supporters did believe in a new, free sexuality—not just for men, but for women. As a young woman, Sanger had been sexually involved with a man who was courting her, a "trial marriage" that she later broke off. After having three children with her first husband, William Sanger, she was never again monogamous, but took more than a dozen lovers ranging from the infamous (and impotent) sexologist Havelock Ellis to the writer and radical H. G. Wells. These men wrote her ravished love letters importuning her for more time and attention. In her case, the gender tables were turned: the men yearned for intimacy, and the woman seemed cold and distant and enjoyed sex without bonds. Even while married to the wealthy Noah Slee—the manufacturer who on her behalf imported spermicidal jelly in his motor oil cans, and later staked one of her old boyfriends in becoming a contraceptive manufacturer —she traveled widely, spent passionate weekends with her lovers, kept up her amorous correspondences. Like male politicians whose outsized passion for power so often spills over into their sexual appetites, Margaret Sanger never seemed to require the emotional precision of one deepening love.

But Sanger's sex life—like the charge that legalizing contraception would turn us into a bestial, orgiastic nation—was a red herring. Sexual choice was shocking only as long as women were denied other choices as well. As women gained rights that ranged from property ownership to education to the vote, as both men and women gained the freedom of choice required by a capitalist society, birth control came to seem as natural as women on bicycles. What was most frightening was the most straightforward effect: female freedom, not the predicted apocalypse. Can we survive in a world without women imprisoned at home to do the mothering, without dads locked to those moms by law? We're still skirmishing over that question today.

Over the next decades—as the children raised in the Jazz Age came to power, much as the 1960s generation has come to power now—the new sexual ideal became the reigning public philosophy. By April 1931 even the conservative New York Academy of Medicine issued a statement that contraception was acceptable, since married sex was "a supreme expression of their affection and comradeship—a manifestation of divine concern for the happiness of those who have so wholly merged their lives." Since legislators were still too frightened to touch the controversial issue of contraception, judges took the lead, poking holes in the Comstock laws and thereby allowing physicians to prescribe contraception as they saw fit. By 1936, in the precedent-setting *United States v. One Package,* a federal appeals court decided that Comstock had been wrong to link contraception and pornography—and allowed diaphragms to be shipped through the mails, Comstock's own turf. The ginger-whiskered crusader was turning in his grave.

By the 1950s, even the Pope agreed that "husband and wife should experience pleasure and happiness in body and spirit. In seeking and enjoying this pleasure, therefore, couples do nothing wrong." Goodby to Augustine! No wonder Catholics started massively defying the Church's contraceptive strictures: the prohibition stopped making sense. If it is only pregnancy that justifies the evil nastiness of sex, then contraception is easy to understand as sin. But if sexual pleasure and happiness are ordained by God, then why should you make babies every time? Sex as spiritual expression: the Refreshing ideal had won the war.

Over the course of this battle, having sex while preventing babies was compared to all the usual suspects. Contraception was worse than homicide, incest, polygamy; was against nature or bestial (i.e., not animal or too animal); disease-ridden, immoral, vice-ridden, equivalent to masturbation, prostitution, adultery, atheism, orgies; it would destroy youth, marriage, the family, the state, and civilization. Of course, all those charges are now used against same-sex marriage, and for the very same reasons—to call up the cultural idea that sexual pleasure is disgusting and sinful if it does not lead to babies. What other arguments can you resort to when your ideology is outdated—except apocalyptic predictions of misery, disease, and God's wrath?

But once that kind of rhetoric is used, the battle is lost. In this society, we believe people should be free to use their own judgment and make their own choices. With no more socioeconomic justification for enforcing the link between sex and babies, with the very idea at odds with the philosophies behind consumer capitalism, the state had to step out of the debate: contraception was up to each individual conscience. By 1998, 75 percent of Americans believed health insurance should underwrite contraception just as it does any other prescription—as if the link between sex and pregnancy was a health condition to be prevented, not a crime against nature or a direct contravention of God's law. In other words, today if you want to have sex without making babies—contrary to more than a thousand years of official Christian teaching—you can still call what you have not a brothel, not a bestiary, not an adultery, not an orgy, not a crime against nature, but a marriage.

Refreshing, 2: Intimate to the Degree of Being Sacred

There are two postscripts to this particular battle, at least in the United States. In Connecticut, Comstock's law stayed on the books so long that there are still women alive today who will talk about how, as young women, they had to show at least their wedding rings, if not their marriage certificates, to get a diaphragm prescribed. They shared the names of contraceptive-prescribing physicians in the same way that, during that era, lesbians and gay men traded the names of illegal gay bars that they knew full well might be raided. As one lawyer marvels retrospectively, as late as 1961 intervening in sex was still "accepted by many as a legitimate exercise of the police powers of the state." Legislators were not about to wade into the political mud of legalizing contraception, not with a powerful and openly threatening Catholic lobby and a lingering sense that enjoying sex was immoral. And so a group of lawyers and contraceptive activists opened a storefront contraceptive clinic, inviting arrest—and launched the test case that reached the U.S. Supreme Court as *Griswold v. Connecticut,* which overturned the last legal enforcement of Comstock's Reproducing ideal.

It's fascinating that in 1965, what the U.S. Supreme Court found shocking was the *opposite* of what had seemed shocking just one hundred years earlier. "Would we allow the police to search the sacred precincts of marital bedrooms for telltale signs of the use of contraceptives?" wrote Justice Brennan. Just a century before, what seemed shocking was the idea that *contraceptives,* not police, would invade a marriage. In the same way, the Protestant Reformation had once reinterpreted Catholic celibacy, turning a saintly act into an invitation to sin. Even more thrilling for observers of history's marriage skirmishes is *Griswold*'s more famous phrase: that marriage was "intimate to the degree of being sacred" *even if it did not create babies.* Its sacredness lay not in its procreativity but in its intimacy. That radical claim was a shocking upset in the marriage wars. The Refreshing ideal had triumphed.

By now even explicitly Christian marriage counseling advises couples on how to improve their bedroom lives, seeing sexual pleasure as refreshing the marital commitment. Tim and Beverly La-Haye of the Moral Majority and Concerned Women for America organizations, and leaders among those conducting the "family values" charge, even wrote a book suggesting that reading the Song of Solomon offers information on clitoral stimulation. They write that the verse "Let his left hand be under my head and his right hand embrace me" can be carried out with "the wife lying on her back with her knees bent and feet pulled up to her hips and her husband lying on her right side." When even evangelical Christians wholeheartedly dispose of the Refraining ideal to prescribe sex *a mano,* which Catholic theologians declared a sin that deserved the fire, the Refreshing ideal has utterly swept the field. And if the LaHayes are correct—if, as that minister wrote in the 1920s, "the sexual act, as a sacramental act, has a value apart from any results which may follow it. . . . [and] is the attainment of that spiritual, mental, and bodily unity with the person beloved"—then my nuptial life most certainly belongs.

From the post-*Griswold* point of view, what is marriage for? For the close companionship and sexual pleasure of the pair. By legalizing birth control, our nation's laws recognized that the goal of sex was now love, pleasure, and that other response so difficult to put into words—that temporary transcendence of self, that deep gratitude of belonging to another, which so many of us—including Madeline and myself—want to surround with a gold band's determined, optimistic promises. Once society has gotten rid of the idea that sex without babies is bad—or to put it differently, once our philosophy and laws protect sex for pleasure and love—how can same-sex marriage be barred?

The new code put in a terrible bind anyone who—upon all that introspection encouraged by the capitalists, Protestants, and that new breed of priests, the psychologists—discovered within herself affections and desires aimed at her own sex. How could she now justify imprisoning herself in a baby-making marriage? In the seventeenth or even eighteenth century she could simply have lay on her back for her husband and then politely greeted him in the morning over breakfast after gathering the eggs or opening the shop. But now simply making babies wouldn't do. Now she had to feel a deep, intimate, personal union with this guy—which made her inner dryness toward him an insupportable hypocrisy, even a sin. But on the other hand, if she wanted not *him* but a woman, she was—in accordance with newly invented theories about homosexuality—sick. Suddenly hers was an impossible conundrum, a shocking difference from her sisters, a difference far more visible and disturbing than it would have been only two hundred years before.

And so, conveniently, she became the latest—and now the

only—scapegoat for the "crime against nature." Sodomy was no longer defined as any nonprocreative seedspilling; instead, the laws attacked only those who loved someone of the same sex—and with terrible consequences. When a Virginia appeals court agreed that Sharon Bottoms' son should be brought up not by his mother but by his grandmother, the court explained that Sharon Bottoms was an admitted felon—that she'd admitted to having oral sex and admitted she'd do it again. Never mind that no police officer was going to arrest Sharon for her felony; never mind that some 95 percent of American women say they have oral sex; never mind that no judge would yank away the son of a heterosexual woman if she "admitted" to having oral sex with her new husband (which does count as "sodomy" in the Virginia statute). The most thoughtful and prominent theorists against homosexuality make clear that they oppose homosexuality on the same grounds that they oppose "the acts of a husband and wife whose intercourse is masturbatory, for example sodomitic or by fellatio or coitus interruptus . . . or deliberately contracepted"—in other words, any sex that cannot make babies. But only lesbians and gay men are now legally expected to live by that early Christian Refraining ideal: know and conquer your sexual feelings. How, in a pluralist democracy, can you draw a circle-and-slash around one group's inner lives? How can only one group be barred from the Refreshing ideology that guides the West's sex and marriage law?

Many people imagine that any sexual act between two women or two men must feel like a loveless and barren perversion—just as sex with men felt, to me, numb and degrading. And of course many young men are afraid of being treated, or even thought of, the way they treat or think of women: Norman Podhoretz wrote in one *Commentary* article that "men using one another as women constitutes a perversion," which is an amazingly open admission of the disgust for women that lies behind much antigay writing. But neither this secret misogyny nor this failure of imagination, this inability to accept others' inner lives as different from one's own, is a justifiable reason to bar lesbians and gay men—and only lesbians and gay men—from testifying that when we love we, too, find sex to be a sacrament, a language for love, a marital bond. As one pundit has written, we want to commit monogamy. If sex is justified by your inner life—whether the high spiritual standard of love or the low pragmatic standard of willingness—then no one else can testify about mine.

The war of the words   And so, naturally, the rhetoric of those opposed to same-sex marriage has grown more and more hysterical—echoing other marriage battles. In the anti-gay campaign of the 1920s, one newspaper pundit charged that, "Once a man assumes the role of homosexual, he often throws off all moral restraints . . . they descend through perversions to other forms of depravity, such as drug addiction, burglary, sadism, and even murder." In the 1970s, Anita Bryant picked the perennial danger-to-children theme when she called her campaign against a human rights ordinance "Save Our Children" because of "fears we now felt of widespread militant homosexuals' efforts to influence children to their abnormal way of life." Some of her allies used that other perennial charge in the marriage wars: that any protection for lesbians and gay men was "a carefully disguised attempt to break down further the moral fabric of society."

And of course, there's the traditional charge that any change in the marriage rules will pollute society and therefore lead to disease. The fact that, in the developed west, HIV has spread especially among gay men—unlike in Africa and Asia, where AIDS is primarily a heterosexual epidemic—has made this charge particularly potent. As one opponent writes, "Vaginal intercourse is the only kind of sexual intercourse that medical research has shown causes no physical or mental damages." Such a sentence entertainingly ignores the facts: because penises are so efficient at dispersing viruses and battering vaginal walls, lesbians have lower rates of gynecological and sexually transmitted diseases than do straight women or men.

Underlying most of these charges is the basic fallback position of those who fear change: God is on their side. As one pamphlet puts it, "Homosexuality is not what God intends for individuals or society. . . . it is the willful sin of human beings which causes homosexuality."

Disease, bestiality, incest, polygamy; a flagrant violation of the very definition of marriage; threats to children, family, society, and civilization; God's coming punishment for sin: These same apocalypse-now charges are hurled in every marriage battle. Are such predictions any more true now than they were, say, when early Christians advocated celibacy; when nineteenth-century women struggled to control their own wallets; or when twentieth-century feminists worked to legalize birth control? Such outcries are always a backlash against social and economic changes that have already taken place. For instance, today's commentators have genuine concerns about what will happen to family life in a consumer capitalist age. There remains an uneasy tension between, on the one hand, marriage as a way to resist consumer capitalism's pressure on the individual soul—and, on the other, consumer capitalism's ideology of individual love and fulfillment. But they wrongly choose those who love among the same sex as their scapegoats. The movement toward same-sex marriage is the consequence, not the cause, of many other changes in Western life—changes like legalized contraception, already inscribed in Western laws. A pluralistic democracy cannot fairly bar as pariahs people who fully fit its ideology of the meaning of sex within marriage. Madeline and I now belong.

THREE:

Babies

———

Marriage has universally fallen into awful disrepute.

—MARTIN LUTHER, "On the Estate of Marriage" (1522)

The family, in its old sense, is disappearing from our land, and not only our free institutions are threatened but the very existence of our society is endangered.

—*Boston Quarterly Review* (1859)

Will the family, that institution which we have long regarded as the unit of civilization, the foundation of the state, survive? . . . The family of our fathers' time has almost entirely gone. . . . The home made by one man and one woman bound together 'until death do ye part' has in large measure given way to trial marriage. . . . [T]he bearing of children, finds less place in the conduct of this generation.

—CHAUNCEY J. HAWKINS, *Will the Home Survive* (1907)

Then your family disintegrated, began to split into groups. . . . the apartment rang with "Dad, I'm taking the car!" from 16-year-old Bill; "Mother, I'm sleeping over at Alice's house—it's too far to come all the way home" from adolescent Mary; "Let's eat out dear, and we'll have time to do something on the outside" from Mother. . . . For one reason or another, the middle class family has been disrupted. Women who will not settle into domesticity and maternity, fathers dispossessed of their sovereignty, children running tangentially

against their parents' wishes, the pull of outside forces, all
have made middle class society homeless. . . . A single generation has marred them completely.

—JOHN H. LAVAL,
"The Disappearance of the Family" (1939)

The American family has, in the past generation or more,
been undergoing a profound process of change. . . . Some
have cited facts such as the very high rates of divorce, the
changes in the older sex morality, and until fairly recently,
the decline in birth rates, as evidence of a trend to disor-
ganization in an absolute sense.

—TALCOTT PARSONS, "The American Family" (1955)

IT WOULD BE SILLY TO PRETEND OTHERWISE: ONE OF MAR-
riage's goals has always been children. However quaintly familiar the jeremiads that start this chapter, it *is* a sign of dizzying
social change, of how profoundly the Refreshing ideology has triumphed, that you can now ask a classroom of college students what
marriage is for—and they can talk for an hour or more before anyone mentions kids. The Egyptians didn't even have a word for marriage, which men and women could enter and leave at will; rather,
a man was said to "establish a household," implying a home that
would include offspring. A typical medieval catechism defined
marriage as a "sacrament instituted in order to have children legitimately and to raise them in the fear of God." Enlightenment
thinkers agreed, although they boldly tossed out God and sub-
stituted the State when defining marriage as "a civil contract
whereby a man is joined to a woman for the procreation of legitimate children." That concept was losing ground by the late eighteenth century, when *The Lady's Magazine* huffed that traditional
marriage was being destroyed by a new romantic ideal: "The intent
of matrimony is not for man and his wife to be always taken up
with each other, but jointly to discharge the duties of civil society,
to govern their families with prudence, and to educate their children with discretion." All these are clues to how *un*familiar that
word "family" gets once you investigate its history.

Whenever today's pundits throw up their hands about society's morals, they point to the disintegrating family as evidence and cause of every other social ill—just as their predecessors have done for nearly two hundred years. Opening marriage to same-sex couples, in this view, would be the final straw that would cause the entire family structure to come crashing down around our heads. The pillar of society is apparently paper-thin. As James Q. Wilson writes, "Marriage is an institution created to sustain child-rearing. The role of raising children is entrusted in principle to married heterosexual couples because after much experimentation—several thousand years, more or less—we have found nothing else that works as well." Such commentators are trying to call up, in our historically unfurnished minds, the flickering ghosts of the 1950s TV family—itself a radically new aberration that was once considered a social horror, not "traditional."

Are they right? Is the family now, and has it always been, one mother, one father, and two or three or ten children? Have children always been raised by their married heterosexual biological parents? These turn out not to be simple questions with obvious answers, but rather, questions with even more questions nestled inside them, like Russian matriarch dolls. Although there are an astonishing number of ways in which "family" has varied in the West, this chapter will look at three key questions, all hot topics in today's debates. When has a group of human beings been designated as a "family"? When was a child considered socially and legally "legitimate," or to put it differently, when were her parents considered properly married—and more important, why did anyone care? Who has society considered to be the most "natural" parent: dad, mom, a legally assigned biological stranger? History's disorienting answers differ depending on who, and when, you're asking.

In other words, the meaning of "family" is shiftier than just about anything else in the history of the marriage wars. And exactly what family *is*, what it has been, and what it can or ought to be, is one of the questions tucked inside this book's main question: what is marriage for?

Many readers may have heard of Philippe Ariès's thesis that "childhood" was only recently invented, that premodern children died in such numbers that most parents withheld their affection lest they be plummeted again and again into grief, that—in Lloyd DeMause's famous phrase—"the history of childhood is a nightmare from which we have just begun to awaken." As it happens, these are hotly contested theories in the history of the family, scholarly minefields into which I dare not step. But even without worrying about whether parents loved or ignored their children before the nineteenth century, we can easily discover that "the family" has never held still but has veered from one conception to the next—its current manifestation vanishing in a way that rightly terrifies a given generation, since family really is just as central to society as everyone insists. Family is where wave after wave of human beings are socialized and cared for, where children are raised to be useful members of society instead of dangerous cast-outs. Family is often an urgent part of how individuals make decisions that affect state, economy, and employer—as when an adolescent chooses a college a thousand miles away to flee his troubled family, or when a woman starts a home-based consulting company because she urgently needs both the income and the flexibility to stay home with the kids, or when a forty-year-old computer whiz turns down that fabulous posting to Germany because his New Jersey-bound ex-lover is ailing and needs care. Without family— without others we are responsible to and for—we scarcely seem human.

And so the questions underlying any changes in the definition of "family" truly are socially urgent. What makes it possible for children to grow up successfully? In what configurations can people best carry out those mutual responsibilities that keep us and society alive? What *is* a "family"? The question puzzles historians far more than it does those involved in today's shouting match over "family values." What they do agree on is that "the family" as we know it was invented in the middle of the nineteenth century—which is when cries about the "death of the family" began to rise in number and pitch. And yet somehow "the family" always seems to reappear in a way that—despite jeremiads—manages to rear children for the duties of the newly onrushing world.

What Makes a Family?

One of the first and most urgent questions that faces any society is: how can we best ensure that children will grow up into a successful adulthood? The contemporary intuition that a child must be raised by his "natural" parents is one about which many feel quite passionately. It's therefore exceedingly disconcerting to discover how recently we got sealed off into the "family" we now call traditional, the one whose goal is to provide a safe and secure nest for the tender young. Of course, the idea that a child belongs to its parents is ancient—but the key phrase in that sentence is belongs *to*, not belongs *with*. In many eras, while plenty of parents raised their own children, they also felt free to ship them off with impunity, from infancy through adolescence.

Most historians warn readers that to grasp "family" history you must first abandon the idea that you already know what "family" means. "Family" seems to be a word invented by Humpty Dumpty, who told Alice that "a word means what I say it should mean, neither more nor less: the question is, which is to be master, that is all." Historians always remind us of the word's etymology. Our *family* is related to its root in the Roman *familia* just about as closely as a Chevy Suburban is related to an elephant- and camel-drawn caravan. Sure, both of them move—but who's inside, and what are they doing in there?

Inside the Roman *familia* was everyone in the household: legitimate children, adopted adults, secretaries and other dependents, slaves of various ages. "The Romans rarely used it to mean family in the sense of kin," writes Roman family historian Suzanne

Dixon. What counted, rather, was ownership. The words for children, slaves, and servants were so often interchanged that historians can't always tell how many of which lived under one roof. And for good reason. The patriarch's rule was complete: he could educate, beat, sell, give, indenture, marry off, endow, or kill any one of them, almost at will.

He could, of course, care for his *familia* as well. Romans lived with their slaves and servants so closely that it "in some ways resembled kinship, even if the slaves were always in the position of poor relations," explains Dixon. Masters might inscribe the tombstones of especially beloved slaves in grieving words that mourned someone expected to care for the masters during old age; ex-slaves might write similar gravestone encomiums to former masters. (Did slaves really feel affection for their masters, or were they hoping to keep those ex-masters' children as patrons? Probably both— although at this distance, it's hard to read between the epitaphs' lines.) Dixon cites one hard-fought custody battle between a freed slave and her former owners over who would keep the ex-slave's daughter Patronia Iusta, a custody battle as vicious as that over Baby M. The masters "clearly wanted to treat [Patronia] as a daughter and were prepared to insist on her servile birth as a means of keeping her from her mother." Could it be that the daughter was biologically the patriarch's?

Maybe—or maybe not. Romans didn't consider birth the only way to acquire offspring. Just as they felt free to expose (in other words, kill) any child they didn't need, they also felt free to adopt— adults, that is. Adoption's goal was not to nurture a child but to install an heir to carry on the house, a goal better served by adults— and so nearly all adoptions were of grown men (yes, men). Adoptees were usually nephews or grandsons or cousins, sometimes adopted through a will. As one historian explains, "A citizen of Rome did not 'have' a child; he 'took' a child. . . . The Romans made no fetish of natural kinship." Choice, not biology, made a *familia*.

Since so much of the Romans' attitude toward human life seems foreign, perhaps it's not strange to discover their families feel foreign as well (except by comparing them with Southern plantation owners who might sentimentalize their extended enslaved "family"). What *is* strange is discovering that the Romans' idea that "family" meant everyone under one roof, biologically related or not, lasted until the eighteenth century's end.

Historians and anthropologists frankly throw up their hands and admit they can't define "family" in a way that works universally. "Before the eighteenth century no European language had a term for the mother-father-children group," one pair of historians writes, mainly because that grouping—although widespread—wasn't important enough to need its own word. A 1287 Bologna statute defined "family" to include a father, mother, brothers, sisters, and daughters-in-law (sons brought home their wives), but Italy was an exception. For Northern and Western Europe, the extended family is a myth. New-marrieds almost always launched their own households—if their parents signed over the farm, the contract often included a clause insisting that the old folks must be built their own separate dwelling—and socialized as much or more with neighbors and work partners as with kin. Rather, the European family, like the Roman, included people we'd consider legal strangers: they were grouped together in that word "family" not by blood but by whether they lived under one roof. "Most households included non-kin inmates, sojourners, boarders or lodgers occupying rooms vacated by children or kin, as well as indentured apprentices and resident servants, employed either for domestic work about the house or as an additional resident labour force for the field or shop," writes historian Lawrence Stone of the British between 1500 and 1800. "This composite group was confusingly known as a 'family.'" A baker might have a family of a dozen or fifteen, including four journeymen, two apprentices, two maidservants, and three or four bio-children, all of whom worked, lived, and ate under his roof, at his table, and by his rules. A baronet might have a family of thirty-seven, including seven daughters and twenty-eight servants. Or was that ten daughters and twenty-five servants? Historians grind their teeth as they try to

figure out from church, census, and tax records which "menser-
vants" and "maids" were children, stepchildren, or nephews and
which were hired labor. Children, apprentices, servants—all were
under the master's rule. In other words, until very recently, not
love, not biology, but labor made a family.

Sometimes, of course, that family's labor was less than voluntary. As Africans crossed the ocean into slavery, they often created
"uncle" and "aunthood" amongst shipmates. Those new-hatched
kinship links were taken so seriously that they were taught to the
children—and even, as much as possible, to the masters—by insisting that a particular woman or man be respected as "Aunt" or
"Uncle," with all the attendant obligations.

While it might seem strange to see hired or enslaved or indentured labor called "family"—not just patronizing but actually
meaningless—it makes more sense when you remember that children, whether bio- or borrowed, were laborers. By age four, a child
might be minding the infants; by age six he or she was herding
geese, fishing, gathering firewood, drawing water, doing laundry,
sieving flour, carrying goods to market, and so on. That might be at
home—or it might not. Depending on era and region, a late medieval or early modern British or French or Swiss middle- or upper-
class man indentured or "fostered out" his children—at age six or
eight or ten or, at the very latest, twelve—as servants or apprentices
in other families. Just as regularly, he took relatives' or friends' or
neighbors' children to be servants or apprentices or pages in his
own. Aristocrats, shopkeepers, artisans, lawyers, butchers, black-
smiths: everyone did it, however rich or poor. The custom seems
to have hung on longer in Britain than on the Continent. One
sixteenth-century Italian traveler wrote,

> The want of affection in the English is strongly manifested to-
> wards their children . . . at the age of seven or nine years at the ut-
> most, they put them out, both males and females, to hard service
> in the houses of other people . . . and few are born who are ex-
> empted from this fate, for everyone, however rich he may be,
> sends away his children in to the houses of others, whilst he, in re-

> turn, receives those of strangers into his own. And on enquiring
> the reason for the severity, they answered that they did it in order
> that their children might learn better manners.

No good father wanted to see his child morally warped by his own,
or his wife's, over-tender affections.

But children didn't leave their parents only at seven or eight;
they often *started* life with "strangers." Until the eighteenth century, in a startling number of Western societies, regions, and eras,
infants and toddlers—except those of the extremely poor—were
sent off to wetnurses miles away on a farm or hidden in the man-
or's back halls, despite (or because of?) the fact that wetnursed children died at a much higher rate. Among Tuscan pre-Renaissance
householders, for instance, three out of four children spent their
first months away from their families—more than half until they
were eighteen months old. Not always, not everywhere, but often enough that, for centuries, the Catholic Church inveighed vehemently against wetnursing—to the point of commissioning
Madonna-and-child paintings as propaganda, one historian believes.

In other words, a child might well live with her own parents only
from age two to age nine, making Mom and Dad just one stop in
her peripatetic family life. And why not? In some ways, which
"family" you lived with didn't matter, since you were always under
someone's authority: you had no local social or political power until you ruled a household yourself. That throws new light on the
word "patronizing": whether your patron or *pater*, the master was
equally able to rule and condescend to you. The difference between
servitude for an upper-class youngster and servitude for everyone
else: the young male aristocrat knew someday he'd be in command. In the baker's or tanner's or husbandman (farmer)'s "family," sons, daughters, apprentices, maidservants, and journeymen
might someday hope to be master or mistress themselves—but
only if they made enough money to marry and found a "family"
themselves. What's different in our own time: today's young people feel free to marry *before* they've finished their apprenticeships

and saved a down payment on a house, whether via medical school or working a UPS route. We get sex and companionship comparatively young; but (except for that blip downward in the 1950s, when making a living was startlingly easy) most of us who believe that our futures can be prosperous wait until we're financially settled before we start making babies.

But the household merry-go-round was not as orderly as those descriptions imply. Often, children spilled into a new family because they lost their own. Even if you and your brother were the two out of three children who lived to adulthood, you probably didn't get there with two parents—either because of desertion, plague, famine, flu, fever, childbirth, or accident. "Less than half of the children who reached adulthood did so while both their parents were alive," explains Lawrence Stone. Marriages lasted, on average, seventeen to twenty-two years, depending on region and century—which is how long my own parents' marriage lasted (a pretty good run when you realize they raced down the aisle at barely twenty-one and twenty-four during the 1950s marriage madness, each a significant five years younger than Europe's historic norms).

Although I was nineteen and off in college when my parents split, my baby sister was only six—and therefore grew up in a stepfamily, making her upbringing more "traditional" than mine. Since Roman aristocrats divorced at will and children always stayed with their fathers—who sometimes sent the kids home to be raised by granddad—most Roman upper-class children grew up alongside step- and half-sibs and cousins, in addition to semi-acknowledged half-sibs born to their father's masters/slaves. At the end of the seventeenth century, 50 percent of all French children had lived with a stepparent at some time in their lives. Roughly a quarter of all British premodern families included stepchildren, or at the very least, orphaned or abandoned nephews and nieces. That's quite a bit more than the 11.3 percent of American children who lived in stepfamilies in 1990. Remarriage was often the time to "foster out" or indenture the first marriage's children, in contracts binding for roughly seven years. Some children did spend their entire early lives with one biological mother and one biological father—but that was not as common as it is today.

Today's families, historians note over and over, are vastly more stable than their predecessors, however defined. To put it another way, children today spend twice as many years with their bio-families than they did in the past. One historian suggests it's no wonder far more murders happen within the family today (only 8 percent of fourteenth-century Britain's homicides were between family members, while today's proportions are 53 percent in Britain and 30 percent in the United States). You have to feel pretty strongly to kill someone—and perhaps the earlier versions of the "family" weren't confined tightly enough to cause our era's nuclear explosions.

In 1996, *Christianity Today* called Gary Bauer, president of the Family Research Council, a "defender of the two-parent family and other radical ideas." The "radical" tag, surely intended as an ironic comment on today's morals, turns out to be historically accurate. In fact, the nuclear family has so recently become the standard household unit that U.S. demographers can't accurately track it before 1940. Bauer and his ideological kin want the definition of "family" to remain static at the recently-minted sense of "people related by blood, marriage, or adoption." But why should the rest of us pay attention to his prescription? The adaptable human young have throughout history managed to grow into successful adulthood under the tutelage of wetnurses, tutors, godparents, stepparents, nannies, uncles, neighbors, masters, lords—whichever version the ever-vanishing family happens to take in a given lifetime, region, and class. We might, however, want to be wary of the tightly confined stationwagon version, which did leave an awful lot of people carsick (or rather, depressed, addicted, eating-disordered) before many women and children burst out of it, gasping for air.

Despite this century's uprush in family stability, the 1930s, 1940s, and 1950s—like our own time—saw a flood of writing about the family's imminent death. As one pair of historians recently wrote about Scandinavia, which today has (as it has had historically) the highest rate of cohabitation and unmarried births, "The irony remains, however, that during the whole period of the 'death throes of the family,' the family continued to prosper. Although we can nowadays establish that the intellectuals were wrong, they were no less anxious about the . . . fall in the birth rate, relaxed divorce laws and premarital sexual relations, etc. What they forgot, however, is that the family is not a thing but a network of human relations, which survive even when their forms change."

What Do We Do about Those Little Bastards?

Among the many places we can see change in family forms is in the changing meaning of the word "bastard." Keeping parents tied to their children—and ensuring that people made only babies that they could and would feed, clothe, and rear responsibly—has always been one of society's key interests in "the family." And so, since marriage was the one and only way to be a fully functioning economic unit, societies urgently worked to confine parenthood within marriage—or to put it more clearly, if you were going to have a baby, you had to marry first. From Murphy Brown to Heather's two mommies to Madonna, this mandate has notoriously collapsed—giving rise to a great deal of political hand-wringing. Not surprisingly, during today's boom in independent motherhood, we may use "bastard" as a bad word meaning an especially bad person—but we no longer use it to mean someone stuck permanently in an outcast (or rather, under-caste) status because of his parents' premarital sex. When and why did that stop being so sternly enforced? What has made possible today's unrepentant and unpunished surge in mom-only childrearing? Have we fallen from a moral order in which virginal brides-in-white patiently awaited their wombs' owners to a moral chaos in which loose women employ their wombs with dangerous recklessness—or have economic changes altered mother- and fatherhood, making the two parents far more equivalent? In other words, inside the book's title question lurks yet another one: what is "legitimacy" for?

Bastardy really did once bar you from your class or caste, from the property and status and possibilities you'd have had if your parents had married. And yet European history teems with a lot more bastards—and a lot more brides preggers at the altar—than most of us would suspect. Or does it? How do you know which child's a bastard and which one's legitimate—or to put it differently, who counts as married? The answer depends on who's counting, and why. Different groups answered that question differently, based on their own worries—worries unrelated to today's psychological concerns about children needing to know their two biological parents.

For ruling classes, the worry was: Can that baby claim my property or power? Almost everyone else was asking: Who's gonna pay for that baby? Among Greek citizens, that first question was a stern one. They wanted to be absolutely sure each new citizen was properly conceived, that he had two citizen-grandfathers who fully approved of sending property and status his way, that no concubine's bastard claimed political or inheritance rights. This concern, shared by the British aristocracy, was put with admirable clarity by Samuel Johnson: "Consider of what importance to society the chastity of women is. Upon that all the property in the world depends. We hang a thief for stealing a sheep, but the unchastity of woman transfers sheep, and farm, and all from the right owner." Besides worrying about wives or daughters who foolishly believed their bodies to be their own, a British aristocrat wanted protection in case some kitchen maid insisted that his philandering (or rapist) son must marry her and legitimate their baby. British jurist William Blackstone wrote that to allow children to be legitimized by their parents' later marriage "is plainly a great discouragement to the matrimonial state; to which one main inducement is usually not only the desire of having *children,* but also of procreating lawful heirs." Clearly that's what the British aristocracy thought marriage was for. As a result, in British law a bastard was *fillius nullius,* literally, the child of no one. No one was obliged to care for her: she could not legally demand food, clothing, housing, or inheritance. In practice, that wasn't much different from the Greeks and Romans who "exposed" or abandoned any child they didn't want. Across medieval and early modern Europe, from 68 to 91 percent of infants sent to foundling hospitals died before they reached age six—and foundlings' death rates actually went *up* in the eighteenth century. And even if the bastards managed to make it to adulthood, their parents had guaranteed them a harder life than usual for a child from their class: premodern aristocracies wouldn't or couldn't pass them a full inheritance, while German guilds refused membership to any child who could not prove "honest birth."

Fillius nullius, of course, meant the most to aristocratic men who wanted to protect their property from the consequences of their brothel-going. Everyone else worried more that the child would, in their language, "fall to the parish." Except for the period when the early Protestants were actively policing souls (whipping fornicators or putting them in the stocks, even if the fallen pair was engaged), medieval and early modern European societies worried less about preventing sin than about controlling costs. Priests trying to convert the Irish complained that mothers didn't think an unmarried daughter's pregnancy was as bad as, say, theft. The French and Germans had a category called "mantle children"— children who were made legitimate by being held under a mantle during their mother's subsequent wedding (not necessarily to the biological father).

Of course, individual interests were always at stake in deciding who was a bastard and who was legitimate. One fourteenth-century English peasant tried to bastardize his older brother "because he was born before the marriage was solemnized at the church porch, but after the plighting of troth privately between them. Robert, the elder brother, says it is the custom on the lord's land in these parts for the elder brother, born after trothplight, to be heir." The peasant jury agreed with Robert—endorsing the idea that a working couple's bodies were their own. Had the brothers been an aristocrat's sons, Robert would have been out on his ear. In just the same way, the Anglican Church was more interested in a child's and her mother's souls than in inheritance rights—and so decreed that a child was legitimate so long as her mother married, no matter when (or, for that matter, whom). Since the child was then considered legit ecclesiastically but illegit civilly, her condition was called "special bastardy." Robert's parents certainly behaved as many of my friends have: living together and having kids before bothering to make things formal. Unlike today's pundits, the peasant jury was *not* shocked; they saw it as customary. The local Church was more concerned that the mother get married to someone, anyone, using her children's legitimacy as a kind of carrot to urge her into wedlock, than it was with punishing their slippage.

So were your parents acceptably coupled or illegally fornicating? Once again, the answer depended on who you asked.

And so who can be surprised that Robert's semi-bastard status was shared by a great many people? In late sixteenth-century England, for instance, one out of three first babies were conceived before—not after—the wedding. That dropped to one out of six in the late seventeenth century, when Puritans were strictly enforcing marriage's boundaries, but bounced back up to one in three at the nineteenth century's end. In postcolonial North America, the number of women whose first children were born soon after marriage was one in three in 1800; this percentage dipped slightly in the Victorian era and spiked back up to one in four by 1910.

What can such numbers mean? In large part, it means that "marriage" was a less formal concept in the past than today. Scandinavians especially disliked the idea that any institution, church or state, had to authorize or bless a pairing, and so often didn't hold the wedding until after the child was born—making the wedding a celebration not just of the pairing but of their fruitfulness. (In other words, Scandinavians' current unmarried birthrates—roughly one out of two, the highest in the developed world—are the result *not* of recent social policies but of stubbornly private traditions). Meanwhile, in most communities the gap between first pledge and final vows—between betrothal and wedding—was a kind of marriage twilight in which the couple was neither exactly married nor exactly single. The engaged pair might well live together under one roof: in early medieval Jewish families, for instance, the prospective groom moved in with his promised bride's family while he got his financial footing, while in many Italian city-states, the bride-to-be was sent to grow up in her future husband's household—at age five, or eight, or ten. Even the northern medieval peasants, the young people who, after saving up a marriage "portion," were finally ready to pick themselves a spouse, often did so via some hanky-panky; they might even wait to see if they were fertile before they got formal. In other words, today's apparently startling habit of getting married only after you're pregnant, or even with your children gathered round, is actually quite traditional. What's more, all these "bridal pregnancies" (as social historians delicately phrase it), trothplight babies, and mantle children reveal that marriage has never been a simple either/or question. Rather, marriage's boundaries are blurry. And exactly what counts as marriage, when, changes according to whose interests are at stake.

So how many children were born entirely outside wedlock—or to put it differently, how many were real bastards? To figure that out from the demographic records, historians have to figure out how to define a marriage—which they wrestle with for pages upon pages. One key social historian, Peter Laslett, throws up his hands and concludes that whatever the local community counted as a "regular union" was—although by that measure, you'd have to include my heterosexual friends who've lived together for sixteen years and are treated as coupled by employers, banks, hospitals, friends, and family (although not insurers or tax law). Across the ocean, Americans hated to bastardize a child (partly for democratic reasons, rejecting the aristocratic British insistence on primogeniture and lineage), and so colonial judges and state legislators temporarily invented "common law marriage"—a form that was widely accepted during the nineteenth century and then outlawed by most states in the twentieth; it exists today in only thirteen states. "If two parties, living together, speak of each other as husband and wife, this public acknowledgment is all that is requisite to constitute their relation in the eyes of the law a perfectly valid marriage," one nineteenth-century legal commentator explained to his audience, *"yet children born from such a union and legitimate in New York, are counted as bastards by every nation of Europe."* Bastardy—in other words, marriage—lies in the eyes (or nation, or class) of the beholder.

For the same reason that most European communities and authorities were willing to legitimate a child *post hoc*—because once the mother married there was a husband helping to feed and house that child—most early modern European law codes made it almost impossible for a husband to bastardize his wife's child. Even if you gave birth three years after your husband had left on a long sea voyage, even if when he finally got back your village held a *charivari* (parading you both on donkeys while jeering and flinging mudballs and maybe covering you with honey to attract stinging insects) to shame you for being a whore and him for being a cuckold—even then, in local law, your husband was your child's father. Period. Somebody had to support that baby, and that somebody was your Mr.—unless he exercised his traditional veto by disappearing.

So what? Why should societies care about children born outside marriage at all? Why not just let women have babies whenever they want? Why pressure men into marriage?

Every historian, anthropologist, or sociologist who writes about bastards mentions anthropologist Bronislaw Malinowski's "principle of legitimacy": the idea that each child must have a "sociological father"—not necessarily the genetic dad—willing to be "guardian and protector, the male link between the child and the rest of the community." In some societies that man is the maternal uncle. In some, it can be a dead man, as when early Hebrew societies charged men with marrying a brother's childless widow and begetting and rearing a child who carries the brother's name. (Onan's famous sin came when he pulled back from this obligatory duty.) In one well-known New Testament family, that man was Joseph, through whom Mary's miraculously conceived son claims descent from King David (or has it claimed for him by his followers). In most modern law codes, it's still the mother's husband, even if (as in one famous U.S. case, *Michael H v. Gerald D*) everyone knows the child was conceived during an adulterous affair, or even if the child was made with the help of a doctor and an anonymous stranger's sperm. According to Malinowski, by punishing anyone who doesn't follow the rule of il/legitimacy, a society ensures it won't have too many mouths to feed.

From this point of view, what is marriage for? Discouraging overbreeding—first, by insisting that each child be assigned to a working wallet, and second, by punishing children not so assigned via abandonment, disdain, and poverty.

This makes sense when your income and status—whether a landed barony or guild membership or tenant plot—must be inherited from some man, because men, and only men, control all resources, financial, social, and political. Or to put it in terms that Samuel Johnson and William Blackstone would understand: if children matter to men because men want and need heirs, then fathers matter to children because children need property and status. Legitimacy is less urgent when each person forges his or her own future from his or her own efforts—whether that's in our frontier past or our capitalist present.

So what happens when a woman can make her own living, passing on property, skills, and status? Shouldn't, then, a mother be able to assign another woman as her child's sociological "father"? To put it simply: if a dead man, or an uncle, or an absent cuckold, or a holy ghost, or a sperm-bank-supplemented husband can be a sociological "father," why can't I?

Will the "Real" Parent Please Stand Up: Mother, Father, Other?

Who's the real parent? Today, some commentators insist that children wither unless they have their biomoms and biodads right there under the same roof; a divorced fathers' lobby bemoans a prejudice toward mother-custody; and many opponents of same-sex marriage recoil from the thought that two moms or two dads might be entrusted with a child. Given their ever-fluctuating family structures, how did our forebears assign a child when there was a divorce, death, or some other dispute? What is it—biology or responsibility, nature or nurture—that makes a person into a *parent?*

Not surprisingly, Western public and legal philosophies over who rightly had charge of a child are as foreign as everything else about our ancestors' families. Among the Romans, for instance, a child always belonged to his father. The Romans had almost a cult of motherlessness: their founding myth of Romulus and Remus includes abandoned twin boys suckled by a she-wolf instead of a human mother. In fact, if not rejected and left out to die, a son of the aristocracy was suckled not by wolves but by wetnurses—to ensure he wouldn't be emotionally weakened by his attachment to his mother. Even when his parents stayed married, they didn't necessarily share a room or even a living area, and so a son might well be quickly moved out of his mother's pavilion to guard against effeminacy. Both boys and girls were assigned a wet and a dry nurse, and then a *paedagogue* or tutor, who together with their father oversaw their upbringing; the tutor, according to one historian, had a tighter bond with and more influence over the child than did the mother. A girl was married off between ages twelve and twenty, but could always come home to Dad. Divorced mothers could still have some relationship with their children—some even left them property in their wills—but could never be guardians. Women weren't full moral beings: only a man could be a legal parent.

Europe and its Western colonies followed the Romans' lead, taking for granted that a child's guardian was his or her father. In the Italian city-states, for instance, it was a father's responsibility to choose a wetnurse and direct a child's education. When Luther, Calvin, and other Protestants launched their campaigns, they aimed their childrearing advice at the male patriarch—whether fathers or masters. Enlightenment writers worried about a child's rearing also talked to fathers, as when John Locke's 1693 treatise advised, "Be sure then to establish the authority of a father, as soon as [your son] is capable of submission, and can understand in whose power he is." Women—being oversexed and undermoral— were scarcely responsible enough to oversee a child's upbringing.

That a child "naturally" belonged to its father was so obvious as to need no gloss in English law. Lord William Blackstone, who in the eighteenth century consolidated and passed on British common law, noted simply that the father had a natural right to his children, while a mother "was entitled to no power but only to reverence and respect." (Ouch.) But of course: a woman couldn't own property, and a child was, above all, productive property. "An orphan in colonial America was defined as a child whose father had died, even if the child had a surviving mother," writes legal historian Mary Ann Mason. Which is not to say that a child was thought to require the presence of his or her bio-father: Dad naturally had the right to assign out his child's labor, including, of course, those of his slave "children." (Since a black slave, according to white law, had no father, his owner was considered his sociological "father.")

And that's how things stood for centuries, until in the nineteenth century remunerative work was vacuumed out of the house and middle- and upper-class children were confined inside it. As men of those top-tier classes marched out to pursue their professions, money, and status all on their own, leaving behind the women who'd once been their economic partners, how were those children—no longer useful as labor, not in the brave new worlds of commerce and corporations—to be reared? And what were those women to do?

The answer: turn women into Mothers, a word that soon had a halo over it—at least, for women in the race and classes deemed worthy of heaven. In the late eighteenth century, all those child-rearing manuals that had been aimed at fathers or "parents" started talking only to moms, with titles like "The Mother's Book: to American Mothers, on whose intelligence and discretion the safety and prosperity of our republic so much depend." As one women's magazine wrote in 1842, "Well may we exclaim THE MOTHER! Oh the significance of the word!" Bereft of all her other duties, Mom was newly exalted as the only right moral guide and "natural" nurturer.

As judges began to absorb these ideals of the Holy Mother and—slowly and agonizingly—started to hand children over to women, they had to strain mightily to justify their radical new doctrines. In 1774, the first time a British court overrode Blackstone and gave custody to a mother rather than a father, it went through logical gymnastics to explain how it could do so "notwithstanding the father's natural right." As American judges began to do the same, they dragged in the Holy Motherhood rhetoric, as when one 1840s Pennsylvania court wrote that its "denial of the father's right" was because a mother's attention "is prompted by deeper and holier feelings than the most liberal allowance of a nurse's wages could possibly stimulate."

Deeper? Holier? Feelings? These shockingly new sentiments—since when had *feelings* been a reason to assign custody?—sounded a battle cry for an ideological war that was being waged across the century. Traditionalists were appalled as the Holy Motherhood ideal was announced in one court after another, appalled that judges were brazenly changing an ancient law in ways that, today, would be called "legislating from the bench." One Mississippi traditionalist judge harrumphed sternly, "We are informed by the first elementary books that we read, that the authority of the father is superior to that of the mother. It is the doctrine of *all civilized nations*. It is according to the revealed law, and the law of nature." An anonymous Massachusetts writer accused the groundbreaking judges of "nothing less than an assumption of power . . . to determine the domestic arrangements of a man's family." Clearly, those nasty old courts have long been out to destroy the family, in the nineteenth century as well as in our own time.

At stake in both battles was the idea of equality of the sexes: could a woman, like a man, have charge of that valuable property, her children? Not as far as legislators were concerned, no matter what those brazen judges might say. When women proposed laws allowing mother-custody, legislators objected that such a move would "weaken the ties of marriage by forcing both sexes into an unnatural antagonism; teaching them to be independent of one another, and to earn their own living apart; whereas God's law points to the family and the mutual intercourse of man and woman as among the strongest safeguards of human happiness."

One 1910 feminist scathingly characterized the California legisla-ture's response this way: "If women had the guardianship of their children, would anything prevent them from taking the children and leaving home? What would become of the sanctity of the home, with its lawful head shorn of his paternal legitimacy?" Would a man be a man if he didn't own his kids? If women had rights over their children, mightn't they pack up the kids and hop on the next train?

But with the shift in the West from a farm economy to an indus-trial economy—soon limned by child labor laws—children were no longer seen as productive labor, especially for the classes who wrote and administered the laws. It's no coincidence, legal scholar Mary Ann Glendon comments, that just as children became an economic burden rather than a profitable asset, mother-love beat father-right for custody of the child.

And so mother-custody got written into laws and legal textbooks in language that made mother-custody sound not like a radical innovation but an eternal verity: "The love of the mother for her child, regardless of conditions and environments, has been proven by the history of the ages ... [while] the tie between father and child is a different matter, and requires the strong arm of the law to regulate it with some degree of humanity and tenderness for the child's good." But the key phrase in that sentence is not "mother"—it's *the strong arm of the law.* Not Mom, not Dad, but the State won the battle for control of child custody. Mothers got their children only if male judges decided they were good chaste women who'd been unjustly abandoned by deserting or adulterous or dead men. If judges decided you were a willful hussy brazenly escaping lawful husbandly authority, Dad got the kids. And so the State began making its Solomonic decisions with a newly invented idea: the best interests of the child.

After 150 years of hearing that phrase "the best interests of the child," it's hard to grasp what an original idea it was. Families were coming, in many minds, to be based not on property but on per-sonality, not on lineage but on love. Yes, of course, the relations of spouses, parents, children, and siblings had always been charged with love and hatred, affection and anger, competition and kindness. But love had not been the main axis on which the family rotated; love was consequence, not cause, of family life. By the nineteenth century's end, the family had been reinvented as the cradle of personality, that new and precious commodity on the postindustrial market. Can it be any surprise that—as emotions newly moved to the family's center—the nineteenth century was when adoption as we know it was invented?

Yes, invented. Which is not to say that children weren't transferred from hand to hand in various ways over the millennia, whether abandoned and taken in in ancient times or indentured and fostered out throughout much of European history. But taking in a child who could be an heir or putting a child to productive use are hardly the purposes we think of for modern adoption. Adoption as we know it has far more to do with family affections—and so was an innovation as feelings took center stage.

Greek and Roman adoption didn't sever biological ties: your mother was still your mother and you stayed in touch with your bio-father—who "gave" you in adoption the way he "gave" a daughter in marriage. Ancient adoption's purpose was to ensure that an older man could pass on his family name and to offer a young man a chance at a brilliant career under the tutelage of a new father/patron. The Christians disliked adoption's goals of transferring power, property, and pagan family worship; besides, adoption might accidentally drag a child away from the bosom of the Church—so it's no wonder Christianity tossed out adoption law. In premodern British common law, formal adoption was an equally abhorrent concept, although for different reasons. As you'd expect from its attitude toward "mantle children," and from Jane Austen's books in which daughters must move out of the estate to make way for the entailed male heir, British law sneered at the idea that inheritance could be voluntarily transferred. The famous thirteenth-century statement by Glanville rang down for centuries: "Only God can make an heres [heir], not man"—and not man's law. Affections did *not* transfer property, and property was the point of parentage.

At least, for the upper classes. For the working folks, the concern was that every child be put to productive use. Once a dad had signed away his child, contract was the pressing issue—not psychology. There was no insistence that a child needed his bioparents, no matter how heartsick that left him. "A Plymouth court severely rebuked parents whose five-year-old son frequently wandered home," Mason writes, "and ordered that if the parents 'do receive him, if he shall again [depart] from his said master without his lycense, that the said Frances, and Chrisian his Wyfe, shall be sett in the stocks . . . as often as he or shee shall so receive him.'" "Family" may always have included emotional ties, even if its members were not biologically linked, but if a family was defined by labor, then of course a work contract was your way into and out of a family. Society and the law dealt with family relations in the language of contract—just as, if tomorrow you were fired from your job, judges would scoff if you claimed a right to your officemates' conversation and affection.

But as Western families began to be seen less and less as work/discipline units and more and more as nests for malleable hearts and minds—as, in other words, parents came to be regarded not as owners but as nurturers—courts and legislatures started looking differently at children. Not only mothers but also concerned others got the benefit of that strange new judicial phrase, "the best interests of the child." The new ideology came in peculiar fits and starts. One early nineteenth-century father left his daughter with her grandparents and then tried to reclaim her—thirteen years later. Too late! The judge's gavel decided that he had "surrendered his rights over the child, by a tacit understanding . . . allowed the affections on both sides to become engaged in a manner he could not but have anticipated . . . [and] permitted a state of things to arise, which cannot be altered without risking the happiness and interest of his child. . . . It is an obvious fact that, ties of blood weaken, and ties of companionship strengthen, by lapse of time."

But of course, judges were merely aligning case law with their era's social beliefs. State legislatures soon followed. In 1851 the Massachusetts legislature passed a statute allowing full adoption.

This new statute—the first of its kind—formalized society's new attitude toward placing a child in a new family. The new law invented a completely new social fiction: a child was to be raised in her new family as if it were her "natural" one—not simply one stop on her picaresque sojourn into adulthood. For the first time, all ties to her old kin were cut, in deference to her own and her parents' feelings. For the first time, a child was moved not because another family needed her labor, not because her widowed father needed a respite or her mother needed income from her domestic service, but because the new parents *would be better for the child.*

You have to pause to see how radical a change this is: the child's feelings, theoretically at least, are being put before the adults' interests. Apprenticeship and fostering-out had been perfectly good methods of providing a child with everything practical: meals, shelter, clothes, discipline, training. But those practicalities weren't enough for an era when children—white ones, at least—were thought to need nurture and love. The family was being turned upside down: no longer first were the child's duties to obey and honor the parents; now on top were the parents' duties to love and nurture the child.

Perhaps even more radical, people were insisting that *affection* was what made a "real" family—a concept that courts and observers couldn't always swallow. One critic of Massachusetts' statute was puzzled—in language that sounds like the language used about IVF today—by the fact that adoption was "irrevocable": if the child didn't turn out well, how were the adopting parents to get rid of him? Wasn't it bizarre, even unnatural, that "the spinster of eighty may rear a thriving family, to inherit at her death"? And so courts kept putting limits on this radical new social fiction. Courts in Pennsylvania, Texas, and elsewhere sometimes disinherited the adoptees after the adopting parent died, in opinions that said, essentially, "Maybe this guy was kind enough to take in this child, but kindness doesn't transfer property." Or they made adopted children pay an extra "collateral inheritance" tax, which blood children did not have to pay (just as Madeline would have to pay more inheritance tax if I were to die). As one court wrote, "why should

... property be subjected to such an unnatural course of descent ... [and] pass into the hands of an alien"? How could the law enforce such unnatural relationships, for such a flimsy reason as *love*?

Adoption simply seemed too unnatural for some nineteenth-century courts to take entirely seriously. And perhaps they were right to worry: once affection, not blood or labor, is what makes a family, all kinds of radical shifts follow—like same-sex couples looking to marry and raise kids.

And yet today we take for granted both mother-custody and adoption, those contested innovations. Even Britain—where lineage had long reigned in the law, where only blood could transfer property—came into the modern era and passed an adoption law in 1926. By the 1970s, custody decisions were being made on an innovative concept called "psychological parenthood": parenthood based not on blood ties but "on day-to-day interaction, companionship, and shared experiences," a role that could never be taken "by an absent, inactive adult, whatever his biological or legal relationship to the child may be." The new concept of the family—the companionate family based on emotional ties, based not on duty but on choice—has so fully triumphed that today even adoption seems "traditional." In other words, despite some of the language being floated in today's family debates, the idea that love makes a family won the battle a century ago—when adoption was invented and mother-custody shoved aside the father's absolute right. Society then decided that nurture and care, affection and attention defined a "real" parent.

So what is parenthood for? If it's for offering a child sturdy and stable affection, two people of one sex will serve.

Why Have Kids?

Adoption was in many ways the flip side of contraception: if you can choose *not* to have a child when you *don't* want one, shouldn't you be able to *choose* to have one when you do? As the 1930s saw its wave of writing about, to quote one famous book title, *The Mar-*

riage Crisis, everyone agreed that "the family, long supposed to be the best anchored of all social institutions, appears at last to have broken from its moorings." While publications, pundits, preachers, and politicians shouted at each other about whether this was good or bad and what it meant for the future, everyone agreed on at least two culprits: woman's emancipation and contraception had overturned all the rules.

The critics had things backwards, just as they do now. Because the economic rules had changed, both women and men felt they should be able to learn and work according to their inclinations, and felt equally free to enjoy their sex lives, try to control their childbearing, and create families as desired. And that meant, strikingly, a new rhetoric about childrearing. Affection replaced duty at both ends of the bond: just as children were with parents not to obey but to be loved, so also parents were to have children not out of duty but love. The Roman law that penalized men who hadn't married and made a minimum number of babies by age thirty; the Jewish rabbis who debated the minimum number of children required to fulfill the biblical injunction to "be fruitful and multiply"; Puritan childrearing tracts enjoining fathers to oversee their children's catechisms: all were full of the same childrearing ideal that it is a man's duty to rear children to be good members of society. Affection had formerly been not a requirement but a bonus. As late as 1926 one *Atlantic Monthly* writer was insisting on the traditional idea that limiting the number of children in your family was "distinctly antisocial, for it enables selfish people to escape their responsibility, ultimately to their own detriment and to the injury of the State."

But soon parenthood was urged almost entirely for the emotional rewards, sometimes in language that sounds like the worst 1970s personal development goo. "A little child is a strongly-uniting bond between husband and wife," sentimentalized one London minister in 1899. A 1925 writer, Paul Popenoe, launched into the psychological age with the biggest rhetorical rockets he could find: "From their offspring the parents derive tremendous advantages that they can get *in no other way.* Man's personality and character (as well as woman's) is an incomplete—hopelessly and pathetically incomplete—thing unless it has included the joys, and the occasional sorrows, of bringing up a family of children."

Parenthood is, of course, an astonishing (and exhausting) thing. But what's more astonishing is that parenthood was being sold by these inner benefits—as a chosen personal experience, not as an inevitable responsibility. As society headed for the twentieth century's end, that rhetoric almost entirely swept the field. The idea that children—like marriage—are a choice, not an inevitable necessity, showed up in book titles like this 1981 volume: *The Baby Decision: How to Make the Most Important Choice of Your Life.* "Which way happiness?" one chapter of *The Baby Decision* asked. "For some couples, children are a necessary ingredient; for others, they would simply spoil the broth." The ideas behind the invention of adoption, behind *The Baby Decision,* and behind all assisted conception services were precisely the same ideas that led to 1985's *Considering Parenthood: A Workbook for Lesbians*—and the lesbian (and, later, gay) baby boom to which that book responded. If the purpose of parenthood is the parent's emotional development— if parenthood is a once-in-a-lifetime chance to revisit childhood playfulness, to love more than you knew was possible, to mature through heartwrenching challenges and joys—why *shouldn't* people have children the way they get married: for love alone? And why should biology stand in the way?

The philosophy behind today's new reproductive technologies—donor insemination, in vitro fertilization, egg donation, and more—are in many ways the philosophies behind both contraception and adoption. To choose to have a child because you want family love is a dramatic shift from the older assumption that a child is both your sexual fate and potentially remunerative labor. The transition to our current era—in which most middle-class folks know at least one family where the new reproductive technologies have helped bring the children to life—did not occur easily. Our society's ethical and legal anxieties today circle around complicated possibilities like surrogacy, or fertilization with borrowed eggs *and* sperm, a kind of pre-birth adoption, so that the child has a

womb-mother, a genetic mother, a genetic father, and a social father—only two of whom register publicly as parents. But even the
simplest of these technologies—donor insemination (DI), borrowing sperm—stirred a ruckus when it was first publicly proposed for married couples.

The question of whether DI was legitimate or not got to court because of the basic question that comes up in every age about children: who has the right and responsibility for a child's care? When
divorcing men insisted that they weren't their DI children's fathers, judges at first agreed that the wife had done something outrageous in conceiving another man's child. "The essence of adultery," wrote one Ontario judge in 1921, "consists, not in the moral
turpitude of the act of sexual intercourse, but . . . . introducing into
the family of the husband a false strain of blood." A 1954 Illinois
court agreed, saying that DI "is contrary to public policy and good
morals" and that DI children were "illegitimate." Some Catholic
theologians wanted to outlaw DI, even proposing jailing DI moms
and the doctors who were inseminating them. After all, some guy
was out there masturbating, and some other couple was having
fruitless sex, and babies were being begotten by strangers: the
world had wandered awfully far from "natural law."

But just as Catholicism lost on *contra*ception—keeping its ability to shake its fingers at its own followers, but losing the ability to
write its theology into law—so it lost on *assisted* conception. After
many years of debate, Western policymaking bodies finally concluded that DI was not, in fact, adultery—so long as the husband
agreed to what his wife was doing. Society's key concern had always
been: who's gonna pay for that child? Wrote one 1968 California
court, "One who consents to the production of a child . . . [has] an
obligation of supporting those for whose existence he is directly responsible." How, in other words, is this case different from any
other guy who made a baby and then tried to skip town? Once a
man agreed to be a dad—whether by having sex with a woman or
by signing papers at the fertility clinic—he'd brought a child into
the world and had to face up to it until the kid was an adult. *You
wanted it? Well, now it's yours.*

Why should the reasoning be any different if the second parent is a woman? According to the most recent statistics, one in eight heterosexual married couples is infertile; of those who pursue biological children anyway, most use donor insemination, as do parent-hopefuls who are both women. Arranging our reproductive and emotional lives by choice, whether through the Pill or petri dishes, donor insemination or cross-continental adoption, is now a social norm. Once feelings—the desire to parent—have been crowned as monarch of both marriage and family, the stage is set for lesbian and gay families. How can the hearts of two loving but infertile parent-hopefuls—even those infertile because they share the same sex—be refused?

> **Item:** Recently a woman in Oregon was running for state representative, accompanied by her pregnant partner. The couple was approached by a man in a conservative rural district. Pointing to the partner's swelling belly, he asked the candidate, "Are you responsible for that?" "Yes," she answered, steeling herself for his invective. "Then I'm voting for you," said the farmer. "If you can do that, you can do anything." The joke, of course, is how dryly he suggested the candidate had balls if she was willing to take on the world as a lesbian "dad."

Should Lesbians and Gay Men Be Parents?

It's one thing to suggest that a lesbian or gay male couple want children for the same reasons any of their contemporaries do—or even to suggest that a pair of same-sex parents fit the egalitarian, loving ideals by which we run contemporary (as opposed to, say, colonial mini-factory) families. But that's not necessarily reason enough for society to endorse us as parents. To many people, marriage is essentially a license to raise a family (albeit a license for which no one has to pass a test). Since the well-being of children is rightly of serious concern to any sensible society, the argument of last resort against same-sex marriage is often that kids need a mom and a dad.

In the cases pending in Hawaii and Vermont, one of the states' key arguments is that same-sex marriage would be bad for children. When the Scandinavian countries, the Netherlands, and most recently Catalonia opened civil registration to same-sex couples, they offered all the benefits of marriage but two: first, no church service, and second, no right to adopt or use assisted fertility services. And yet the Netherlands, Canada, and several Scandinavian countries are now opening parenthood to same-sex couples, while several American states—including Vermont—allow two parents of one sex to jointly adopt. Are they right to do so? To use the phrase that nineteenth-century American courts invented to fit their new Victorian families, can having two parents of one sex possibly promote "the best interests of the child"? That larger question breaks down into a series of smaller, complex questions—most of which are clues to social attitudes not about same-sex parents, but about something else entirely.

Don't children need fathers?   This is an incredibly hot social question—and when phrased like that, tremendously threatening. The viciousness of the battle over whether Heather should have two mommies is often a proxy for deeper cultural battles about men, women, and parenting. Does society really want to suggest to men that once they've spawned, they're vestigial as an appendix and may return to their wild bachelor lives (preferably, of course, remitting a monthly check)? If parents break up, should the mother automatically get custody, or do children require the involvement of both parents even when those parents are no longer married?

Usually—and rightly—the debate and data about whether kids need fathers centers on the unnerving trend of men abandoning their offspring, which has so clearly been shown to be destructive for many kids. For instance, children of divorce, when compared to children in undisrupted families, drop out of high school twice as often and have three times as many teenage pregnancies, two gross measures of misery that suggest many more subtle problems. I'll confess here to my bias: my siblings and I were so thrown by the deterioration and breakup of our parents' marriage that even today, whenever friends with kids tell me they're divorcing, I launch like the Ancient Mariner into an obnoxious lecture about protecting their children. But my bias may not entirely be accurate; researchers find that half of the "divorce effect" is actually not an effect of the divorce but of a bad marriage: if you look back through school records, boys' bad behavior and lousy math and reading scores come well *before* the parents split—which suggests that it's the bad marriage, as much as the divorce, that damages kids.

Since most Western children in the late twentieth century are left in the custody of their mothers, many commentators turn to post-divorce stats, and to stories like mine, to insist that children need their bio-fathers *and* bio-mothers. But asking how kids do after a divorce is *not* the same as asking whether kids need to grow up with parents of two sexes. When looking at the effects of divorce, how can you tell which of them have to do with abandonment, disruption, anger, and a sudden drop in income—most of which usually accompany divorce, at least temporarily? Kids of divorce have to live with parents who are furious at each other, whether out loud or silently. They may feel abandoned by a father who rarely calls (or with whom they have an awkward weekend relationship, which somehow upsets their mother). They may live in chaos for awhile, grabbing meals out of the fridge and searching fruitlessly for clean underwear, while their custodial parent succumbs to grief, or stays out dancing all night to prove she's still attractive, or tries to figure out how to work *and* get the kids to dentists' appointments. And they almost always live with a heightened and corrosive anxiety about who will pay for heat, orange juice, car repairs, and new shoes. Measuring the effects of a divorce, in other words, does *not* measure the effects of living without a father: it measures the effect of conflict, disruption, and loss. In fact, if what harmed kids was simply the loss of their biological father, then widows' children would do much worse than children of divorce—since someone under six feet of dirt is more definitively gone than someone who's moved to another address. But widows' children do vastly *better*, with, for instance, no more likelihood of dropping out of high school. Divorce stats, in other words, may tell us that having one parent ripped out of your life hurts (surprise!)—but they can't help us decide whether or not children need to start with both a male and a female parent.

Nor do stats on children of single mothers—who usually have higher dropout rates and more delinquency—necessarily point to the need for an XY-parent: as one *New York Times* article observed, "while an absent father might be the reason, so could poverty, or bad schools, or the lack of a family backup system, or something else altogether." In fact, when researchers control for money and the mother's age—i.e., if a single mother is no richer or poorer than a mom-and-dad pair, and if she isn't a teenager or is matched with other teenage moms—they find that a child raised without a dad can turn out just as well.

Until the 1970s, psychological researchers trying to understand how infants and children developed into successful adults focused almost entirely on mothers and their babies. With the women's movement, a host of mostly male researchers wanted to overcome that mother-bias and began trying to find out how, exactly, a dad's effect on a child is different than a mom's. Their surprised answer: it's not.

Which is not to say that fathers make no difference: two involved adults are better for a child than one. When children have mothers *and* fathers who are both very involved with them, their "separation distress"—that period that all parents dread, when toddlers scream at being left with a stranger—starts later and doesn't last as long. According to current psychological theory, that's a good sign that a child trusts his or her emotional bonds. But then, if the children have *more* than two adults to whom they're close (aunts, granddads, nannies), "separation distress" comes even later and lasts even less long. Having more "psychological" parents, in other words, is very helpful: the additional adult's sex or biological relationship is not necessarily what makes the difference.

Looking further, researchers found that infants did treat their parents differently, but the differences did not divide up by sex: rather, infants treated each parent as an individual, responding to individual temperaments. The Victorian hymns to the irreplaceability of "Mother," however politically convenient for keeping her home, were false.

One common belief is that children need fathers because real men help children develop strict consciences, show boys how to be men, and generally prevent delinquency—or to put it differently, children without fathers grow up to be rampantly destructive ids, stealing and getting pregnant and joining gangs and becoming social nightmares. But when researchers look closely, they find that what makes the difference is *not* simply having a male parent, but rather how involved and affectionate those fathers are. Which boys behave well? Boys with involved and affectionate fathers. Which boys become delinquents? Boys whose fathers neglect or ridicule them or are distant or travel a lot—especially boys with military fathers. Which boys rate more highly as "masculine" and identify more comfortably as men? Boys with warm and involved relationships with their fathers—*even if those fathers are not rated as very "masculine."* Which boys score lower on *feeling* masculine and make up for it by behaving in more stereotypical (i.e., aggressive) male ways? Boys whose fathers are missing *or* authoritarian *or* distant (especially those in the military)—but *not* boys whose fathers are *really* absent, i.e., dead. Meanwhile, having an affectionate, involved second parent does more than prevent male delinquency: it helps boys and girls in other ways as well. Which children do better in school, feel more in control of their lives, are more comfortable and confident socially, are more cheerful and take more initiative in school and in their lives? Children whose fathers are more involved—while children whose fathers hold back, or are authoritarian and "controlling," do *worse*.

But if an *affectionate* father helps, and a *nasty* or *distant* father hurts, then researchers still haven't discovered something essentially *male* that a child needs: they've simply discovered that children do better with closeness and reliability than with ridicule or rejection. Maybe children, especially boys, just do better when they have more than one parent who's affectionate and involved from birth. Maybe involved fathers are a sign of a happy household, a definite plus for any child. Maybe boys are more likely to obey the cultural model of manhood if they like the guy nearby—and to flout it if he's nasty. So how do you stop measuring the effects of having a good second parent, or having two stable and happily married parents, and start measuring the effects of having at least one parent who's *male*?

Are moms and dads different?   Researchers also try to measure differences in how mothers and fathers—*as* mothers and fathers—treat their children. The problem here is that what researchers measure is extremely culture-bound, since different groups—even today, within the West—actually hold opposite ideas about what makes a good father. For some, a good father brings home the bacon and holds himself as a distant moral authority, while in others, a good father shares both the financial responsibilities and the day-to-day diapering, listening and playing. (In just the same way, of course, what's considered "a good man" differs among groups, eras, and cultures.) As a result, differences in how fathers and mothers *behave* are even smaller and harder to generalize than the differences in their effects on children. For instance, some researchers find that fathers (Western, white, middle-class) talk in more complex language to their daughters, and mothers to their sons; but then other researchers find that mothers pay more attention to their daughters, and fathers to sons. All researchers find that fathers are much more likely than mothers to encourage their children, especially sons, to "play with sex-typed toys"— boys with trucks, girls with dolls—but then, some fathers *don't* chastise or hit their sons if they become enamored of, say, sewing. (The result here is that boys with fathers in the house tend to be more gender-stereotypical, and more hostile toward effeminacy, than boys whose fathers are away. Is that a *good* thing? Is it simply that Western fathers are trying to protect their sons from the hostility and violence they remember being directed at soft boys? Or— given that girls today have vastly more latitude than fathers would have given them a hundred years ago, and certainly more latitude than boys—is it a temporary blip as our culture shifts away from

strict gender-roles?) All researchers do find that, as a group, contemporary Western fathers spend less time with their children
than do mothers. But of course, since *some* fathers spend *more* time
with the kids than do *some* mothers, this doesn't tell us anything
about the elusive father-effect.

Researchers most consistently agree that Western fathers, besides seeing to it that their sons behave as boys should, spend a
higher proportion of their time with the kids playing than do
mothers; even if the mothers spend more *actual* time playing, it's a
smaller proportion of their time together, since mothers also do
most of the bathing, dressing, feeding, and so on. And when they
do play with the kids, most researchers agree, fathers "tended to
provide staccato bursts of both physical and social stimulation,
whereas mothers tended to be more rhythmic and containing." Fathers, in other words, toss their kids up in the air, or growl that
they're coming to get them, or play touch-football, making kids
squeal; moms hold and nurse and coo and listen thoughtfully.
Some theorists decide that *this,* then—this thrilling alternation of
fear and happiness, this more challenging and demanding play—
is how (good) fathers help children become more autonomous, socially skilled, willing to take on challenges, confident, and so on.
But is it? While researchers find this difference consistently between American and British dads and moms of various races and
ethnicities, they find *no* such difference between Swedish and Israeli kibbutz dads and moms, who play with the children equally.
If that staccato father-play is so distinctive and important, how
come the Israeli army is such an impressive fighting force and
Swedish society is so harmonious? Once again, researchers might
be discovering only that two parents are better than one—not that
male and *female* parents offer something distinctly different. In
fact, after offering pages and pages of the most minute data, one
father-researcher after another throws up his hands and concludes
that he cannot demonstrate specific effects from fathers as *fathers,*
not just as good people.

The lack of fundamental differences between fathers and mothers shows up in a most unlikely place: studies of postdivorce cus-

tody. Children in father-custody and children in mother-custody turn out equally well on every measure: self-esteem, maturity, independence, anxiety, behavior problems, psychosomatic complaints, and relationships (although teenage girls in father-custody were slightly more at risk for pregnancy—so much for father-discipline). Apparently neither Roman aristocrats, British common law, nor Victorian judges were right in suggesting that fathers/mothers were "naturally" the superior parent.

You have to read these hundreds of pages of studies to quite believe how thoroughly researchers have tried to measure a difference between moms and dads and how thoroughly they've failed to find one. Clearly, it has come as a surprise. "In sum, very little about the gender of the parent seems to be distinctly important," writes Michael Lamb, the dean of the father-researchers, who sounds like he's scratching his head as he summarizes the last twenty years' research. "Fathers and mothers seem to influence their children in similar rather than dissimilar ways. Contrary to the expectations of many psychologists, including myself . . . the differences between mothers and fathers appears much less important than the similarities." They write it over and over, as if they can't quite believe it and don't expect us to. Writes another, Charlie Lewis, "If there are differences between mothers and fathers, these are not easy to measure and do not have demonstrable effects on the child's development, as was once simply assumed."

So what *does* help kids? Although researchers have to stand on their heads and squint to find any distinctive father-effect, they very *easily* find a few things that have a powerfully good effect on children. Enough resources (like food, shelter, clothing, healthcare, and schooling) make a big difference. Happily married parents who get along well and feel that chores are shared fairly have a powerful effect on both infants and children (even if the father is *not* actively involved with the kids, presumably because the mother is more attentive and affectionate when she herself is happy and less stressed). Children need the basics—food, shelter, clothing, healthcare—and they need reliable warmth, affection, and attention. When they get that in double doses, of course they do better—

but not in ways that differ dramatically based on which sex gives the second dose. Which, if you want an evolutionary explanation, makes sense: given a world in which either Mom or Dad or both could disappear at any moment—and, until the twentieth century, often did—why would nature overspecialize in who we needed to grow up, so long as we were fed, sheltered, and treated reasonably well?

So most of the current "children-need-fathers" rhetoric—or at least, the research upon which it draws—can really be translated as "children-need-two-parents-with-enough-resources." It does not really tell us anything about whether children need one parent of each sex. But maybe dads *do* offer something unique that simply can't be teased out so long as both parents live at home, or even if fathers were around only while their offspring were infants. Which is why some researchers have turned to examining lesbian and gay families: to understand whether male and female parents offer something distinct. But before we look at those studies, we have to ask a (perhaps prurient) question: how, exactly, do homosexuals become parents?

How lesbians and gay men become parents, 1: divorce

There have been two waves of research on children who grow up with lesbian or gay male parents. The first wave was conducted in the 1970s and early 1980s, just as the movement for lesbian and gay rights was beginning. These studies were done on children who were begotten the usual way, then came to be the children of lesbians or gay men when their parents divorced and one (or both) found a partner of the same sex. Those children, of course, respond to the new parent as warily, angrily, wearily (or even, if they had a vile ex-parent, hopefully) as to any parental revision. Any anger—and it's not universal—at Mom or Dad for saying he or she is gay would be difficult to untangle from the anger of having the family roof ripped off, of being exposed to the chill of separation and loss and change. That's why the researchers who originally studied the children of divorced lesbian or gay parents usually compared them to children of divorced heterosexual parents: if they compared chil-

dren of divorced lesbians or gay men to children of still-paired heterosexuals, they would be unable to tell whether any differences
should be attributed to the divorce or to one parent's sexual
orientation.

Whether or not you fully accept psychology's criteria for measuring who we are and who we become (and the professionals themselves debate their system of measurements with a fair amount of
heat), their studies uncover only minuscule differences between
children of divorce whose parents are heterosexual and those
whose parents are lesbian or gay. For instance, one study of one
hundred children of divorced lesbian and heterosexual moms
found no difference in the sex-typing of their favorite television
shows, characters, games, toys—in other words, both groups of
boys were more likely to play with balls and guns, both groups of
girls played with dolls—and no difference in their sense of themselves as male or female (measured by such tests as whether, when
asked to draw a person, a boy draws a boy or a girl draws a girl). Another showed that although daughters of lesbian mothers were
more likely to be described as joining in "rough-and-tumble"
play—arguably good, allowing girls to learn the famous fairness,
hard-work, resilience, and team-player lessons that boys usually
get from sports—or as occasionally playing with "masculine" toys
like trucks, no differences could be found among their sons. Aside
from these results—and the differences were very small—the children looked the same in terms of gender identity, sex role behavior,
and the whole gamut of psychology's measures of well-being, from
rates of psychological disturbances to moral judgment, "locus of
control," intelligence test results, social relationships, and popularity. A more recently published longitudinal study, methodologically superior to those done earlier, traced children of divorced lesbian and divorced heterosexual British mothers from age ten into
young adulthood: this study found no differences in mental health,
education, or employment.

Perhaps the most scrutinized results are on sexual orientation:
do gay parents turn out gay kids? So far, the answer appears to be
no, although commentators argue over how to interpret the scant

evidence. The proportion of divorced gay people's now-adult off-spring who call themselves gay (or whose parents say they think the kids are gay) wavers from study to study. In one study of thirty-six adolescents between thirteen and nineteen, half of whose mothers were lesbian and half heterosexual, one daughter (no sons) of the *heterosexual* mothers identified as gay; none of the lesbians' kids were gay. In another study, two out of nineteen adolescents with gay fathers called themselves gay. In the more recent and methodologically superior study, two of twenty-five adult children of lesbian mothers considered themselves lesbian, gay, or bisexual, while none of the twenty adult offspring with heterosexual mothers did.

What can such tiny numbers mean? Some doomsayers have insisted that the numbers from that last study meant that having a lesbian mom increases the "risk" of being gay astronomically: two out of twenty-five is many more than zero out of twenty, especially when contrasted to the conservative estimate that roughly 2 to 3 percent of us are gay. But can you really make meaningful predictions about sexual orientation from two out of forty-five kids? If so, you might conclude from the earlier study that daughters of *heterosexual* mothers, not daughters of lesbian moms, have a higher "risk" of being gay themselves. Or maybe you'd conclude that when gay parents' offspring are also gay themselves, they're more willing to be contacted by researchers than are the gay offspring of straight parents. Or you might conclude that gay parents' influence is biological, not environmental, since during the youngsters' formative years their parents were modeling heterosexuality by living with spouses of the other sex. Or perhaps, among youngsters who grow up in gay homes, a few are more willing to be open to all their possibilities, free of shame—which is, to some minds, not a bad thing. Or maybe you'd decide that, if that's the best gay parents can do at "recruiting" their kids—to use that old slander—they're doing a pretty lousy job. Or you might decide that, whatever the influence, the huge majority of *everyone's* kids tend to fall in love with someone of the other sex: does it really matter if there's a two- or four-point difference either way? Or perhaps you'd decide, sensibly, that nature, nurture, and culture cannot be teased apart in such tiny studies—if, in fact, those threads will ever be teased apart at all.

But there's a problem with those early studies on divorced lesbian and gay parents: their results can be—and have been—criticized on any number of grounds. Sometimes samples were small and recruited by word of mouth, and so are not "random"; sometimes the divorced lesbian moms lived with partners although the heterosexual moms did not (giving the lesbian moms' kids the extra boost of their mothers' happiness and an additional parent, two things that tend to improve kids' well-being). Most important, while all those children were infants and toddlers—apparently when our sense of gender, sex role, and sexual orientation are forged—they did have parents of both sexes. And so these studies *still* do not answer our main question: do children need parents of both sexes to grow up okay? The only way to answer the question accurately, it seems, is by looking at children who have been raised, since birth, by two parents of one sex.

How lesbians and gay men become parents, 2: the "gayby" boom Which brings us to the second wave of research on children who grow up with lesbian or gay male parents: research on the children of the lesbian and gay baby boom. This boomlet is hard to measure, since many parents hesitate to identify themselves as lesbian or gay for fear of losing their kids. But everyone within the community has noticed that this boom is growing dramatically: more and more, lesbians and gay men are starting families *after* settling down with partners of the same sex.

The boom started among lesbians, since women have the more complicated equipment right there at home, in a handy duplicate set. It can be dated to the mid-1980s, when the generation who'd "come out" in the 1970s—a time heady with rhetoric about pride—started hearing their biological alarm clocks ticking and decided to start families. When lesbian couples in Boston and San Francisco were turned down by mainstream medical providers unwilling to inseminate women who weren't legally married, those communities launched donor insemination (DI) programs catering to women unsupervised by men. Thousands have gone through their doors; thousands of others have made babies without medical help, asking a brother or friend to donate. In cities with large lesbian populations—like Boston, San Francisco, London, and New York—some HIV-negative gay men report wearily that they've been asked up to a dozen times to be donor dads. Some don't mind the role: as a kind of thank-you for lesbian help during the AIDS crisis, one group of British gay men has an informal network that helps lesbians find donors who match their hoped-for specs.

The consequence: parents' contingents head the latest lesbian and gay pride parades, and gay havens like Provincetown or Park Slope are teeming with paired moms or dads strapped to papooses or pushing strollers. Younger women, who are more likely to "come out" without the dour belief that being gay means forgoing other life hopes, are especially likely to plan for and conceive babies once they pair up. For lesbians and gay men who want to "co-parent," or share the efforts of conceiving and rearing a child with someone of the other sex, there are Internet lists, websites, gay community center "maybe baby" groups, and matchmaking services. What's fascinating is that those looking for coparents sound much more like prospective partners in "traditional" matches than in twentieth-century marriages: their ads seek someone stable and reliable, with compatible genes (i.e., Jewish but no Tay-Sachs), temperament, and values. In other words, the way these families are formed sounds more like the matchmaking between Tevye and Golde than Mike and Carol Brady.

Finally, some adopt. Both gay men and infertile lesbians (like their heterosexual sisters) are adopting through social service agencies or privately. Lately gay men, in particular, have been adopting in larger and larger numbers, as they, too, see that it's possible—that their life hopes were not dashed by the fact that they're gay. Depending on where they live, some couples adopt jointly; others do so as sole legal parent and later add the other parent, if their state allows. The trend is so ubiquitous in some circles that recently I ran into an old friend who—after realizing how long Madeline and I had been together—blurted out: So do you two have a Chinese baby named Lily yet? (We do not.)

XX, XX/XX, XX/XY: same difference?   It is on the first wave of these children—the children born to the early lesbian baby boom, from the mid-1980s to today—that the latest research is being done. And because our era's questions about sex and gender are so hard to answer, a surprising amount of the research is being done by nongay psychologists and sociologists who've realized that these children are a natural way to learn whether kids do need an adult's XY chromosomes at home. Examining lesbian families allows people to ask basic and provocative questions about what children need, about masculinity and femininity, about trucks and Barbies, about sensitivity and discipline, about competence and kindness. Here there is no need to adjust the results for one group's abrupt loss of income or grief over the family's shattering: these children can fairly be compared to children in the general population. And chastened by earlier public criticism over research methodologies, these new researchers are being far more meticulous in a variety of ways to ensure that their results are valid.

With all this care, studies of the lesbians' DI kids show much the same things as the studies of the kids whose parents divorced: kids raised by two moms and kids raised by a mom and dad turn out just as well, on every conceivable measure. For instance, lesbians' preschool children form "secure attachments" to both moms; have neither more nor fewer emotional problems or "separation distress"; show no differences in measures of social competence, behavior problems, gender identity, sex-role behavior (i.e., whether girls like the toys, characters, and games that girls usually like, and boys like those of boys); and are equally likely to see themselves as sociable or as enjoying attention. There is, however, a little variety among the results—as you'd expect from a discipline that looks at people instead of, say, H_2SO_4. For instance, one study found that children of lesbian parents saw themselves as less aggressive and more likable than children of single heterosexual moms; that doesn't show up in the other studies. Another study found that lesbians' kids reported both more symptoms of stress and a greater sense of well-being than those of comparable straight moms: in other words, the lesbians' children more often said they were angry, scared, upset—*and* also said more often that they were joyful, content, and comfortable with themselves. Is that because having two moms brings you more stress and more happiness; or does being around two women give you more practice talking about your feelings; or can this not be generalized, since it hasn't been tested in any other research? In either case, neither effect can be considered a problem—unless you're dedicated to turning out only unflappable silent types.

Since so much of today's pro-family rhetoric insists that children need two bio-parents, we might wonder whether the very fact of having only one biological parent handicaps those children in any way. Probably not—not only have a good large proportion of children in history grown up with just one biological parent, but also most studies of DI children born to heterosexual parents show no extra (in fact, less) pathology or developmental problems. And yet some studies on lesbian moms go the extra mile and compare children born by DI to two women with children born by DI to one woman and one man. All the children, in other words, have only one bio-parent but two emotional parents involved with them from birth, parents who are comparable on other measures, with the only variable the nonbio-parent's sex. Once again, results are a big yawn: researchers find no differences in cognitive, emotional, behavioral, or gender development. (The kids in these studies are no older than nine, so no one can yet measure their leanings in love.) Interestingly, all the children feel more strongly about their bio-mom and just about the same amount of warmth toward their second parent, whether a mom or a dad, even though the nonbio-moms spent more time with the kids than did the nonbio-dads— suggesting that neither gender nor time together, but rather gestation and suckling, may give youngsters that extra bond with mom.

The most consistent difference is one most women would predict: in aggregate, the "other mothers" get much more involved in the nitty-gritty of childrearing than do fathers. The co-moms score as having a "superior quality of interaction" (warmer, when rated by outsiders; more likely to be there when you need her, as rated by the children themselves) than either biodads or social dads, and they're much more involved in practical childcare and day-to-day discipline. One study found that—possibly as a result of having that extra support—the lesbian biomoms are warmer and more involved with their children, and less likely to fight with their daughters, than the heterosexual biomoms; another study found that children with two moms were more "securely attached" to their parents than children with a mom and a dad. It's particularly interesting that the children of lesbian moms are not scoring any *higher* on any of these measures of well-being: perhaps so long as you have two reliable parents, it doesn't really matter exactly how involved, day to day, the two of them are—so long as they're there and they care.

Some people think only of sex when they think of same-sex couples—as if lesbians and gay men, simply by being in the same room, expose children to unseemly urges. But most contemporary parents—of the same or different sexes—go to extreme lengths to keep their sex life private and are more at risk of being too exhausted for sex than of having the kids walk in. Some people are edgy about the idea that children will grow up in a household where Mom and Mom cuddle in the family room while everyone's watching *The Lion King*. But if you remember seeing your parents hug and kiss affectionately after a day apart, you're lucky: warmth is good for children. And that's proving to be true whether the parents are the same or different sexes.

In other words, the father-researchers and the lesbian-mother researchers are finding the same thing. What's key about a second parent is *not* sex—either the sex they are or the sex they have—but behavior toward the children. A warm (read: caring, in whatever way they show it) parent turns out a happier and better-adjusted child than does an unkind (read: cruel, alcoholic, arbitrarily ridiculing) parent.

And there's an even stronger result: when parents are more happily mated, share household tasks more equally, and find parenting less stressful, their children have fewer behavior problems and a greater sense of well-being. The parents' behavior toward each *other*, in other words, matters a great deal: happy parents raise happy children. Which makes sense: we've all seen—whether from being a child or knowing a child—how excruciatingly responsive children are to adults' emotions. Put children in a room where the adults are at swords' points, and—even if everyone's perfectly well-behaved—infants wail, toddlers throw tantrums, older children grow sullen or silent or aggressive. Conflict and stress are hard on kids, and harmony is good. To put it differently, *how* households are run affects children more than *who* runs them.

Or is it too soon to draw that conclusion? As those fatherless children get older, will measurable differences show up in such things as "aggressiveness" or sexual orientation? Reading those who insist it will, I'm surprised to discover that—since they have no research or statistics on their side—they keep lapsing into the mantra that it's "common sense" that every child needs a mother and a father.

But their sense and my sense are not held in common. Really, how could you group all "fathers" or "mothers" together as if they were the same? If there are "innate" biological differences between men and women, there are also "innate" variations among men and women: just as one father is five foot tall and another six foot six, so one father is mild and another quick with the belt. What does my tough little mother—who as a tiny thing beat up the boys on her Brooklyn block, who was for years the mayor of our town, who loves nothing better than a political fight—have in common with yours, besides the fact that yours and mine (probably) bore us, fed and clothed us, and launched us into adulthood, and perhaps that you are also endlessly proud of your mother's strengths and sometimes frustrated by her flaws? What does my father—who diapered and doted on me, who insisted I aim high, whose sarcasm can still make me wince—have in common with the junkie that my (heterosexual) friend Susan called a dad, or the kindly and mild-mannered guy who raised my (heterosexual) friend Laura, or the battered Holocaust survivor who fathered my (heterosexual) friend Jon? What do any of our late twentieth-century dads have in common with Roman aristocrats who refused to let their sons see their mothers, or the tenth-century father who committed his youngest at age three to the local monastery for life, or the twentieth-century Japanese salaryman who briefly stops home to sleep? What do 1950s mothers who fed their babies on a strict schedule have in common with Yucatan or Japanese mothers who believe the child must never cry or be put down? The idea that one XX and one XY per roof could possibly have the same effect across all this personal, historical, and cultural variety is simply magical thinking.

And so, as necessary as they may be for our era's public debate, perhaps all these "measurements" are beside the point—something like the exceedingly careful Harvard study I have on my desk of "anthropometric" data on "cephalic index, length-height index, nasal index" in "Negro" and "Negro-White" families done in the late 1930s, in which teensy-weensy differences in head size or hair nappiness "prove" that children born to mixed-race parents are (a) inferior or (b) just fine, depending on the researchers' point of view. Perhaps having two parents of one sex is something like having parents who are both doctors or janitors, Republicans or Baptists: you may grow up with a worldview slanted by the fact that your parents share many experiences and points of view, but you still benefit from the variety in their personalities and histories, their complementary weaknesses and strengths, their love or lack of it—in other words, from the "two-parent" advantage. But who ever said that every pair of parents must be precisely the same? This can be a hard concept for those of us who *were* raised by one mother and one father, to whom we are still passionately attached—whether with love and gratitude, frustration and anger, or all of the above. But why shouldn't children feel strongly about whoever does the real, daily work of making their lunches, managing their crankiness, and insisting they can and will learn algebra?

Of course children need to know a wide variety of women and men, to learn how many ways there are to be human. Lesbian and gay parents, particularly sensitive to the charge that their children might grow up warped by not knowing someone of the other sex, often go out of their way to compensate for that cultural paranoia. One study finds that, like children of heterosexual parents, children of lesbian mothers usually stay in touch with grandparents, aunts and uncles, and other adult family friends—giving them more models than their parental units. And many lesbian families make sure they bring in a gay or straight "godfather," or gay men a lesbian or straight "godmother," who'll widen the child's world in more ways than just gender modeling. These strategies are hardly new. Parents and communities have long found ways to help children stay involved with role models of all kinds, whether or not both sexes live in that particular home: whether formally, by "fostering out," handing a kid over to a nanny, sending him to military school, or requiring certain duties of the godparents; or informally, as when an uncle plays basketball with his widowed sister's sons, or a much older half-sister raises the youngest after their parents are dead, gone, or overwhelmed. If such variety were detrimental, if "maleness" or "femaleness" are so fragile as to require daily observation to learn—and as important as many commentators insist—how could those qualities have survived?

Fear of fathers: or, won't gay men abuse children? One concern that springs quickly to mind when people talk about gay parents is rooted in the cultural confusion between homosexuality and pedophilia: are two dads more likely to molest their child?

What's true is that it is men, far more often than women, who sexually abuse children. If you open your newspaper, you will almost certainly find an example like one that's in mine, this spring of 1998: a report of a male high school soccer coach who, from 1973 to 1997, never went six months without either seducing or raping at least one of his underaged athletes (but since his athletes were girls, his superiors object that his fifteen-year prison sentence is too long). Another article, about a South African epidemic of child rape, describes police heading out to round up dozens of accused men at a time—men who've raped girls ages two to twelve.

Gay men are men, and so, in roughly the same proportions as do heterosexual men, some gay men abuse children physically or sexually. About 90 percent of substantiated child sexual abuse is by men—almost always by men who are married, have girlfriends, or otherwise identify or behave as heterosexual. Usually that man is someone within the family. A 1998 study of American adolescent boys found that one in eight had been abused—most physically, some sexually—and that among those who were sexually abused, 45 percent reported their abuser was a family member. In a 1994 study of all the sexually molested children examined at Denver Children's Hospital during one calendar year, the abusers of eight out of ten girls and three out of four boys were either men who were involved with the children's mothers, or some other family member; only one of fifty boys was molested by a gay man. That puts the percentage of child molesters who identify as heterosexual at 97 percent, roughly their proportion in the population. But while no newspaper headline ever reads "heterosexual man kills wife, children, and self"—heterosexual being the default assumption, and murder of a wife or ex-wife depressingly common—adding the word "gay" to a particular crime adds enough shock value to sell papers.

The complication here is how to define those adult men who abuse male children—but who, in their adult sexual lives, are heterosexual. "Straight" and "gay" are words for adult attractions to other adults (or, perhaps, adolescent attractions to movie stars). We all know that adult relationships can include anything from loving consent to coercion to rape. But "straight" and "gay" are terms inadequate for discussing sexual abuse of children who cannot reasonably consent. Some men have a sexual fixation on adolescents or children—and those men, who may or may not distinguish between girls and boys, are a separate category. Other men seem disturbingly willing to abuse the children of their wives, girlfriends, sisters, or sisters-in-law—again, often without distinguishing between boys and girls. For instance, in one study of 175 Massachusetts men who were imprisoned for child sexual assault (and therefore arguably *more* likely to be gay, since male/boy abuse arouses more social fury), *none* had relationships solely with men. Just under half were exclusively "fixated," to use the researchers' term, on children; another 40 percent were heterosexually paired men who also molested children; the rest were men whose adult involvements were primarily with women and occasionally with men, and who also molested children. In other words, pedophiles are their own category. Whether stepfathers, priests, married soccer coaches, or the creep next door, pedophiles are less likely than men with a strong adult sexual identity (whether straight or gay) to distinguish between boys and girls. Men willing to marry other men would be more likely to have a strong adult sexual identity—and would be, arguably, *less* likely than other men to abuse the children in their care.

Perhaps the fear of gay fathers is a sign of our current fear of unsupervised fathers in general—a fear that would have been incomprehensible to our ancestors, who believed women morally incapable of raising kids. But just because XY is a big risk factor for child abuse—in the most methodologically sound studies, roughly 20 percent of adult women report having been sexually abused as children, about half the time by men in their families—our society doesn't insist that all men stay away from all kids. Why should only *gay* men be blamed for the sins of *some* men—men who do not mainly behave or identify as gay—and thus be barred from being parents?

The fact that stepfathers abuse their wives' children significantly more often than do bio-fathers has been taken as evidence that children need their biological fathers—which would rule out adoption by any man, including gay men. But when you look closely at the evidence, you discover that what children need is *not* bio-parents, but parents who get involved while the children are still infants. Significantly, American war babies born while their bio-dads were away in World War II did badly when their dads came home—just as badly as today's divorced kids do under stepfather-rule. An extensive study found that returning dads were far less fond of these wartime firstborns, disliking these strange children who came between them and their wives. The vets criticized their warbabies far more often and were far nastier disciplinarians toward them—scolding, threatening, slapping, and spanking—than the very same men were with their *later* children. Once those fathers had children born while they were home, they softened up, babying them and referring to them as "their" children. In other words, toward their warbabies these men acted like stepfathers— since they'd been grafted in too late to feel like "real" fathers. On the other hand, DI and adopting fathers who *do* get that early bonding are no more likely to abuse than are bio-dads.

Biology, in other words, is not what makes fatherhood: involvement is. What seems to turn grownups into parents is the chance to hold, nuzzle, soothe, and agonize over those wrinkled, milk-and-poop-fragrant bundles while they're still tiny and cuddly. How could it be otherwise? Even evolutionary biologists don't believe men have some mysterious psychic sense that instructs them a child is biologically theirs, any more than infants have some psychic sensor for their bio-parents: being around each other is how we know who's "ours." And since it's not a biological link but intimate and early involvement that softens men into fathers, it would be best to treat gay men like other parents—and to get them close to their future children as soon as possible in the kids' lives.

The related fear about having two dads is that a child would miss out on a mom's essential nurturing. But the father-researchers and custody-researchers both find that mom's monopoly on kindness and caring is a myth. A good father behaves very much like a good mother—with kindness, attention, affection, and nurturing that affects the child in more or less the same ways, regardless of the parent's sex. As one Yale psychiatrist says, "We know for certain that men can be competent, capable, creative caretakers of newborns. . . . The research . . . says it over and over again, in data from many different disciplines." My own earliest, delighted memories are of my father (I was a daddy's girl) waking me so we could have breakfast, cuddle, and watch "Cap'n Roo" before he went off to teach his morning classes. One pair of dads I know reports that bringing their son to preschool perfectly clean and well-behaved, day after day, has first amazed and then infuriated some of the moms, as they realize that their husbands *can* do things they've simply refused to. Our culture may have assigned babies mainly to moms, but dads are fully qualified for the tasks.

In fact, many pro-father and pro-family writers insist that men need to have children in order to grow up, to leave behind their profligate or violent or otherwise wayward youths. "Under the magic of family responsibility, even the painted doll often grows into a woman and the callow stripling into a man," wrote moralist and eugenicist Paul Popenoe in 1929. Or as his son David Popenoe writes in less dated language, "[Y]oung men say that they gave up certain deviant or socially irresponsible patterns of life only when they . . . felt the need to set a good example for their children. . . . [M]en found that fatherhood promoted male maturity, especially the ability of men to integrate their own feelings and to understand others' sympathetically." In other words, who has time to stay out cruising the strip joints, drinking and brawling and trying to score, when your little one needs new mittens, when he won't go to bed until you read him *Goodnight Moon*, when he thinks you're the greatest thing on earth?

Is it right to expose children to prejudice?   Another objection is often posed to lesbians or gay men who plan families: is it fair to let children be stigmatized by their parents' homosexuality?

Most studies of lesbians' and gay men's children don't find the kids scarred by teasing or ostracism; the kids hardly report any at all, and—so long as they're strong in the usual ways—they get along fine with other children. Sometimes, in fact, adult children of women who'd divorced and then come out as lesbian spoke more proudly about their families—especially when their mothers had been easy and open about being gay—than did the children raised by divorced heterosexual moms. Is that because having a happy and proud mother makes for a happy and confident child, or having a stepmom is nicer than having a stepdad (the lesbians' children in this study all got along better with their stepmoms than the straight women's kids did with their stepdads), or that being in a minority forces forward your family loyalties?

But there's a larger, more important idea at stake. Could anyone but Pharaoh imagine suggesting that, say, Jews should not have children because someone might scrawl a swastika on their notebooks? As the only Jewish child in a semi-rural Bible Belt school, I suffered annual agonies over whether to sing the Christmas carols in music class or sit through class prayers that were not mine. Should I not have been born? Hardly. Because my parents had no qualms about being Jews, I was left with a ferocious pride in my family and culture. Kids from any minority group know that such tests can leave scars—and can also incise pride, self-reliance, and strength. When people of different races wanted to marry, the outcry about their children's psychological well-being—how would they identify? wouldn't they be outcasts, belonging nowhere?— was really a cover for the speakers' own biases. So are the fears about prejudices toward children with two parents of one sex. It's every parent's job to teach children to handle ridicule and disrespect, whether from being called fatso, four eyes, nigger, or faggot. And it's *all* our jobs to go to bat for those children. From elementary to high schools, words like "gay" and "faggot" are among today's most common insults—and are unfortunately permitted by many teachers and adults. People who worry about the effects of stigma on children of lesbians and gay men have a moral duty to intervene, as they do when the playground's insult of choice is any other slur on humanity. Truly concerned adults can help *erase* the stigma—by making it possible for those children's parents to marry.

But the deepest objection to same-sex parents is the same one seen throughout history. Whenever a previously forbidden family arrangement starts to look reasonable, those who still recoil—and can't find a rational argument—thump their chests about "the children," projecting anxieties onto a cultural ideal so pure and shiny we can't squint past it to see the particular facts. Medieval Christians accused Jews of slaughtering a Christian child as their annual Passover sacrifice—as if Jews were interested in reenacting Easter—and used that as a reason to go on a spring pogrom. Protestants called Catholic priests babykillers. Late nineteenth-century reformers insisted that unloving couplings produced defective and retarded children, or quoted Shakespeare that a "dull, stale, tired bed" would create a "tribe of fops." People opposed to interracial marriage "scientifically" explained that "The offspring of these unnatural connections are generally sickly, effeminate, and . . . inferior to the full blooded of either race in physical development and strength." It's the same old charge: *if you disobey me, you and your children will wither and die, and civilization itself will collapse.*

Of course, the impulse to save children is humanity at its best. But we have to be cautious when noble sentiments are invoked on behalf of bigotry—especially when it means restricting dissenting or unconventional parents from raising children as they believe right. From Mennonites to survivalists, a pluralist society allows people to raise their children in freedom. Only totalitarians want some central authority to decide precisely which values and models every parent offers. When there's no neglect or abuse, do we really want to have one ideology intervene, via the state, in individual decisions to create families?

There is no one standard of success by which every child should be measured, and those who think there is do not take into account the real, messy, exhausting, invigorating plurality of human life through history. Even investigating the psychological "best interests of the child" is a wonderful luxury compared to the concerns most societies have had for their children—fears of famine and drought, epidemics and plagues, pogroms and murders, invasions and civil wars. Given the basics—food, shelter, clothing, education, encouragement, and a sense of belonging—children grow up successfully in an unbelievable variety of circumstances. How could the human race have otherwise survived?

So what do children need to be protected from? Given Western democracies' bedrock belief in pluralism, family choice will not go away. The question then is: how will society deal with it? Will we try to define it under the rug, leaving an unsightly lump? Or will we legally recognize the families that actually exist—and truly protect those children?

Because make no mistake, those children do need protection—not from any special homosexual threat, but from the same things that all children need protection from: hunger, cold, disruption, instability, and poverty. Which, not incidentally, is the goal of much marriage law. Any state's marriage laws includes scores of statues allowing spouses to handle each other's property "as if they were sole." That's critical for parents, since it lets them build their children a single shelter from their two incomes, benefits, tax returns, pensions, health insurance, and more. Imagine raising your children without marriage's protections: knowing that if your spouse died in a car crash, you'd be taxed heavily for inheriting his or her "half" of the house, refused his or her pension benefits, your custody challenged by the grandparents. Imagine being refused the ability to govern your child's schooling or visit her hospital bedside. That's what most same-sex couples with kids face. Heather may have two mommies, but her legal mother—whether her bio-mom or the one officially granted adoption—better go quickly back to work, because the other's healthcare insurance won't cover Heather's booster shots and tonsillitis.

Legally recognizing those parents' partnership offers more protection to that child than simple financial security. If, as child expert Anna Freud wrote, "a child can handle almost anything better than instability," then today's laws can be bad news for children with two moms or two dads. Today's laws sometimes bar children from the parents who raised them—as can be the heartbreaking case when a lesbian bio-mom dies and grandparents legally kidnap the child from her other mother. In one such case, argued for years in Florida courts, the girl plaintively told judges that "for Christmas I don't really want a present. All I want is to live with Neenie [her other mother]." That particular girl finally got to go home. Not every child does.

Some states and countries do allow two parents of the same sex to share legal custody. As one Ontario judge wrote in 1995, "When one reflects on the seemingly limitless parade of neglected, abandoned and abused children who appear before our courts in protection cases daily, all of whom have been in the care of heterosexual parents in a 'traditional' family structure, the suggestion that it might not *ever* be in the best interests of these children to be raised by loving, caring, and committed parents who might happen to be lesbian or gay, is nothing short of ludicrous." Not all states or judges agree, finding same-sex parenting to be unnatural—just as, not so long ago, some judges refused to fully recognize adoption statutes or DI fatherhood, believing those innovations to be unnatural.

But even if every jurisdiction allowed both moms or both dads to be legal parents, the children would *still* need the extra protection of their parents' marriage. Because there's another thing to protect children from: a household that falls apart. One expert in adult sexuality, Pepper Schwartz, has testified that marriage's very public nature—the gifts and celebrations of its ceremonies, the hurdles of its divorce laws, the formal involvement of extended families—does help couples stay together when their relationship is tough. And so she argues that letting same-sex couples marry would be better for the kids. Any legal zipper that holds parents together during those difficult early years when time, sleep, sanity, and commitment can be seriously strained is arguably better for the kids (unless you've reached the point of all-out war).

But though everyone has high hopes, not every marriage (legally recognized or not) works out for the best. Many breakups—most, one fervently hopes—put the kids first and work hard to ensure they're not ripped away from either parent. Not all do. A very depressing way to measure the lesbian baby boom is the recent wave of no-holds-barred, teeth-bared, mom v. mom custody battles, just as nasty as any to be found in heterosexual splits—but without divorce courts to adjudicate. Sometimes the biomom tries to pretend that the woman who held her hand during labor, who patiently sliced grapes into bits small enough for a toddler, who may even have voluntarily paid child support after moving out—that this mom was just a babysitter or a family friend that the "real" mom temporarily let into the family. And whenever a parent gets angry enough to shut his or her ex off from the child, twisting the law to destroy their shared family, things can be nasty—especially for the kids. What *ought* to count legally for these families is precisely what counts in defining rights and responsibilities in heterosexual DI or adoptive parenting: Did they together plan for and consent to the pregnancy or adoption? Were they both involved in the child's daily life from the start? To decide such larger questions, it would help if courts could ask a simple one: Were the pair married, signaling a desire to share their lives (and, not incidentally, childrearing)? Marriage—with its hard-won history of custody rules—would simplify those children's lives.

There's one last question to be asked about children and same-sex marriage: Is the *option* of same-sex marriage good or bad for kids? That question gets many people nervous, because in some minds it invokes the myth that gay people "recruit" by going after youngsters. That libel is why childrearing has been a subject many lesbians and gay men prefer not to raise. And yet the very existence of same-sex marriage *would* send a message to young people—a good one. It would offer visible evidence that there's nothing wrong with being gay, that "sodomy" is a sin only in the eyes of the beholder. Some commentators would much rather see outré urban queers throwing drunken kisses off bar floats than have two nice married girls move in next door, with or without papoose, demonstrating to every neighborhood kid that a good marriage is defined from the inside out. Which is not to say every child with lesbian neighbors will grow up to be lesbian, any more than every neighbor of heterosexuals will become one herself. But perhaps those children *will* learn a basic and important lesson about our society: that we get to choose our life course based on our inner gyroscopes, and must respect others' choices. Whether for girls or boys who come of age with the sudden realization that they're falling in love with another girl or boy, or for those who find in themselves a heterosexual attraction, the possibility of same-sex marriage offers a lesson good for any child: One's own heart counts.

FOUR:

Kin

———

Therefore shall a man leave his father and mother, and shall cleave unto his wife, and they shall be one flesh.

—Genesis 2:24

What, would you like to marry your sister! What is the matter with you anyway? Don't you want a brother-in-law? Don't you realize that if you marry another man's sister and another man marries your sister, you will have at least two brothers-in-law, while if you marry your own sister you will have none? With whom will you hunt, with whom will you garden, whom will you go to visit?

—Arapesh man to Claude Lévi-Strauss,
in *The Elementary Structures of Kinship* (1949)

Let the sharp question pierce the national heart: "Shall I or shall I not blend my Caucasian, world-ruling, world-conquering blood with the servile strain of Africa?"

—WILLIAM BENJAMIN SMITH,
The Color Line: A Brief in Behalf of the Unborn (1905)

The chief excellence of the religion of heaven consists in . . . giving to faithful servants a plurality of wives by which a numerous and faithful posterity can be raised up and taught in the principles of righteousness and truth.

—Mormon leader (1852)

The honor and faithfulness that constitutes an ideal marriage, may exist between two hundred as well as two.

—Oneida Community Handbook (1871)

THE STORY SO FAR: DURING THE PAST 150 OR 200 YEARS,
Western society has dramatically reshaped three basic pillars
of marriage—money, sex, and babies. The triumph of urban capitalism over agrarian feudalism has made it possible, even mandatory, for most of us to make a living on our own—without
needing the investment or approval of our parents or the assign-
ment of a spouse as essential work partner. That economic
earthquake has shaken apart the traditional "family," releasing
each of us to choose not just our jobs but also our loves. Today
we each (in philosophy, if not always in practice) have the choice
of when, who, or even whether we will marry, and of when, how
many, or whether we will have children. These radical individual
freedoms, most of which seemed sinful to our ancestors (and
still do, to some) now strike society as simple justice, the necessary corollaries of Western economic reality and democratic political philosophy.

And yet despite these upheavals, money, sex, and babies are
still recognizable as marriage goals. Still more revolutionary has
been the almost complete overthrow of perhaps *the* fundamental
reason for marriage: creating kin.

Westerners have heard *ad nauseum* about how anomalously in-
dividualistic we are. Because our reigning ethos *is* so individualis-
tic, kinship sounds to many of us like a quaint or faintly oppressive
reason for marriage. And so we may never be able to grasp how
fully the institution of marriage has been about kinship—horizon-
tally creating bonds with other families as well as vertically seeding
new descendants. Marriage-for-kinship was politically key for
early medieval clans like the Franks, Vandals, Ostrogoths, Visi-
goths, Merovingians, and Carolingians, for whom the demands of
kinship were as powerful as the demands of citizenship today—
and just as non-negotiable. How would you feel about your own
or your brother's marriage if it involved your town council in a

NATO-like alliance with a nearby town council—committing you and your sons, siblings, uncles, and cousins to lifetime military and economic obligations? You might well rank making kin above making love.

Marriage, in other words, was long a clan project, not an individual pursuit—so long as your family had *any* property or status. An eighteenth-century Angiers official noted of a French widower, "since he could not have the eldest daughter, he wishes for the youngest daughter, out of his attachment to the families." Doesn't matter which daughter, so long as it's the same family: It hardly sounds like the way we think of marriage today.

Of course, the idea that marriage creates kinship—not just between the couple but among their families—still lingers in our cultural rituals. What else is the wedding except a way for the families—whether family by blood or family by friendship—to work and play together in effort and celebration? Kinship is more voluntary today than it once was: today's kin-by-marriage may never see each other after the wedding, or they may become each other's main social circle with barbecues every weekend and a shared vacation house at the beach. True, exchanging birthday cards or even underwriting the aging parents-in-law is not *quite* the same as buying a docile adolescent (a bride for your son) to do the household scut work. Although we don't see creating kin as a *reason* to marry, many Westerners still expect marriage to extend our families.

But if you put kinship at its center, marriage has very different rules and boundaries than does marriage for love. On one edge of the circle is the limit on how far out you can marry—or, as we know it, the race taboo—while the other edge is the limit on how far you can marry *in,* or the incest taboo. That circle of permitted intimacies can have still another dimension: the question of whether your society will allow or even require more than one spouse per person, whether because of traditional—or shall we say, biblical—polygamy or because of a utopian vision. Where should we draw the boundaries of our tribe? If marriage is about making kin, should we create *more* kin with *more* marriages? When and why do societies allow people to marry in, or out, or often?

In other words, what kinship should be permitted? This question comes up in the debate over same-sex marriage: proponents say that banning same-sex couples is as unjust as banning interracial marriage; opponents insist that, to the contrary, banning same-sex couples is as righteous as banning incest and polygamy. If same-sex marriage is allowed, must we strike down every other marriage taboo? Your answers will grow from what you think marriage—and human life—are for.

Marrying Out: Barricading the Tribe

If marriage is for creating bonds among families, what is to be done about those who defy the circle of designated equals, bleeding away the tribe's human capital to people who aren't "ours"? That's the question that was debated in the most infamous scar in the United States' history of marriage laws: the ban on "miscegenation," a word invented in the social turmoil just after the Civil War. At one point, forty-one American states and territories barred marriage between the races. The mixed-marriage battle is full of rhetoric that is, word for word, interchangeable with the rhetoric hurled today against same-sex marriage. Can the American battle over interracial marriage fairly be compared to the fight for same-sex marriage?

To answer that, we need some historical background. Most groups throughout history have insisted that their daughters (and yes, the rhetoric is always about whether "their" men should be allowed to have "our" daughters) keep their wombs inside the tribe. One Old Testament man named Phineas speared to death a fellow Hebrew who married a "Midianitish woman"—an act reported in a Numbers verse that some white supremacists today use to justify murdering mixed-race couples. Over time the Jews' punishment of out-marriage became more muted, although emotions remain high: when I told my rabbi's wife I was a lesbian, she urged me, if I were ever to have a child, to be sure that the father/donor was a Jew (and if you're Jewish, you've heard this language a thousand times) because "Hitler tried to wipe us out. Let's not finish the job ourselves." Whether the threat's Hitler, Haman, or the Midianites, the Jews' recoil from mixed marriage has always been intensely tribal —and explicitly political.

But the Jews are merely the example I know most intimately. We've all, by now, read about Serb/Croat marriages sundered in that region's recent genocidal civil wars. Just after Ireland's Easter peace accords in 1998, a Catholic woman's house was set on fire and her children murdered—apparently because she lived with a Protestant. We needn't agree with such terrorism to understand its logic: If you believe urgently in your group's solidarity, identity, and strength, how can you *not* react when your members marry out? How is the tribe to continue if it gets mixed up with those who aren't "us"—who aren't fully *human,* in the way *we* are human?

In the United States, we have the unfortunate distinction of being able to trace the invention, enforcement, and then destruction of one such out-marrying taboo. Marriage between black and white was *not* always unthinkable. According to one historian, the upper- or merchant-class British immigrants in the American colonies looked down equally on enslaved Africans and indentured Irish, assigning them to the same tasks and holding them equally in contempt. Sharing their lives in their owners' kitchens and downstairs, Irish or lower-class British indentured servants and African enslaved servants often married. Learning how they came to be severed by the "miscegenation" sword reminds us that group borders are far less permanent or inevitable than, even today, we imagine.

The story starts with British laws, which the colonies took as their legal model—and which had no race bar. And so, when the colonies began, it was not yet clear what would be the difference between slavery and indentured servitude, except that one was for a set period—seven or eleven years—and the other was for life. Nor was it immediately obvious that Africanness would become an inherited caste, overriding any other ancestry. Why should someone whose parents were African and Irish be more "black" than Irish (especially if the child was as white-skinned as her Irish mother)? Some colonial courts even decided that European ancestry trumped African: presented with the puzzle of a slave woman who'd given birth to a white man's child, one eighteenth-century Connecticut judge freed the boy, reasoning that he "has English blood in him, and therefore was born free."

Legislators rolled up their sleeves to clear up such confusions. Between the 1660s and 1725, Virginia, Maryland, Massachusetts, North Carolina, Delaware, and Pennsylvania enacted laws that prevented "abominable mixture and spurious issue." Legislators revised and refined these laws repeatedly throughout the 1600s and early 1700s, trying to get just the right punishment for the "crime." Eventually the colonies and states found the rule that was most useful for perpetuating the institution of slavery (and African heritage, with which it was soon confused): inherited status. First, a slave woman's children inherited their mother's "condition," unlike a free woman's children, who got their name and class identity from their father. That meant that *all* a slave woman's children were always slaves and officially black, no matter how European in features and skin tone ("bright," in the jargon). Conveniently for whites, this meant that no matter from which side you got it, African heritage overrode European—allowing white men to increase their property by having sex with or raping enslaved women with impunity, while white women who had sex with black men were out-caste, their children visibly bastards (and the men in danger of lynching).

The rule, in other words—like the British rule of *fillius nullius,* which insisted that a child could never be legitimated by his parents' later marriage—protected ruling-caste men from the consequences of sexually using lower-caste women. Legal commentators, in fact, justified the laws via an old British legal ruling that a particular countess could not possibly have married her footman but had merely had a seamy affair. Sure, you might have sex with menials, but marry them? *That* was too degrading to be thinkable.

And yet feelings against intermarriage were not, at first, as ferocious as they later became. When slavery was fully in place and thoroughly enforced, or when black migration from the South to the new territories or northern states was only a trickle, free men and women could occasionally acknowledge African ancestry and still marry someone of European background—in colonies or states as different as Virginia, North Carolina, Massachusetts, and New York. Wealth, particularly, made a difference. In South Carolina in 1731, one committee assigned to investigate a new resident of color—Gideon Gibson, "mulatto"—even took his marriage as a proof of his reliability: "The account he has given of himself is so Satisfactory that he is no Vagabond that I have in Consideration of his Wifes being a white woman." The legislature allowed the Gibsons, like some other mulatto/white pairings, to settle on the South Carolina frontier; their children married into rich (white) planter families. In other cases, there was simply no penalty unless the marriage was free/slave. Alabama, for instance, allowed marriage "between any free persons" throughout colonial times and early statehood, and as a result had a variety of mixed-race marriages—both between white men and women of color, and between white women and men of color.

Border skirmishes—the insistence on patrolling a sharp difference between black and white—increased as slavery began to crumble and abolitionism rose—and, not coincidentally, as less and less colonized territory remained available for new settlers' use. From the beginning of the nineteenth century to the Civil War, frontier territories like Indiana, Illinois, and Tennessee tried to ban freed blacks or escaped slaves from moving into their states—and thus threatening their control of land. As one Illinois opponent of black migration into his territory said, "If we would allow the negroes any kind of equality we must admit them to the social hearth . . . and also, if they desired it, must not object to proposals to marry our daughters." That fear wasn't *entirely* spurious: Although land was the main resource for which whites wanted no competition, another equally essential and limited commodity was the pioneer wife, since men seriously outnumbered women on the colonizing frontier. And so when attempts to ban black migration failed, state legislators instead passed interracial marriage bans.

Many intermarriage laws, especially in the South, were briefly repealed or suspended at the Civil War's end—but then returned with a vengeance. A sense that slave equalled African equalled inferior had deeply stained the white psyche, which propped up its beliefs with a notorious range of tools from violence to segregation, among them the interracial marriage bans. The new laws were complicated by the near impossibility—by the nineteenth century—of clearly defining race. Plenty of people in the South descended not just from Irish maidservant/African manservant marriages—consensual and perhaps even equal—but also from illicit or forced relationships between white male owners or overseers and black female slaves whose offspring had escaped or been freed and who "passed." Even prominent "white" families might know, suspect, or merely fear a mixed ancestor or two. One 1850 Alabama court rejected the idea that "mulattoes" must be defined as anything more than the children of one black and one white parent, writing, "if the statute against mulattoes is ... to include quadroons, then where are we to stop? ... are we not bound to pursue the line of descendants, so long as there is a drop of negro blood remaining?" Alabama and other legislatures hastened to correct the judge's misconception, defining "quadroons" as black. And yet white Southern legislatures didn't dare, until very late, define "black" as being any more than one-quarter, or one grandparent, of African descent.

Even that definition was so ridiculous that many people wound up in court over racial identity. In North Carolina in 1832, two Caucasian grooms—after their apparently white wives gave birth to apparently "mulatto" children—tried to annul their marriages. In the first case the judge refused, saying that "persons who marry take each other as they are." Faced with community outrage, he ruled differently on the next case, writing, "This is a concession to the deep-rooted and virtuous prejudices of the community." Is yours a legal marriage? *Yes*, if seven of your great-grandparents are Caucasian, but if only six are, *no*. It sounds abominable if you believe that affection and commitment make a marriage—but it's quite serious if you believe that marriage is to fortify and barricade your tribe.

The enforcing of racial boundaries via antimiscegenation laws actually escalated after slavery was abolished. As legal historian Lawrence Friedman puts it, "What was at first a law for the servant class developed deeper and deeper overtones of color. The slave laws then became laws about the fate of a race." Alabama, for instance, first passed an intermarriage ban in 1863. Meanwhile, legislators responded to the racial-identity crisis by issuing increasingly stringent definitions of race. By the end of the nineteenth century and early in the twentieth, Southern states pushed the definition of "Negro" beyond the quadroon to one-eighth African heritage, one-sixteenth (fifteen European great-grandparents and one African made you "black"), and finally, the infamous "one drop." In other words, people legally "white" in the nineteenth century became "black" in the twentieth—revealing as utter fiction any ideas about the races' fundamental difference. That one drop was taken quite literally, as if people could sift through corpuscles to find the contaminating "Negro" blood. One writer insisted that "under certain conditions, Negro virus, like other poisons, has a power of diffusion superior to pure blood"—an infection that could make you sick, that traditional and irrational fear of sexual plague. One Louisiana statute declared that every white person should have the right to refuse transfusions from "coloreds," an ideology that at its most extreme might be interpreted "better dead than brown." Still others used the blood metaphor to their advantage: one white New Orleans cashier transfused himself with blood from his beloved, a black woman, and then, claiming to be black himself, legally married her.

The more social equality seemed possible, the more intermarriage hysteria mounted. In the year 1913—in the infancy of the NAACP—twelve separate state legislatures were considering anti-interracial marriage bills, including California, Michigan, Nebraska, Washington, and Wisconsin. When in the 1940s Gunnar Myrdal asked white and black Southerners to rank the importance of various segregation rules, whites "nearly unanimously" ranked the ban on intermarriage first, with economic discrimination in jobs, credit, and housing last. Southern blacks ranked the same items in exactly the *opposite* order, with jobs on top, even before the vote, and at the bottom "the marriage matter . . . of rather distant and doubtful interest." Which is not to say black folks were *for* intermarriage bans. W. E. B. Du Bois wrote in 1913, "to prohibit such intermarriage would be publicly to acknowledge that black blood is a physical taint, something no self-respecting colored man and woman can be asked to admit." But for most black people the ban rankled only symbolically, since they mostly fell in love with and married other black folks. Jobs, voting rights, education, and the daily threat of death for walking into the wrong restroom were far more urgent and immediate. Besides, why would anyone proud of his or her race fight for the few individuals who wanted to abandon the tribe—which only confirms the ruling caste's smug belief that what your kind *really* wants is a taste of *their* kind? No wonder, when the NAACP Legal Defense Fund planned its attack on segregation laws, or when the 1960s civil rights movement turned TV cameras like neon arrows on Southern buses and lunch counters and schoolrooms, or when Malcolm X urged freedom from the white devils by any means necessary, intermarriage—with its high public relations cost and negligible benefit—did not rank on the black political agenda. Even today, *Loving v. Virginia*—the court case that brought down antimiscegenation laws—does not even rate an index entry in books about the civil rights movement.

Meanwhile, segregationists sounded the intermarriage threat incessantly. When Walter White, director of the NAACP in the 1950s—a blue-eyed and white-skinned "Negro"—married a white woman, Herman E. Talmadge, former Governor of Georgia wrote, "There it is for anyone to see. The ultimate aim of the National Association for the Advancement of Colored People is the complete amalgamation of the races." Mixed-race marriage, in other words—however *individual* couples might have desired it, however blatantly unjust the ban against it—was no group's goal. In this way, the battle over mixed-race marriage is unlike the battle over same-sex marriage: it was useful to very few black people, since most of them could marry the person they loved. No lesbian or gay man can.

And yet some of the reasons for the bans are similar. Inflammatory as mixed-race marriage was and is—literally inflammatory, at times inciting riots when mobs realized a black man and white woman were living together—the threat was not what lay at the end of equality's road, but the road itself. Social equality wasn't frightening because it led to intermarriage; rather, intermarriage was frightening because it implied social equality. Or as one anthropologist writes, "One can usually take for granted that families consider themselves to be roughly equal economically or socially if they believe it is acceptable to join together in a marriage." At a time when segregationists could still insist with pride that "to hold a superior race, with all its material, intellectual, and moral interests, under the heel of an inferior race . . . is, every way, such an outrageous proceeding, that it staggers belief," no wonder they could also write that "intermixture of the two races is contrary to nature and the well-being of man; that it brings corruption of blood and confusion; breeds a class of deficient mongrels, generally short-lived, and in a few generations sterile." If I believe you're that far beneath me, I must protect my superiority and its privileges by banning you from my tribe—because marrying would mean you were my equal and therefore deserved equal treatment in every other way. The parallel in the same-sex marriage fight is that many of those opposed believe that "to permit persons of the same sex to marry is to declare, or more precisely to be understood by many people to be declaring, that homosexual marriage is a desirable, even a noble, condition in which to live."

And so it wasn't until the civil rights movement had won the moral battle for the nation's conscience that mixed-race marriage laws could fall—not because it was an item on the civil rights agenda, and certainly *not* because most Americans yet believed that mixed-race marriage was "a desirable, even a noble, condition in which to live," but because of a subversive pair of individual hearts. Two separate fights are worth noting—since one "activist" (to use the imprecation hurled by today's conservatives) state court raced ahead of its populace in striking down its intermarriage ban twenty years before the Supreme Court followed. In 1948, Andrea

Perez, a white woman, and Sylvester D——, a black man, argued that they were both Roman Catholics—and that banning their marriage violated their freedom of religion. They were backed by the Catholic Church, which had always been especially interested in erasing the out-marriage taboo, treating us all as "neither Greek nor Jew" but united in Christ. The California Court decided—far ahead of its time—that if a *white* man could marry a white woman, then it would be discrimination to say that a *black* man could not, based solely on his race.

Over the next decades some state legislatures repealed their intermarriage bans. In others, notably the former slave-owning states, individuals challenged the ban in the courts—and saw these bans upheld. Some state courts all but dared the Supreme Court to decide that "the newfound concept of 'social justice' has outdated 'the law of the land.'" The Court refrained until it had dismantled more important props of segregation.

In 1958, Richard Loving and Mildred Jeters drove to Washington, D.C., to evade Virginia's ban and get married, then drove right back home. Within six weeks, they were arrested by a Virginia sheriff at 2:00 A.M. and hauled off to jail. After being convicted of their felony, they were released—on the condition that they leave the state for twenty-five years, or face a year in jail. As the ACLU pursued their case in both the Virginia and federal courts, the Virginia judge who ruled against them wrote, "If the Federal Government can determine who can marry in a State, there is no limit to its power." Only sixteen states still had bans on their books in 1967, when the Supreme Court agreed to hear the case. In *Loving v. Virginia,* the Court ruled that the ban on Richard's and Mildred's marriage violated the Fourteenth Amendment, resting as it did "solely upon distinctions drawn according to race."

It was not a popular decision. According to one contemporary Gallup poll, 72 percent of Americans then disapproved of interracial marriage (far more than disapprove of same-sex marriage today); perhaps more shocking, 48 percent believed interracial marriage should be a *crime.* And yet there were no race riots, no mass movement for repeal, no courthouse sit-ins. Unlike integrated schools or affirmative action, if you opposed mixed-race marriage all you had to do was not marry someone of another race—or, as happened in my own family, inflict pain by refusing to speak to those who did.

The war of the words   The jeremiads against mixed-race marriage will sound familiar—although since this fight was about marrying outside the tribe (and since so many people suspect that those beyond their tribe aren't fully human), accusations that mixed-race marriage was actually bestiality were especially prominent. Turn-of-the-century pseudoscience "proved" that Europeans and Africans were nearly separate species with scrupulously gathered data on such comparative "measurements" as "nasal index," hair "distinctly woolly, not merely frizzly," and "a peculiar rancid odor, compared . . . to that of the buck goat," all of which made sexual relations between the races "disgraceful and almost bestial." The comparison of African-Americans to the lesser animals was sounded incessantly, in the most "respectable" quarters. A Florida judge wrote in 1955,

> segregation . . . is and always has been the unvarying law of the animal kingdom. The dove and the quail, the turkey and the turkey buzzard, the chicken and the guinea, it matters not where they are found, are segregated; place the horse, the cow, the sheep, the goat, and the pig in the same pasture and they instinctively segregate . . . when God created man, he allotted each race his own continent according to color, Europe to the white man, Asia to the yellow man, Africa to the black man, and America to the red man, but we are now advised that God's plan was in error and must be reversed.

No matter that it had been the "white man" who had violated God's plan by invading continents and either kidnapping or "buying" human beings. This rhetoric was repeated so widely that you'd think they were all reading from the same secret white-supremacy handbook, passed out at birth.

But though bestiality and God's plan were favorites, all the usual suspects were dragged in. In 1872, one Tennessee judge issued a ruling against a racially mixed couple who'd moved to his state, suggesting that if he allowed this, the tide of contamination would never stop:

> ... we might have in Tennessee the father living with his daughter, the son with the mother, the brother with his sister, in lawful wedlock, because they had formed such relations in a state or country where they were not prohibited. The Turk or the Mohammedan, with his numerous wives, may establish his harem at the doors of the capital, and we are without remedy. Yet none of these are more revolting, more to be avoided, or more unnatural than the case before us.

Of course, children of mixed-race pairs would wither and die, since "hybrids are never healthy or vigorous, and vanish with the third or fourth generation." One Georgia court famously stated that "the offspring of these unnatural connections are generally sickly, effeminate, and that they are inferior to the full blooded of either race in physical development and strength." The words are surely familiar from the accusations hurled against two moms or two dads raising kids. As we've seen before, when a marriage rule is outdated, there's nothing much to say except, *You and your children will sicken and die, and God will punish all of civilization.*

The codes and emotions barring marriage to outsiders remain eerily similar from one group to another. There seems to be, inside us, some horror at mixing whatever seems essentially *us*—in the same way that Leviticus prohibited you from wearing a garment that mixed two fibers, or eating any food that was not clearly fish or mammal, or blurring your gender by lying with another man. Mixing reveals that your group identity is a mirage, fictional as the Emperor's new clothes. It poses a vertiginous question to anyone who believes in their group identity: Am I not, after all, so separate and superior, so endowed with a "world-ruling and world-conquering" destiny?

So *are* the battles for interracial marriage and same-sex marriage comparable? Not in the kinship sense: mine is not an out-marriage. Like most of our heterosexual siblings, most lesbians and gay men find someone of a similar cultural background: our marriages do not *necessarily* push the boundaries of our ethnic, racial, class, or religious tribes. From the point of view of the out-marrying taboo, marriage is for demonstrating equal status between two families. And if that is the case, then marriages between two women or two men can either observe—or violate—the taboo, just as a marriage between a man and a woman can.

What *is* comparable—and comparably frightening—is that civil marriage would imply that lesbians and gay men are our heterosexual siblings' social equals. Even more significant, same-sex marriage will imply that the *sexes* are deeply and fundamentally equal. In the spring of 1998, the Southern Baptist Convention passed two closely linked rules: that a wife must "submit" to her husband and that homosexuality must be opposed by every possible means. Those ideas are twin sides of the same coin. If a woman marries another woman, who's in charge? Restricting marriage to husband/wife pairs is an essential symbol of *male* supremacy—just as restricting marriage to one race was an essential symbol of *white* supremacy. It's no mistake, in other words, that those most vocally against my marriage to Madeline are also against abortion rights, divorce, childcare, laws mandating postpartum leave, or anything else that might let women escape the nineteenth-century hearth. Same-sex marriage reveals that marriage need not be hierarchical at all, that biology is *not* destiny, that marriage can be about not obedience but love.

And there is another comparable fear: the fear the tribe will disappear. Segregationists charged that legalizing interracial marriage would "make this country a brown race"—committing race suicide, to quote Teddy Roosevelt. In a similar way, some opponents of same-sex marriage fear that with Melissa Etheridge and Julie Cypher up there as an optional model, suddenly *all* women will flee their husbands and marry their best girlfriends, or that after learning about the long and contented life together of Allen Ginsberg and Peter Orlovsky, *all* men will escape to an all-male subculture—and that our society will no longer reproduce. Melissa and Julie *are* parents, but it is true there are far fewer surprise births among same-sex pairs. But this threat is actually quite ridiculous: by far most human beings are heterosexually oriented, and will remain so. More than 95 percent of twentieth-century Americans marry heterosexually sometime in their lives—and even more simply live together at some point. At the beginning of the Reformation, approximately 40 percent of all women were single (especially in Germanic central Europe—half spinsters, half widows); 15.9 percent of the women and 12.1 percent of the men in one eighteenth-century American Quaker community never married. Ours is a rampantly marrying society: the very small percentage of us who partner with the same sex do not threaten the tribe.

The point here is that same-sex marriage is neither precisely like, nor precisely *un*like, the out-marriage taboo that our laws have so firmly rejected as unjust. Only two things are truly comparable: first, the more that social equality seems possible, the more hysterical the threats against it become; and second, just as it was a step toward social justice when all the United States recognized my uncle's marriage to my aunt, so it would be a step toward social justice for the West to recognize my marriage to Madeline.

Marrying In: Protecting the Family

What about the *in*-marrying taboo? Is same-sex marriage like incest, something that we still agree must be prohibited lest the tribe be permanently polluted? The answer depends on what the incest taboo is for.

Say the word "incest" in conversation today, and—unless you hang out with anthropologists—most of your listeners' minds will skip to the sexual abuse of children. Late twentieth-century prosecutors invoke incest laws only as an extra-nasty charge against child-rapists, so that most of us think of "incest" as a synonym for daddy-dearest forcing himself on his fifth-grader. But the debauching of children was *not* what horrified our ancestors when a twelve-year-old was married to her wealthy uncle, or an eight-year-old was sent to live with her fiancé. How did "incest" come to mean violations of consent more than violations of consanguinity? How can a word so fundamental as "incest"—a word hissing with horror, a word from which everyone recoils—have almost entirely changed its connotations? If the violation of children was *not* the sin that worried our ancestors, what did?

The theme has some startling variations. Some tribal societies allow a man to marry his younger sisters, although not his older ones; others, like the Egyptians, allow royal sibs to marry each other—considering it natural that childhood intimacy should grow into marital intimacy, and equally natural that royalty should not marry someone of lower status. On the other hand, many societies have *far* more comprehensive incest codes than our own, such as the complicated rule of cross-cousin marriage: you *must* marry cousins by your father's sister or mother's brother, but you must *never* marry cousins by your father's brother or mother's sister, which would be incest.

Then there are the Old Testament Hebrews, that notoriously clannish bunch. The anthropologists call them *endogamous:* they enforced muscular rules against marrying foreigners—but had only the barest of rules against marrying within the family. Their founding pair, Abraham and Sarah, shared a father. That marriage was *not* considered incest: in a world in which your father's various wives raised children in separate tents, sib-marriage was incest *only* if you two shared a womb, and therefore an upbringing. Remember that Jacob married a pair of sisters, Rachel and Leah, whose children presumably married each other. After they fled Sodom (and watched their mother turn into a pillar of salt for looking back), Lot's daughters apparently thought that keeping the tribe safe from the foreign hordes was pretty darn important—because they got their father drunk and into bed with them, so that he fathered their children.

Seen from today's genetic point of view, the Leviticus incest rules—directed only at men—seem entirely arbitrary. Yes, there's a long list of women forbidden to a man because "none of you shall approach to any that is near kin to him, to uncover their nakedness: I am the Lord." But—surprise!—a man's daughter and nieces are *not* banned, although his aunt and his brothers' or father's wives *are.* Why? One scholar explains that a daughter is her father's sexual property: he can use, sell, or give her away. But his brother's wife was some other man's sexual property. What counted was the need, in a clannish world, for brothers to stay unified and to refrain from muddling the ancestral line, their sperm incestuously touching in one womb.

There was one interesting exception: the rule called "levirate." If a man died and left a child, the widow was forbidden to the surviving brothers as incestuous. But if the same man died *without* fathering a child, his surviving next-in-line brother *had* to marry the widow and create a child to bear his brother's name. Onan's sin was refusing to impregnate his dead brother's childless widow, refusing to work the family property—her uterus. The only escape clause the Hebrews gave the brother who refused his responsibility was a formal ceremony in which—in Deuteronomy, at least—the widow got to spit in his face. Over the years, as the tribe grew into a people, the Jews slowly expanded the rules against marrying in (a man who touched his daughter, for instance, was punished by burning)—although not as enthusiastically as they enforced the rule against marrying *out*.

In-marriage let your family consolidate its property and power: if your grandchildren married each other, your inheritance stayed intact and your bloodline was never diluted. And so the Old Testament Hebrews and the early medieval Jews—with their in-marrying habits and their skimpy incest rules—were far from exceptional. The Romans allowed first cousins to marry, while the early Germanic clans gave the nod to uncle/niece marriages. Unofficially, Roman patriarchs and their slave-daughters, or the patriarch's legal son and his slave half-sisters, were notorious for their liaisons, which couldn't be incest since they had no legal relationship as kin.

You can guess what the early Christians thought about this all-in-the-family attitude toward orifices and wombs, property and power. When they weren't out-and-out rejecting this tainted world by declaring celibacy, they were vehemently denouncing all this incest—and radicalizing the marriage rules.

It took awhile—but *radicalizing* is exactly the right term. As

Christianity consolidated from a lot of squabbling sects into a unified Roman Church, it pursued an astonishing mission that, eventually, all but brought down the Church. As it gained power across
medieval Europe, the Church attempted to break open the tightly
intermarried clans by insisting that it was illegal for them to "approach to any that is near kin to him, to uncover their nakedness"
(Lev. 18:6). But what counts as *near* kin? Leviticus had been pretty
explicit—but not, the Church decided, comprehensive enough,
when it decided around 385 A.D. that that verse barred cousins
from marrying. For the next thousand years, the Church kept
changing its incest prohibitions, occasionally pulling back in to
allow some individual to manipulate power by marrying close by,
and then pushing it out wider and wider again. That included an
extremely creative interpretation of the Genesis verse saying husband and wife became "one flesh": because you and hubby were
now one, your husband's brother (even once you were widowed)
and uncle and cousin and so on were just as off-limits as your own.
The exegesis got even more creative: since you became "one flesh"
by having sex, even if you'd had a single illicit roll in the hay with
some boy, all *his* relatives were forever off-limits. And let's not forget your godparents—or your parents' or your brother's godparents—and all *their* relatives, *also* one flesh with you in Christ. By
the eleventh century, the Church was banning marriage as far out
as the seventh degree, or fourth cousins—via blood, marriage, sex,
or godparenthood.

Picture this geometrically, spinning out like a Calder mobile:
you're barred from marrying anyone, out to fourth cousins, to
whom you're related by ancestry, marriage, sex, or godparenthood.
That might not mean too much in today's Los Angeles, but for
eleventh-century peasants it could easily bar everyone in the village and scores of miles beyond; for feudal lords, everyone within
the clan; for aristocrats, just about every other aristocrat in Europe.
Or as one historian puts it, men were forbidden to marry "all the
marriageable girls they could possibly know and a great many
more besides."

Why? Why did the Church let its incest rules—based on the very same verses from which Jews created such skimpy prohibitions—get so ridiculously vast? Historians have speculated endlessly. The Church wrinkled its nose at marriage to begin with, of course, so making it hard for you to find a spouse might not have struck theologians as a problem. And—as a theological matter, at least—the Church disliked the earthly piling up of goods and power, precisely the goal of marrying in. What's more, the Church was concerned about protecting the individual spirit: if individuals had to marry out instead of into the family, theoretically they could be treated less as pawns in the family power strategy and might even have some say in their partner. But most important, the goal of the Christian Church was the opposite of that of the Jews: it wanted to break open families into a wider society, bound not by ethnic or clan or tribal solidarities, with "no Greek or Jew, male or female," united only in Christ.

And the Church succeeded. In forcing people to marry beyond kinship, to traffic emotionally and financially among many groups, the Church changed the face of the West. In flinging society open wide, it forced the West to find a way to organize society based on something other than clans. To put it differently, in part because incest rules barred people from putting kinship first, we now live in a world based on capital and the nation-state, an anomaly in world history and culture.

Catholicism also won a smaller political victory: with almost everyone forbidden, rulers across Europe had to bargain with bishops and popes to marry their chosen spouses. After all, Church administration was reasonable: you could always apply for a dispensation and—after paying enough fees—marry your brother's godmother's niece after all. Meanwhile, for people in unsatisfactory marriages (say, a marriage in which the wife was not producing any sons), the incest rules were a godsend: almost any marriage could be annulled. All you had to do was pay: pay some lawyer to dig up or invent a seventh-degree relation, pay enough dispensation fees to your ecclesiastical authorities to review your case, pay more dispensation fees to be free to marry again. Which is one reason the Church started asking, right there in the marriage ceremony, whether anyone knew a reason you two should not be married.

The incest system seriously backfired. The Protestants insisted that this side of Church doctrine—a scandalous and constant source of ecclesiastical litigation, ever-flowing dispensation fees, loopholes, manipulable decisions—was so far from reality as to be rotten, and they diminished incest back to a somewhat expanded version of the Leviticus limits. And yet it should be no surprise that changes in the incest rules can and have brought on the same fever-ish language of abomination and family collapse that we've seen elsewhere in this book. The late nineteenth century, for instance, saw a bitter debate over whether kinship by affinity—i.e., relation-ships through your spouse, living or dead—should be forbidden as incest. One nineteenth-century American quoted the Bible as say-ing that to allow a man to marry his dead brother's widow "is an unclean thing. . . . Is there no danger of pollution to the soul, to the church, and to society from acts, for which Canaan vomited out its inhabitants? . . . It would destroy all order and morality in society to allow men to marry their relatives." Less feverishly but with no less vehemence, an American judge insisted that marriages between in-laws were horrifying to consider, since "prohibitions of natural law are of absolute, uniform, and universal obligation . . . founded in the common reason and acknowledged duty of mankind, sanc-tioned by immemorial usages." In 1840, the American Presbyteri-ans, in an uproar, defrocked a North Carolina minister who "inces-tuously" married his dead wife's sister.

But by the nineteenth century, the financial and emotional reali-ties of family had shrunk down to the new, nuclear version—and so there was no longer any justification for allowing outdated bibli-cal strictures to guide secular law. "Natural" law or not, no one would any longer consider actually *out*lawing marriage to your in-laws.

So what? Why, except for its entertainment value, should we care about these blips in the marriage wars, a battle that has nothing to do with "real" incest—dad/daughter, mom/son, brother/sister? First, they remind us that the most fundamental marriage rules—

even the rules of incest—are not natural but social, revised by each culture to match its sense of justice and purpose. Which means that, throughout history, groups with profound disagreements over what counts as a "real" marriage nevertheless acknowledge each other's marriages. For instance, from the Christians' Year Zero to our own times, Jews governed their own marriages. Which meant that, on the very same acreage and at the very same time that their next-door neighbors were trooping past priestly courts for annulments because of some fifth-degree relation-by-marriage, the consanguine marriages of this troublesome archipelago through Christendom were honored. A few centuries and an ocean away, a similar thing happened in the American plantation South. The white land- and slave-owners "were most amazingly interwed, the marriages of cousins being almost the rule rather than the exception," consolidating property and power by staying close. But enslaved Africans and African-Americans living on the very same territory flatly refused to marry first or even second cousins. Are you and your spouse legitimately married? The answer—as always—depends on whose social map gets superimposed.

Second, the shifting boundaries of incest force us to think about the *real* purpose of the incest taboo. We usually explain it as based on genetics and family psychology, scriptures our society subscribes to more widely than Leviticus. But neither genetics nor family psychology can possibly be the reason for incest rules that let you marry one brother or cousin while barring the other—or to use the Hebrews' example, lets a man marry his niece but not his aunt—or to use the medieval Catholic example, forbids you to marry your husband's or godfather's relatives. Meanwhile, in a small community, marrying your niece and marrying your neighbor are genetically not that different: premarital genetic testing would do more to prevent, say, Tay-Sachs disease than a law that automatically separated Sam and Fannie May. Nor can family psychology—the idea that allowing Dick and Jane to marry would cause too much household tension—have mattered to the many societies that sent an affianced girl off to her future husband's house at a young age.

So why *do* human beings ban incest—however it may be defined at the time? Anthropologists insist that it really doesn't matter what the incest taboo is, so long as your society has one. The point, they say, is to force families to break open, every generation—to force families to give up their children, to force you to leave your father and mother—in order to create new kin, and therefore, a common society. Families thus become fluid cells in a larger society rather than sternly defended turrets—tied to others, loaning their members out, sharing obligations that range from delivering all your yams to your new brother-in-law or babysitting the new nephew every Thursday. The incest taboo insists that the basic human impulses toward sex, affection, food, and mutual support must be routed in a way that weaves a larger social web.

But *how* that breaking apart and weaving together must happen—exactly *how* family units might turn inward, like bad toenails, hobbling the larger society, and therefore what rules must guide families out of their self-absorption and into a common civilization—varies according to how a society is organized. Some groups want to keep marrying inward as closely as possible, like the ancient Hebrews, letting each marriage strengthen tribal power (while refusing to let any given father horde his daughters, cutting the small family off from the tribe). Others do *not* want to pull up the drawbridge to outsiders: they want to build power by having a far-flung network of kin, tied to a wider human community. The incest rules that keep turning a group's members outward—whether Africans' careful prohibition against marrying "parallel" cousins, or Catholicism's outrageously broad sense of family—can have surprising effects. According to historian Herbert Gutman, under American slavery, the African prohibition on marrying cousins turned into a wide network of kin to turn to in extremis, a kind of cross-plantation resistance network.

Our own society scarcely worries about the power problem that preoccupied the early Church: clans marrying inward so often that they consolidated too much power and didn't have to recognize other families as human. Rather, now that our public ideal of individual freedom has been translated into the sexual values of willingness and consent—and now that feminists have spoken up about being used by brothers, fathers, uncles—the West worries about those too young and powerless to say no. If we really believe that marriage must be a meeting of peers, and if we believe that each person should grow up with a sense of personal integrity, emotional security, and bodily independence—urgent concepts to an economy whose motor is the individual personality—then we must be especially concerned about that invisible abuse of power, about adults who take advantage of the vulnerable ones in their charge.

If the anthropologists are right, and the point of the incest taboo is to force us to leave our parents and create new kin, then the incest prohibition really *is* the very fiber of civilization—the basic rule that prevents the war of all (families, that is) against all. Or as anthropologist Claude Lévi-Strauss puts it,

> if each small biological unit does not wish to lead a precarious existence, haunted by fear and prey to the hatred and hostility of its neighbours, it cannot remain turned in upon itself. It must instead sacrifice its identity and continuity and open itself up to the great game of matrimonial alliances. By resisting the separatist tendences of kinship, the prohibition of incest succeeds in weaving networks of affinity which give societies their framework and without which none could sustain itself.

So what is marriage for? Seen from this angle, it's for creating obligations beyond one's own household, for creating a society that's wider than blood. Marriage between two people of one sex—who are just as likely to visit the in-laws, send birthday cards, and take on all the other family obligations of our era—will serve.

Marrying Early and Marrying Often: Polygamy

Perhaps the most famous way to make kin is to make babies—seeding heirs to carry on your personal tribe. And if making children was good in God's eyes, then traditionally, making *more* children was even better. We all know that men have a far greater ability to fertilize than women do to grow new life. And so if you put that vertical proliferation of kinship at the top of marriage's to-do list, it's easy to guess the resulting marriage rule: polygamy. Is polygamy, as many suggest, the next stop after same-sex marriage? Or is it a form that firmly endorses male power, a form we've outgrown, in which women are not the moral equals of men but are treated as incubators, a social arrangement in which fertility trumps love?

Polygamy (or to be verbally strict, polygyny) is one of the most traditional marriage forms: one man, several wives. Most of the ancients took it for granted that if a man's wife was not producing children, she should hand over a surrogate—as Sarah offered Hagar—to handle the job in her name, or he should take on an additional wife; early medieval Jews considered a second wife mandatory if a marriage hadn't produced children within ten years. Jacob launched the twelve tribes with his two wives—the sisters Leah and Rachel—and two concubines, his main wives competing with each other to "give" him more children from their own and their handmaids' wombs. As time went by, the Jews frowned more and more on that agrarian and tribal marriage form. Some Jewish families actually wrote into their daughter's *ketubah,* or marriage contract, that she was to get her dowry back if her husband ever took another wife—although officially the tribe kept the polygamous possibility until roughly 1300 A.D.

The Romans were a bit appalled by Jewish polygamy, in part because they felt free to make heirs via adoption. And yet the Romans excelled at serial polygamy, or as we'd know it, divorce, and unofficial polygamy, what with the panoply of slave and semi-free males and females available to each Roman patriarch and his sons.

Polygamy was a given among early medieval Germanic and Frankish clans. Since no ambitious or powerful man could afford to lack an heir, and since half your children could easily die before adulthood, one wife was never enough. A powerful man had at least a chief wife, second wife, and a back-up chorus of concubines. One well-known Carolingian lord had seven simultaneous wives and concubines—or more, reports one historian, if you count adultery and rape. And all those marriages and their offspring were "legitimate," in the sense that any one could inherit if necessary.

Christianity's most controversial marriage innovation was the idea that marriage was an either/or proposition. You were married or not: there were no more grades of marriage, no more wives of different ranks. A woman had just one husband—and a man had just one wife. Period. Male or female, lord or laborer, everybody had to play by the same marriage rules: one spouse at a time, forever. Adultery no longer meant invading another man's sexual property but straying from your own; keeping a concubine was now as adulterous as shtupping another man's wife. Part of what fueled the Church's new doctrine was its dislike of two things: first, sex for pleasure's sake, and second, marriage's grubby interest in dynasty-building. But also important was the Church's respect for women. The early Church's vision of marriage may have been far from egalitarian, but it did offer a step up from women's status in the past: frankly opposed to seeing women treated like meat, the Church insisted on monogamy as an acknowledgment that their inner lives were as valuable as their husbands'.

We take monogamy for granted now as "traditional" marriage, but at the time it was such an outrageous and radical leveling of society—taking away such key political (let alone personal) options from the men in power—that imposing this concept took more strength than the Church had for hundreds upon hundreds of years. *One* wife, and *only* one, was an incredible—not-to-be-believed—concept. No concubine? No repudiation? No way out? Explains one historian, the older world's key distinction had been between freeborn and slave-born; the Church changed that into a line between legitimate and illegitimate, which "can be considered as no less than a social revolution."

Jump forward more than a thousand years to a time when monogamy had become synonymous with morality. Certainly by the time of the Protestants, serious Christians believed fiercely in monogamy's mutual respect and sexual control. Meanwhile, as the West shifted from a farm-based to an urban world, families no longer needed that vast tribal brood. By the late nineteenth century, during the sentimentalizing Victorian era, young people chose their mates for themselves, falling in love with another's unique inner spirit, then joining their hearts and souls and bodies in a romantic fusion. In the midst of a world like this, what possessed the Mormons to try to resurrect polygamy?

The story of Mormon polygamy is instructive in part because of its wholesale rejection of the Western beliefs in individual emotional freedom and gender equality that undergird today's political and marriage philosophies. What the story also tells us is how opposed are the impulses toward polygamy and same-sex marriage. Or to put it differently, for the very reasons that polygamy was so definitively trounced in the nineteenth century, recognition of same-sex marriage is edging into Western law.

But first, some background. The nineteenth century, aboil with political and economic upheaval and with disturbing shifts in the roles of women and men, saw a proliferation of sects, revivals, and religious and political utopias that puts the 1960s to shame. The next section will look at some that believed in personal, social, and sexual emancipation, including such radical ideas as that husbands and wives should be fully equal. The sect focused on here, the Church of the Latter-Day Saints (LDS), had an entirely different vision: a hope of eliminating its era's chaos by returning to the clear and crisp patriarchal rules of the Old Testament.

In 1823, Joseph Smith found and translated golden plates (lost before anyone else saw them) that explained that Israel's lost tribes had long ago come to North America, and were now commanded to "restore the ancient gospel spirit" of Christianity in all its fullness and purity. Toward that end, the Mormons aimed—among other things—to rescue marriage. Marriage, in LDS theology, was the *only* way a person could achieve the highest glory and status in its very hierarchical heaven. The Church of the Latter-Day Saints had (and has) an incredibly complex marriage theology. You could marry for "time," which was valid only here on earth, involved sex, children, and household responsibilities, and could be performed by anyone, Mormon or secular. You could marry for "eternity," which had to be "sealed" by Mormon priests in private Temple rites, was valid only in heaven, and included no earthly sex (although a man was still financially responsible for an "eternity" wife, if alive). And you could, under the auspices of a Mormon priest, marry for both "time and eternity"—valid *both* on earth and in heaven.

Here's the key: your earthly marital status defined your status in heaven. In "eternity," men who'd had properly "sealed" Mormon marriages became angel-patriarchs ruling over their wives, children, grandchildren, and so on. A woman's rank in this system depended on how senior her husband was in the LDS Church. Anyone who, while on earth, had *not* married for "eternity" spent the afterlife serving those who had. Meanwhile, as angel-patriarchs' children went on to have properly sealed marriages and offspring, the clan's senior patriarch "eventually would move on to rule over whole new worlds, achieving full godhood in conjunction with their wives in what could easily be seen as a kind of cosmic 'manifest destiny.'" The Mormon vision of marriage was quite openly about male rule—on earth as in heaven.

Once you believe marriage to be about eternal male power, making you the ruling patriarch of a heavenly tribe of angels, why stop at eight or nine children by one wife? Why not go the whole way and ensure that your tribe's heavenly seed will be as numerous as the sand on the seashore and as numberless as the stars? We know how the Mormons answered the question, but at the time it was far from obvious. Because the accompanying question is: how in the world did good nineteenth-century Protestants, raised in an urbanizing world, retreat back to agrarian polygamy? How could nineteenth-century Americans or Europeans (Mormons were and are indefatigable missionaries) raised in strict monogamy possibly turn to something so reviled by Christianity, their families, their neighbors, and themselves?

It was far from easy. Joseph Smith's charismatic prophet-status—he was regularly handing down new revelations from the fierce angel Moroni—had drawn thousands of folks into this spiritual elite. And yet when Smith secretly told his coterie of top leaders that God had ordered them—like the Hebrew patriarchs—to take up "plural marriage," many rebelled. Some had to be flatly ordered to obey. Some left the sect rather than, as instructed, take another wife or hand over a daughter to be sealed as one of Smith's "plural wives," of whom there were soon dozens. But the Saints were already cut off from the outside world by their own belief that they were the Chosen and by neighbors' intense hatred and persecution. How could they refuse their Prophet's direct revelation, endangering their salvation and solidarity? Meanwhile, once they *were* doubly or triply married, how could they ever leave the Church without admitting that they or their daughters had been licentious sinners?

Smith was not so rash as to openly introduce the drastic new doctrine of "plural" or "Bible marriage" to his ordinary flock. And before he got around to it, he and his brother, also a church leader, were jailed—and then dragged out and killed by a mob of Illinois militiamen. In the resulting crisis, some Mormons fled the Church. Others joined Brigham Young's famous covered-wagon trek into Utah's Martian landscape, during which many died. All this—Smith's martyrdom, attacks by the "gentiles," exile into the desert far from their birth-families—steeled the spines of the Mormons who remained, making it far easier to cut off their childhood training in monogamy. And once Brigham Young introduced it, "plural marriage" was a way to prove one's stern Mormon commitment.

Its first purpose was to restore men to their superior position. The Saints (as they thought of themselves) believed, as historian Lawrence Foster writes, that "polygamy would allow men to reassert their proper authority and leadership. It would free them from the unnatural sexual influence women hold over men in a monogamous system [which leads] to ungoverned and ungovernable children . . . thereby undermining the whole family organization and resulting in social chaos." Or, as Brigham Young put it, "Let the wives and the children say Amen to what he says, and be subject to his dictates, instead of their dictating [to] the man." Being a patriarch, of course, wasn't pure pleasure. Multiply-married men had to support those wives and children, an especially heavy load because wives usually balked at sharing their household or children and so each required a separate house. Even at the peak of plural marriage in official Mormon theology, only about 20 percent of Mormon men lived polygamously.

Polygamy also allowed men many sexual outlets while still forcing them to take responsibility for the consequences of their drives: it was usually Mormon elders who were rewarded with fresh sixteen-year-old wives. But most interesting to us is, perhaps, that "at the deepest level, [polygamy] was a fundamental protest against the careless individualism of romantic love, which seemed to threaten the very roots of family life and social solidarity." There was almost no courtship for these plural marriages, since it would be slightly scandalous to see a married man hanging around a young woman too much: an elder simply sent a proposal to a potential wife via her family, and she responded yes or no. Nor was there modern intimacy *after* marriage. You can't get *too* personal if you see each other only once or twice a week—or if you know that one of you will be with someone else the next night. As one plural wife wrote to another, she must be as "pleased to see [her husband] when he came in as she was pleased to see any friend"—neither more nor less. Wives treated polygamy as a kind of religious renunciation, while husbands had to avoid favoritism and work hard to keep harmony lest they be exposed as unable to govern. You weren't making love: you were making kin. Just as polygamy, in other words, was explicitly antifeminist, so it was explicitly anti-individualist.

But it was pro-community. Since polygamists could not retreat into the gauzy haven of personal sexual love, a lot of energy—male and female—could be harnessed to build the new Jerusalem. Martha Hughes Cannon, the United States's first female state senator and a fourth wife, argued that polygamy was a feminist's dream: "If a [woman's] husband has four wives, she has three weeks of freedom every single month." And think how the kin ties multiplied! One nineteenth-century elder "was related by blood or marriage to over eight hundred people"—making one's family and one's community almost interchangeable.

But while all this made sense to the Mormons themselves, LDS polygamy was shocking to outsiders. One British commentator said it was "incompatible with civilization, refinement, and domestic felicity." Others attacked it as sowing despotism and undermining a republic: all that male rule over small clans had explicitly kingly implications. (Although Elizabeth Cady Stanton was heard to mutter that most Senators were polygamists, even if they hadn't married their second wives.) And many people linked polygamy with slavery, insisting that both turned women (willing or un-) into concubines.

The polygamous side of Southern slavery, of course, was very much on nineteenth-century Americans' minds. How polygamous was the South? Every bit as much as the Romans, their counterparts. Young white plantation owners or heirs could go to New Orleans' annual octoroon debutante balls, where they could choose a young woman and then haggle with her mother over the exact terms of the concubinage contract: in what part of town she would live, how large her house or apartment would be, what she'd get for annual maintenance, all written and signed before consummation. Less formally, of course, slaveowners did seduce, coerce, or rape their female slaves. Plantation polygamy was based on the feudal idea of father/lord/master, a more sensual and exploitive system than the Mormons' biblical father/patriarch. But the two did get conflated in public debate.

And so in 1862, President Lincoln signed the Morrill Act, which outlawed polygamy in American territories. In 1874 Brigham Young's personal secretary challenged the ban as violating his religious freedom: he got two years of hard labor and a whopping $500 fine. By 1882 Congress passed the Edmunds Act, which criminalized a man's *cohabitation* with more than one woman; stripped anyone convicted of polygamy of the right to vote or hold office; and barred you from jury duty if you so much as *said* you believed in polygamy. In 1887 Congress annulled the Mormons' articles of incorporation, confiscated their assets, and imposed test oaths on Utah citizens. In all, almost 1300 Mormons were criminally prosecuted. Finally the Church of the Latter-Day Saints capitulated and officially renounced polygamy. Although some polygamous marriages still existed and some new ones are still being made, the official battle was over. Polygamy had been driven from the public field.

Why? Because Mormon polygamy was aiming in precisely the opposite direction of Western society. Privately, it stood for the opposite of sexual equality and individual choice. Politically, plural marriage was precisely opposed to a democratic system. It explicitly consolidated theocratic and tribal—or kin—power, shutting out outsiders and knitting in insiders; it installed the male as patriarch, officially superior, a monarch instead of an elected legislator; it subordinated the individual to the group and strictly disciplined emotions; it stripped away individual uniqueness and equality and replaced it with clan discipline; it opposed capitalism's urbanizing trend toward smaller and more intimate families; it elevated constant procreation and the making of kin over personal love. Mormon polygamy was trying to push back the oncoming tides of the modern world. It aimed in the *opposite* direction as the forces that lead us today toward same-sex marriage.

To put it more simply, those who fear that same-sex marriage will lead to incest and polygamy aren't looking at the facts. Tribal and despotic societies put kin first, allowing in-marriage and polygamy. Democratic egalitarianism, on the other hand, implies that the individual is who counts in marriage. The first insists that women are subordinate to men, either to be exploited or overruled, and reduces *both* to their reproductive functions. The second treats women and men as equals in morals, politics, sex, and marriage—and treats their inner lives as what matters in sex. Polygamy endorses and grows from the first; same-sex marriage, based firmly on gender and sexual equality and individual choice (to be explored more fully later), endorses and grows from the second. Philosophically, the two stand perfectly opposed: the same social system could not stretch to admit both.

Such a statement may seem to contradict one of this book's running themes: that throughout history, different marriage rules often overlap on the same ground. But societies cannot tolerate marriage rules that oppose their most fundamental political, economic, or philosophic values—which is why, for instance, the battle to legalize contraception (and to recognize individual choice in sexual life) won despite centuries of official Christian opposition. The LDS attempt to revive biblical polygamy was a defiant stand against the West's most basic political and personal values: the movement toward same-sex marriage, on the other hand, grows out of precisely those values. For the very same reasons that the Mormons lost their marriage battle, same-sex couples belong.

Marrying Everyone: Utopians

There's one more attitude toward marriage-for-kinship: those who object to marriage at all. History is littered with visionaries who have wanted to overthrow family ties—whether by blood, adoption, marriage, or friendship—so that we could *all* be kin. Within the lesbian and gay communities remain some who recoil from today's campaign for same-sex marriage, who came of age with a revolutionary sensibility and thought marriage was one of those oppressive institutions that should be overthrown. Their antimarriage philosophy comes from a long and venerable tradition. The intensity of the human sexual bond has always been disturbing to any utopian vision, since it drags our attention away from the needs and hopes of the collective to the selfish desires of the few. Utopians regularly wish we could love everyone equally—which is roughly the same as loving no one particularly. It's worth looking at what happens when you try to erase kinship and individual bonds—to wipe out the selfishness of marriage—in order to build a vaster human solidarity.

Plato's *Republic* is famous as (among other things) the first recorded intellectual utopia that aimed to throw out marriage whole hog. Writing in the fourth century B.C., Plato proposed that "women shall be wives in common to all the men, and not one of them shall live privately with any man; the children too should be held in common so that no parent shall know which is his own offspring, and no child shall know his parent." Since Plato aimed at a perfectly harmonious Republic, he wanted all private property—emotions included—utterly banished. There would be no marriage and no ownership: mating would take place at semi-annual festivals, with partners eugenically matched by benevolent overseers. Plato insisted that if a man had a particular family to whom he was attached, "one man would then drag into his own house whatever he could get hold of away from the others; another drag things into his different house to another wife and other children. This would make for private pleasures and pains at private events. Our people, on the other hand, will think of the same thing as their own, aim at the same goal, and, as far as possible, feel pleasure and pain in unison. . . . Will not lawsuits and mutual accusations disappear from among them . . . since they own nothing but their body, everything else being held in common?" Great idea—if you're an ant, not a human being.

Unfortunately, it's been tried—repeatedly. The sexual forms may differ but the totalitarian impulse remains the same: guided by some philosopher/tyrant, erase individual emotions and replace them with a bond to the whole. Not only did the early Christians want to escape marriage, sex, and birth to bring on the millennium; they wanted also to shed their bodies and care for everyone equally, not as flesh loves but as God loves. Writes one scholar, "Jesus commanded his followers to forget ordinary concerns about food and clothing, 'sell your possessions, and give alms,' divest themselves of all property, and abandon family obligations"—or in the New Testament's words, to be his follower each man had to "hate his own father and mother and wife and children and brothers and sisters." It was a goal much like Plato's: one can have a pure and undivided heart only by refraining from the selfishness of individual love. Why? As an early Christian theologian wrote mournfully, marriage distracted a man from Christ "because anxiety for those he loves fills his heart." Heaven forbid! No wonder generations of theologians warned against loving one's wife too much, "like an adulterer," drawing attention away from God and the collective good. As one commentator writes, "The

Sermon on the Mount is a wonderful, intoxicating sermon. But it is a sermon for bachelors."

That millennial fever burned itself down to an ember once the Church became established, although, as we've seen, its antagonism toward marriage hung on until the Protestants came around. But the Protestants' encouragement of marriage—especially when combined with the newly rising powers of the nation-states—included its own internal contradictions, which burst onto the scene in the nineteenth century.

The nineteenth century was a stomach-churning rollercoaster of economic and social change, with everyone suddenly tossing up and down, here and there, from one class and trade, job and region to another. And just as all traditional controls were taken off the economy, leaving individuals at the mercy of larger forces, suddenly the new and rising nation-states decided to flex their muscles by clamping down more on marriage than had any earlier social authority. During this wild socioeconomic ride, this best of times and worst of times, many individuals had the same impulse as did the State: reform marriage and the family—instead of vaster and more significant forces like, say, Andrew Carnegie. And so the nineteenth century was frenzied with millennial sex-and-marriage hopes, with communities that fervently believed brave new sexual forms could cleanse us of the messiness of being human. We can group the more formal of these utopian seekers into three groups: the celibates, the patriarchal polygamists (or the Mormons, visited in the last section), and the pluralists or sexual socialists.

The celibates   You have to feel for the Protestants: once they broke off from Catholicism with their trumpet-chorus about holy matrimony, those drawn to a celibate life no longer had the option of checking into a monastery or convent. However peculiar it seems to a post-Freudian consumer culture, the celibate impulse is a regular human variation: in every generation some get the call. One of the more famous is the eighteenth-century British woman

Ann Lee, who had always recoiled from sex; even after marriage she lived in her father's house. She gave birth four times in terrifying and traumatic deliveries, and all four children soon died. She looked for redemption in pentecostal religion, until in a 1770 vision she saw clearly—as clearly as had Augustine—that lust and sex were the true sources of sin. The dynamic Mother Ann took charge of a Quaker splinter group called the "Shaking Quakers," soon called the Shakers, a group whose root beliefs included both equality and separation of the sexes. Together they migrated to the American states, haven for religious dissenters.

By 1822 there were nearly four thousand Shakers in a variety of American communities. Their religious boot camp accomplished exactly what Jesus had called for: separating parents from children, husbands from wives, all reorganized into "families" of 30 to 150 under a single roof. Strictures included a daily schedule that ran with military precision, hard work, ecstatic pentecostal religious services, absolute celibacy, and owning "all things common"—all things, as Plato had envisioned, including everything from children to meals to emotions. That last required some serious effort: every letter, or feeling, or decision had to be checked with the elders, and everyone submitted to group confession. The long-held human ideal of a transparent, unified heart—everyone committed to the group rather than to the few—could be reached only through total obedience.

Ah, that terrible little word, obedience. Although essential to the monastic life, it can backfire spectacularly. Everyone who has ever worked with a visionary organization knows how easily it eats its own, how the demand for religious or moral or political conformity can become a kind of cannibalism. For the Shakers, this implosion came during a tumultuous few years around 1845, when some left or were purged, and the flow of new members slowed to a trickle. Outside, mainstream Christianity was making its peace with sexuality and individual love—with individual courtship and contraceptive use both on the rise. The Shakers could not, and so left us mainly their beautiful songs, chairs, and fertile material for graduate theses.

The pluralists   The Shakers were merely the most successful and consistent of the nineteenth century's celibate utopians: others who attempted the celibate approach to heaven include the Rappites and the Zoarites. The flip side of this impulse moved the sexual pluralists, who believed that *restraining* sex caused sin— and yet who agreed with their fellow utopians that the goal was to love all, equally and transparently, holding nothing back for self or partner.

The most successful pluralist was John Humphrey Noyes, who called his system "complex marriage"—as if marriage were not complex enough already. Noyes preached that "communism in love" would be superior to "egotism for two," that "in a holy community, there is no more reason why sexual intercourse should be restricted by law, than why eating and drinking should be." Marriage, in his mind, was the source of all sexual evil. "It provokes to secret adultery, actual or of the heart. It ties together unmatched natures. . . . It gives to sexual appetite only a scanty and monotonous allowance, and so produces the natural vices." And so Noyes founded a community in Putney, Vermont, then fled after being charged with adultery, only to reorganize and expand in Oneida, New York.

"Oneida" became a nineteenth-century American synonym for a snakes' nest of immorality, a Sodom of illicit and unnatural sex— because every man and woman within the community was considered the heterosexual partner of every other woman or man. Noyes and his followers tried earnestly to explain that their community was not a bacchanal: "Free love with us does not mean freedom to love to-day and leave tomorrow. . . . We receive no members . . . who do not give their heart and hand to the family interest for life and forever." It couldn't be adultery, in other words, because they were all married to each other for life—not just sexually but emotionally and financially as well.

How in the world could such a system—at its height, more than three hundred people belonged to the Oneida communities, which lasted from its founding in 1843 to 1879—not collapse in a hysteria of mutual jealousies and accusations? There were quite a number of rules to keep the community functioning. Noyes and a committee of elders had to approve or decline every proposed sexual coupling. When concerned that a particular pair was getting too close, the committee would separate the pair or even assign them to other partners. Then there was that very necessary element, group crit. The inverse of confession, mutual criticism put each Oneida member successively in the hotseat to have her character flaws and behavior aired by her fellows. There was a complex rule of "ascending" and "descending" fellowship, which meant in practice that the male elders got the young women (as early as age thirteen) while female elders trained the young men. But the most startling rule, to contemporary minds, was Oneida's special contraceptive practice, which Noyes called "male continence" or *coitus reservatus.* Men were never—*never*—to ejaculate, not before, during, or after sex. It's hard to imagine, but historians seem to think that dedicated believers really followed the rule almost all the time. "Between 1848 and 1869," writes one, there were "at most 31 accidental births in a community of 200 adults having frequent sexual congress with a variety of partners . . . fewer pregnancies . . . than there would have been with the pill." But "complex marriage" depended on the benign oversight of its philosopher-king John Humphrey Noyes. When an aging Noyes's authority was challenged (a disgruntled follower went to the police and charged Noyes with statutory rape), he fled—and Oneida dissolved.

The socialists A variation on the sexual pluralists would be the sexual socialists. Marx, Engels, and their followers offered their revelations not in the fading language of religion, as did the Shakers, Mormons, and the Oneida community, but in the up-and-coming language of economics and politics. And yet their goal was also that of Plato and Paul: replace the selfishness of individual love with the utopian love of all for all.

The need to transform marriage was a socialist given. Many believed with the anarchist Michael Bakunin that "in abolishing . . . civil and juridical marriage, we restore life, reality, and morality to natural marriage based solely upon human respect and the freedom of two persons . . . who love each other. . . . rejecting in general the interference of any authority with that union—we make them more closely united to each other." A commonplace among nineteenth-century leftists was the idea that a wife was just a legitimized prostitute, except that, in Engels's words, "she does not let out her body in piecework as a wage worker, but sells it once and for all into slavery." This was an especially piercing truth in an era when a wife actually had fewer rights and less legal personhood than a single working woman, when she could not say "no" in bed and had almost no legal way to leave her husband, when for a man to beat his wife (within reason, of course) was still considered not just acceptable but at times necessary for discipline.

But the passionate utopians who founded the U.S.S.R. would never have been satisfied with the private solutions, the limited-membership communities, of the nineteenth-century sex-and-marriage experimenters like Oneida or the Shakers. They believed profoundly that marriage and the family would wither away with the state, leaving behind a purer and entirely voluntary "sex relation," "based solely on mutual affection" and to "be dissolved if that affection cools." Because everyone would take care of everyone else—child, woman, man—according to each individual's needs, marriage would fade as an unnecessary obligation that perverted both individual integrity and collective responsibility.

Or that, at least, was the ideal that revolutionaries tried to embed in the 1919 Soviet Civil Code. Alexandra Kollantai and others began by writing revolutionary feminism into the proposed Soviet marriage code: civil instead of religious registration of marriages; equal rights for both women and men to child custody, name, inheritance, property ownership, and divorce; and no distinctions between children who were legitimate and il-. None of this—now standard in Western law—shocked the socialists. What did: recognizing marriage at all. Wrote one, "They screamed at us, registration of marriage, formal marriage, what kind of socialism is this? . . . the interference of the state in the business of marriage . . . is completely incomprehensible." And so early Soviet marriage was stripped down even further, so that almost any sexual involvement was equivalent to almost any other, with divorce and alimony freely dispensed.

We all know that this particular utopian vision quickly became a totalitarian juggernaut: collectivized freedom scarcely went as planned, resulting in millions upon millions of deaths from famine, civil war, and the Stalinist terror. Among the many sources of misery was the newly enlightened marriage and family code, as local tribunals, courts, and administrations tried desperately to figure out how to apply the elegant free-love theorem to practical social engineering. What should happen to women who were abandoned as soon as they became pregnant, who still couldn't find work in male-run industries? Did they count as "wives" and therefore get alimony or child support from their deserter, or did that allow some brazen adventurer to unfairly thin out the alimony of a once-committed ex-wife? What happened when families who owned nothing but a cow were ordered to sell it to pay alimony when their son threw his wife out? What happened to the millions of children abandoned and stealing on the street? In fact, people did *not* behave as if, stripped of individual bonds, they were committed to all: rather, they behaved as if they were committed to none.

When, in the 1920s, writers of a new Family Code wanted to eliminate marriage registration entirely, one member of the U.S.S.R. Supreme Court asked, "Then who will decide what is marriage?" How will serious sexual commitments be separated from frivolous ones? Given that some unions—some with children, some without—*did* in fact involve mutual reliance and obligations, given that the penurious State could not in fact take care of everyone's bed and board, how could a court decide which sexual unions gave rise to whose obligations to whom? Within two decades, of course, Soviet social chaos was being cleaned up by the twentieth century's chief totalitarian, albeit one who saw marriage from a right-wing rather than a left-wing extreme. Stalin reinscribed marriage and the family as pillars of the Soviet collective and mothers as heroes of the state—leaving the West to carry out the more necessary feminist reforms.

The imposed and contradictory "freedoms" of a totalitarian state are, perhaps, unfair examples of utopia gone wrong. The anti-marriage utopia that has the best reputation might be that of the early Israeli kibbutzim. In the kibbutzniks' early years in the 1940s and 1950s, no pair registered their marriage with the state; spouses depended on the group instead of each other for financial support; children were raised in shared dorms; everyone ate in a collective dining hall rather than privately, freeing individuals from nightly kitchen duties. And yet marriage never did wither away. Even during the earliest years of the kibbutz, a couple was recognized as such by the group, expected to be faithful, and given private living quarters—basic aspects of marriage. And after a few decades, marriage returned in full force, with elements the social-ist pioneers would have considered abominable: big celebratory weddings; couples who live, eat, and watch TV privately with their children; and the end of the group dining hall.

The more things change . . .   And these were the *successful* utopian sex-and-marriage experiments, the ones that lasted long enough to make it into the history books. However wildly different their diagnoses, remedies, and aims, they all set out to eliminate the evils of private love and marriage—and succeeded, for a time. Yet all disappeared within a generation—except the Mormons, who actually inscribed marriage as *more* honorable than did the outside world. Writes Amos Oz, "the human condition in its conti-nuity and its perversity is complex enough to shatter any scheme and to confound any 'systematic' system." Except for the chosen and dedicated few, most human beings seem to have an inability— or lack of desire—to live up to utopian visions of the withering away of individual love. Nor, given the hundreds of ways in which a couple's commitment to and behavior toward each other affects society's life, has it appeared practical for society's interest in that love and its social consequences to wither away: whenever a uto-pian society attempts to banish rules, the human tendency toward disagreement once again bursts through and makes marriage rules necessary.

Or to put it differently, there's a very good reason that most people have not embraced such visions, so that the Shakers, Oneida, and the kibbutz all faded back into privacy. The history of utopia—in marriage as in everything else—is the history of dystopia: the two are the same. And most people can smell that before they step too far in, like those who described their disillusionment with nineteenth-century utopian communities in words like these:

> After some years of quiet householding in the Connecticut countryside we suddenly found ourselves forced to sit down to three meals a day with eighty-five to a hundred people . . . we had to live, eat, sleep, and work in the midst of all those people and we even had to be polite to them before breakfast. The result was that we lost our appetites, slept badly, and did no work at all. The baby caught our jitters like a disease and filled with her screams the only hours we had alone. . . . We stayed only because we were too broke to move. Every morning we walked up the mountain—the only escape from the people who seemed to have no understanding of two unregenerate individualists—and desperately discussed a way out of this mess.

You could look at this as a failure in changing consciousness, or simply as human reality. Living up to a communal ideal is too much for most of us: we *do* end up being individuals, sticky and particular, hard enough to love individually, much less en masse. Considering how painfully hard it is simply to thrash out a commitment to one peculiar other—not to mention one's children, or parents, or intimate friends—how could any but the most dedicated and saintly human beings actually expect to become intimate with two hundred or two million? And even were it possible, who would have the *time*?

Some lesbians and gay men are still attempting to fit within this utopian tradition. I understand their impulse: I'm an apostate from the utopian faction, someone who grew up hoping for a perfect communal world. Having seen what the 1950s version of marriage did to my mother, I announced at age ten to her and the neighborhood moms that I would never get married; my first love was a girl with whom I excitedly invented socialist worlds at the edge of a lake. Although I was never actively *anti*monogamy like some of my 1970s contemporaries, my younger self would have been horrified to imagine writing a book in favor of marriage. But the more carefully I've examined marriage's practical purposes—combined with utopia's tendency to leave the weaker to be exploited by the worst—the clearer it is that marriage rules are necessary to bring justice to human commitments. Those marriage rules often need improvement—but the fact of marriage and its ever-shifting rules seems to be an eternal social necessity.

So I am a bit startled by those who can still write that "the desire to marry in the lesbian and gay community is an attempt to mimic the worst of mainstream society, an effort to fit into an inherently problematic institution that betrays the promise of both lesbian and gay liberation and radical feminism." Sometimes such rhetoric treats those who want to marry as if they weren't "really" part of the lesbian and gay community, interlopers who didn't pass the political science section of the homosexuality entrance exam. It's easy to see why the right wing would pretend that being lesbian or gay makes one "naturally" a radical outlaw, innately interested in forging a new social, sexual, and political world: it's much easier to marginalize people you portray as innately strange. But why would lesbians and gay men promote such a fiction? Simple: those who get involved in public lesbian or gay politics are often those who are also critical of conventional social forms. But not every lesbian or gay man comes out in a radical immersion, or believes that marriage is "an inherently problematic institution": most stay home in Omaha or Spokane rather than move to Boston's lesbian-feminist political hotbed or San Francisco's gay male sexual frontier. And so antimarriage rhetoric wrongly groups lesbian and gay liberationists with other lesbians and gay men—when really they belong with other sexual utopians in history, or with the heterosexual cultural-leftists of their era who have also been trying to invent new, alternative kinds of families.

A variant of this vision comes from another group: those who believe that being gay means endorsing an endless bacchanalia.

Queer-studies academic Michael Warner, for instance, writes that "the appeal of queer sex, for many, lies in its ability to violate the responsibilizing frames of good, right-thinking people." Novelist Edmund White echoes this sentiment when he writes that marriage is "hopelessly dreary," a "monogamous air lock" that stands in utter opposition to his very definition of gay life, since, as he writes, "being gay seemed at first like another way of being a bohemian," freed from "the most narrow, creepy, selfish sort of conformism." Often, these sexual "radicals" can believe such drivel because they've moved away from their hometowns into a highly sexual gay subculture, and so they never see those lesbians and gay men who *do* live in the "middle-class respectability" that White pshaws, the long-monogamous couples whose lives never touch the urban party.

More important, these professors and bohemians willfully ignore their heterosexual siblings' comparable urban party. Have they never noticed the (straight) men who spend all their money with the local red-light district's prostitutes and peep shows and porno stores, the high-heeled (straight) women hunting for a pickup at the single bar's closing time, the Madonnas and Courtney Loves making careers off their bad-girl reputations? Neither het nor homo has a lock on either urban "bohemian" or ranchhouse "respectable." Lesbians and gay men come from every background, impulse, religion, class, race, ethnicity, and profession in the West. We have far less in common with each other than either queer-theorists or radical rightists like to pretend. Why should lesbians' and gay men's sexual choices—our individual decisions about what counts as good and what counts as chaos—be any more similar than those of the rest of the country, of our parents and high school peers, our pub mates and politicians?

I'm baffled by those who think living a bacchanalian life is in any way politically defiant, since it so obviously endorses our era's reigning corporate theology, the one sold by every sponsor from MTV to Pepsi: consume, consume, consume. With Westerners' personal integrity under attack by the selling of desire, the worm of dissatisfaction constantly wriggles within us, wanting us to want everything, wanting us to refuse to choose. We can declare our resistance by announcing a commitment to something beyond temporary pleasure—such as caring for another human being. That declaration can be conservative in the best sense: conserving the limited energy in one or two hearts.

But even for those who disagree, opening marriage to same-sex couples would scarcely force marriage on *all* lesbians and gay men. "I advocate complete freedom for sexuality the same as for religion," declared the infamous free-lover and presidential candidate Victoria Woodhull in 1874. "I advocate sexual freedom for all people—freedom for the monogamist to practice monogamy, for the varietist to be a varietist still, for the promiscuous to remain promiscuous. Am I, therefore, an advocate of promiscuousness, variety, or monogamy? Not necessarily either. I might do all this and be myself a celibate and an advocate of celibacy." Woodhull's theology of sexual freedom (preached, may I add, to heterosexuals) shocked her contemporaries—and reigns in our country today. Twenty-five percent of today's American households are single individuals (surely not all celibate)—the same percentage as the mom + dad + kids households. The 1950s marriage that rightly stands like a nightmare in White's and others' memories has lost its stranglehold on the majority. Why would it suddenly sink its talons only into lesbians and gay men? Opening marriage to same-sex couples would leave alone those who prefer their leather bars—while allowing the home-and-hearth couples to have their gold rings. It would thus expose that lesbians and gay men are just as various as our heterosexual sibs. No wonder it's a vision disliked by liberationists, queer-theorists, and the right wing alike.

In other words, the option of civil marriage will indeed, as some people predict, split the incredibly multiplicitous lesbian and gay communities in two. It will expose that the varietists and the promiscuous are most properly grouped with other sexual dissidents of whatever orientation—that Edmund White and Michael Warner stand with Victoria Woodhull, Margaret Sanger, Isadora Duncan, Hugh Hefner, Bertrand Russell, J.F.K., and so many others. Opening marriage to same-sex couples may well shift our society's sexual dividing line from the current and temporary line between homosexual and heterosexual back to one more historically familiar, a divide between monogamous and promiscuous.

Utopians have always been somewhat arrogant in their desire to impose new social forms on everyone. A dedicated few always attempt to transcend the pair—whether through celibacy or pluralism, through an austere socialism or an ecstatic sexual vision. But most of us have stubbornly continued as we are, refusing to have our emotions reformed away. For many people, sharing sex is an exceptionally powerful bond, one we want to dedicate just to each other. Why must the entire society abandon a form that most people seem to crave rather than reform it from within? Given the times in which we live, anyone who wants to live in a sexually complex universe—an Oneida of their own making—is certainly free to do so. Why should that therefore overrule the more common human desire to pair off, for two people to dedicate themselves to one another, to build a shared life and a home—and have it recognized by those around them, whether parents or governments? Nor could anyone rightly suggest that marriage is merely about the pair. In fact, marriage insists that the pair is never isolated—whether at the wedding celebration or in daily life, marriage recognizes that the pair is always intertwined with others, which is why society needs to impose some order on the form.

From this angle, what is marriage for? To recognize that a given pair has chosen each other as kin. Coupled lesbians and coupled gay men—if they so choose—belong.

FIVE:

Order

Everywhere a distinction exists between marriage, i.e., a legal group-sanctioned bond . . . and the type of permanent or temporary union resulting from violence or consent alone. This group intervention may be a notable or a slight one, it does not matter. The important thing is that every society has some way to operate a distinction between free unions and legitimate ones. . . . it remains true that marriage is not, is never, and cannot be a private business.

—CLAUDE LÉVI-STRAUSS, "The Family" (1956)

Nothing is more gratifying to the mind of man than power or dominion, and this I think myself amply possessed of, as I am the father of a family . . . I look upon my family as a patriarchal sovereignty in which I am myself, both king and priest.

—*The Spectator* (1712)

I desire you would Remember the ladies . . . Do not put such unlimited power into the hands of the Husbands. Remember all Men would be tyrants if they could.

—ABIGAIL ADAMS, letter to John Adams (1776)

Marriage is a coming together for better or for worse, hopefully enduring, and intimate to the degree of being sacred.

—U.S. Supreme Court, *Griswold v. Connecticut* (1965)

UNTIL NOW, THIS BOOK HAS TREATED TWO INTERLOCK-ing visions of marriage as if they were interchangeable: marriage as a socially defined institution, and marriage as an inner experience. This chapter looks at marriage from the outside in: at the social apparatus that defines and enforces marriage's rights and obligations. To marry, in the public sense, means to expect the world to treat your life as shared—to announce that your sexual partner has first claim on you and your efforts. For the couple to fulfill the wedding vows that make mothers and strangers weep, that claim must be honored by others in things large and small, from holiday invitations to burial instructions. From conversation to finance, the couple's bond can never entirely be severed from the *polis,* the collective, the society in which they live.

Usually those claims are made and honored day to day, in the private social circle: for instance, everyone at the office understands and pitches in when a particular employee is preoccupied and less than productive during his wife's months of chemo. But now and then the larger institutional machinery is invoked to enforce a claim. You may go to court to insist that your parents were legitimately married and that you therefore count as an Athenian citizen—a status you get only because both your grandfathers fully intended to send money, power, and status your way. Or you may insist that you really *were* married and therefore should, after he dies, get to keep not only your two dresses and one cookpot, but also one-third of the land in his name. Or eight years after you moved out and left him to raise the kids, you may go back to court insisting that he's unfit because he's now living—unmarried—with another man, while you're properly and heterosexually remarried, not just in your heart but in the eyes of the law. Society has a stake in seeing that each of those disputes are settled justly, based on some larger social consensus—partly because everyone else's property, or citizenship, or relationship to their offspring may be redefined depending on how *your* dispute is resolved.

Given, in other words, that human beings are flawed—that we do not always treat each other as we should, and worse, that we disagree over what it means to "treat each other as we should"—marriage is not merely an inner experience but also a political institution, an accretion of decisions about how to order a couple's promises and obligations. Whenever two parties disagree—a father wants to marry off a daughter who refuses; a wife says she was raped by a husband who insists her body is his property; a couple demand health insurance from an employer who says they're not married—society must make some reasoned judgment about their dispute. And so marriage's borders are always critical political territory, roiling with such questions as: Which sexual bonds or private promises create publicly policed commitments? On what grounds do we decide what's just? When can society intervene to right private wrongs? Who adjudicates when those involved disagree? Most politically significant, whose interests define marriage, how, and why?

Inside Out or Outside In:
Who Says You're Married?

One of the most basic tensions in the history of marriage is between those two interlocking sides of marriage: marriage as a publicly policed institution and marriage as an inner experience. Which one turns your bond into a marriage: a public authority or your heart? Are you married when the two of you decide to care for each other for life, a decision you live out day to day, a decision only afterwards recognized by your community? Or is it the other way around: does the family, or church, or state pronounce some words over your head, write your names side by side in a registry, and bestow upon you a marriage, a license and legal obligation to carry out the responsibilities of affection and care? This may sound like one of those faces/vases illusions, and for good reason: marriage doesn't exist unless both parts happen—two human beings behave as married, and everyone else treats them as such. But it *does* matter which side you think counts more: the decisions made about individual marriages will be quite different if you think marriage is a publicly conferred status or an immanent state. And each position's internal contradictions can—and have—caused social havoc when unchecked.

In history, this debate is almost inextricable from the debate over which authority rules marriage. *Who* decides where the enforceable marriage is made—in your heart, or in a registry—and why? That decision might be less complex if the only people who have to recognize your marriage live within twenty-five miles, when the people who see you two behaving as married are also the ones who oversee the granting of the widow's dower. And it might be *more* complex in our world, in which each of our daily lives goes beyond our circle of acquaintances to touch dozens of strangers and anonymous entities, from the motor vehicles registry to our children's schools. The story of the public/private marriage line is therefore also a story of how marriage has shifted, in comparative legal scholar Mary Ann Glendon's words, from custom to law.

Roman marriage was the immanent kind: when challenged in court (over, say, whether a widow inherits or whether a child is legitimate), a marriage could not be proved by anything so simple as a public registry. A judge had to investigate whether the two lived together with *affectio maritalis*, "the intention of being married." To be married, all a couple had to do was "regard each other as man and wife and behave accordingly." What does that mean, "behave accordingly"? The Romans may never have defined it, but (like Americans and pornography) they knew it when they saw it. A judge sized up the couple's "marital intentions" by such signals as whether she'd brought a dowry, or whether he openly called her his wife. Augustine and his concubine, for instance, were living together without *affectio maritalis*, since he was intending a later power-marriage. But had the same pair *intended* to be married—with no change in their behavior—they would have been. Marriage was a private affair: the state could police only the consequences, not the act.

While the Jewish configuration changed over the millennia, what remained central is marriage as a private act: only bride and groom could say the magic words that turned them into husband and wife. After many centuries the rabbis inserted themselves and their seven blessings into the ceremony, before the big feast, but even they knew they were not essential: the pair made the marriage within themselves. Which is why, in Jewish law, a court could neither "grant" nor refuse a divorce. If a husband's inner willingness to be married evaporated (sometimes hers counted but often it did not), then the marriage *itself* had evaporated: the rabbinical court or *bet din* could merely decide questions of fault and finances.

Christianity, as we know, wanted nothing to do with marriage for centuries. When asked, some priests might come by and say a blessing as a favor, just as they'd say a blessing over a child's first haircut. No one considered marriage sacred, as celibacy was: marriage was one of those secular and earthbound forms rendered unto Caesar. But as centuries rolled by, an increasingly powerful Church saw that marriage was central to ordering Europe's civil and political life—not so much those few called to sainthood, sacrifice, and martyrdom, but the many ordinary folk who needed to be told how to behave.

And so the Church launched a battle for power over marriage's rules, a battle that lasted roughly a thousand years. Today we have the peculiar impression that Catholicism has always had one vision of marriage, but for every marriage rule eventually imposed on Europe, the Church's own debates were abundant. It first formally ruled on marriage in 774, when one pope handed Charlemagne a set of writings that defined legitimate marriage and condemned all deviations. After another five hundred years of struggle, the Church came up with a marriage liturgy and imposed its new and radical rules—the ballooning incest rules, the one-man-one-marriage rule, and most controversial, the girl-must-consent rule—on the powerful clans. "It is clear," writes one historian, "that this attempt to impose order on matrimonial practice was part of a more ambitious plan to reform the entire social order. . . . regulating the framework of lay society, from baptisms to funerals," the most intimate acts of most people's lives. The Church's push to rule marriage was slow and uneven but very determined. Here and there it would issue a decree and struggle with local nobles over whether it would be observed; now it would retract a bit to permit a lord to marry his dead wife's sister or annul his existing marriage; then it would push forward again.

It was not until 1215 that the Church finally decreed marriage a sacrament—the least important one, but a sacrament nonetheless—*and* set up a systematic canon law of marriage, with a system of ecclesiastical courts to enforce it—*and* had a fair amount of people willing to observe those rules. By 1215, the year that the Fourth Lateran Council issued its matrimonial decrees, the Church had "broke[n] the back of aristocratic resistance ... after lengthy individual battles with the nobility, kings included."

And according to the Church, what turned two individuals into a married couple? It was—drumroll, please—the couple's private vows.

Why a drumroll? Because the Church insisted that a private promise was an unbreakable sacrament—that marriage was an *immanent* experience, a spiritual reality created by the *pair's* free and equal consent. That was practically a declaration of war against the upper classes, a radical and subversive idea emphasizing the sacredness of the individual spirit. Marriage, the Church insisted, was not just about land and power and wombs, but about human feelings.

Unfortunately, saying that *consent* makes a marriage can leave courts in as awkward a position as saying that *affectio maritalis* makes a marriage. How do you define consent? At precisely what point does marriage become "What God has joined, let no man put asunder"—an indissoluble sacrament? This second question was especially important, since—bucking all human precedent, and even going against the example of the Church's own early decisions—the Church started to insist that consent once given could *never* be revoked. After a great many theological volleys and debates, theologians decided that a marriage was made and permanently sealed at the moment that the pair knowingly and willingly said "I marry you." Even if they said their vows in absolute secrecy, with no witnesses. Even if they never actually consummated their union (how could a Church based on a virgin birth elevate sex to the marriage sacrament?). *Words* made the marriage—not family agreements or contracts, and not sex. It was a dramatic break with custom. The Church divided these words into two complex formula—*verba de praesenti* and *verba de futuro*—that no one but theologians and lawyers fully understood. The basic principle, however, was clear, at least to the Church itself: did you two say you are married? Then poof! You are.

That principle caused social havoc. For the upper classes, there were three problems: disobedience, disobedience, and murkiness. Disobedience 1: a balky adolescent could thwart carefully planned mergers and acquisitions, although locking her up and beating her usually brought her around. Disobedience 2: from age twelve and fourteen respectively, a girl and boy could simply meet in a back hall and say those foolish *verba* to each other—and be irrevocably married. (Romeo and Juliet, are you listening?) In one fifteenth-century British landed family, the Pastons, a seventeen-year-old daughter pledged herself to the family bailiff. For three years Margery's parents shut her up in her house, until her fiancé somehow got a hearing with the local bishop. The bishop flatly commanded the young woman's parents to bring her in—and after talking to her, ruled that Margery was married. (The Pastons disinherited her and her children and never spoke to her again—although they didn't fire her husband the bailiff.)

The third upper-class *verba* problem was murkiness. Since not sex but *words* made a marriage, you couldn't always tell when you were merely betrothed and when you were actually married. The Pastons' eldest son John met a woman with whom he exchanged vows. But what kind? *Verba de praesenti,* meaning they'd already married each other, or *verba de futuro,* meaning they were engaged? Neither was sure. After that meeting the pair never spent a night under the same roof, rarely saw each other, and treated each other so coolly that he had trouble getting an appointment to see her—and yet when he finally decided to break things off, her "conscience required an annulment from Rome." *That* took six years and a thousand ducats. If private consent makes a marriage, and if you're not sure whether you consented, who but God—or God's representatives in Rome—can say whether or not you're married?

For the working classes, those *verba* could be just as problematic—but for more personal reasons. Individuals exchanged vows "under an ash tree, in a bed, in a garden, in a small storehouse, in a field, in a blacksmith's shop, in a kitchen, at a tavern, and in the king's highway"—to use some examples that got into English ecclesiastical court records—and then wound up in court having violent "he said/she said" arguments. Had they gotten married after all, or was one fabricating? Most female readers will grasp immediately how much men will promise (and later deny) to get a woman into bed—and most men can testify how women's memories can expand vague sentiments into definite commitments. But women could also be the ones who changed their minds, as when a certain John was about to travel overseas and Agnes begged him to marry her first. They said their vows in front of witnesses. On his trip John lost most of his money, however, and Agnes broke things off. He took her to the ecclesiastical court, saying they were already married—but she countered that, since they hadn't had sex, they'd been only engaged. Which was, the Church notwithstanding, how most people saw things: *verba* put you under contract, but only sex transformed words into marriage.

The *verba*'s murkiness overflowed the court dockets. What happened when a man promised himself to one woman but then promised *and* bedded another: Was his first promise a marriage, making his second tryst adultery, or did the second's consummation make *it* the marriage, eclipsing the first? What happened when a family lured another (wealthy) family's adolescent son on a weekend outing that ended with the girl's parents putting the two young people into a single bed for the evening, by candlelight "witnessing" the boy's "vows." Was he sacramentally bound by his sexual temptation, or could his parents have their tryst annulled? The questions stacked up for centuries; when it comes to marriage, it seems, there is no escape from lawyers.

How was such a mess to be cleaned up? While the working folk stumbled in and out of secret "precontracts," the aristocracy and nobles constantly attacked the Church's idea of marriage-by-consent. By the time it was instituted into canon law, the Church had already run into trouble with its concept that consent-makes-a-marriage—and so at the same time, the Church tried to control the damage by issuing requirements for a *licit* marriage. You had to post the banns, an announcement that a given couple was to be married, three weeks in a row—thus giving plenty of time for someone to come forward and object that, for instance, she was already contracted to John. You had to say vows *in faciem Ecclesiae*, before priest and people, either in front of or even *inside* a church. Both innovations were so disliked that they took centuries to be accepted, and their acceptance was uneven at that. The English middle and upper classes went to church fairly early; the Italians shrugged the demand off entirely, keeping their traditional family wedding procession from bride's to groom's house without so much as a wink at the priest. Everywhere folks kept the bawdy custom (strongly discouraged by the Church) of seeing the couple to bed, where they stood by with a raucous celebration and suggestive toasts, and then checked in a few hours later to see how the sex had gone. Sex, not the priest, was what married you.

The Church got very little cooperation in its attempts to turn marriage into a soberly witnessed event—in part because its decrees were toothless. Not just in the eyes of the community but even in the eyes of the Church, your marriage was still *valid* even when *illicit*—even if you hadn't met marriage requirements like banns or public vows. Despite itself, the Church had created a new in-between marriage category: illicit but indissoluble marriages.

Most were no problem. One historian notes that in one fourteenth-century English town, "of 101 unions mentioned in the register, 89 were of this 'irregular' kind," meaning private rather than public promises: few wound up in court. According to various records, up to one-third or one-half of European adults in the sixteenth century were officially unmarried. Yes, many of these were young unmarrieds, widows, or widowers—but others were cohabitants who believed that *they,* not any outside authority, made their companionship into a marriage. Writes one historian, "The real hurdle for the courts was the persistent idea that people could regulate marriage for themselves."

But while most people might be quite content with their private vows, 70 percent of ecclesiastical court cases were over the *verba* problem: private marriage created public mess. And so what started as the Church's championing of the individual spirit in defiance of clan control became an international scandal. Across Europe people didn't know whether they were married or un-, what with engagements or annulments tied up in court for years; secret vows and seductions that might or might not be binding for life; priests paying annual fees for concubines who were not wives; and of course the proliferation of marriage taxes for dispensations, pronouncements, annulments, and what have you. And so in swept the Protestants, with their ferocious appetite for sexual order.

The reasons that on October 31, 1517 Luther pounded his theses in Wittenberg's church door—and the reasons his protest caught fire across Europe, turning into wars both theological and bloody—are far beyond the scope of this book. But reforming the marriage rules was high up on the Protestant agenda. The Protestants considered their marriage reform to be urgent in part because marriage is both an intimate and a politically urgent act, framing most homes and lives: the religion that won the battle to define marriage had closer control of Europe's souls—not to mention its finances. Unlike the old peasant or aristocratic societies, the rising merchant class needed order across families, borders, and seas. More and more people were trading (and marrying) beyond their old ten-mile radius. How could you run a family business if some pretender suddenly showed up and insisted he was your daughter's husband and therefore had a lien on your possessions? Marriage had to be governed by something larger than one village's communal memory—and something less costly than endless suits in ecclesiastical courts. The Protestants were sick of marriage ideals that—however spiritual in theory—caused nightmares in practice. Besides, they had ceased to believe that private consent was sacred. As one Protestant reformer wrote, "when two young people secretly and without the knowledge of their parents, in the disobedience and ignorance of youth, as if intoxicated, wantonly and deceitfully . . . join themselves together in marriage, who would not agree that such a union has been brought about by Satan and not by the Lord God?" The result: the Protestants ushered in a revolution in the very *definition* of marriage—from announced to pronounced, from privately made to publicly bestowed.

Depending on the region and jurisdiction, what the Protestants usually required were a priest, several witnesses, a public ceremony, parental consent up to age twenty-one or twenty-five or so, even a register of all births, deaths, and marriages. Yes, the Protestants still believed that the *moment* of marriage was when the two said their vows. But that moment was no longer a mystical sacrament, a concept the Protestants ridiculed openly. Rather, the Protestants insisted, marriage was—by definition—a secular status conferred by an outside authority. No Protestant group had the power to control that public recognition, or was prepared to spend a thousand years building that power. So they handed off marriage to their running mates for power, the rising nation-states. In 1525 Zurich flatly denied that private vows were valid, instead insisting that a marriage legally required at least "two pious, honorable, and incontestable witnesses." In 1537 Augsburg and Nuremberg started fining or jailing those who "mingled themselves sexually" before the church ceremony, while clergy living with concubines had to marry or separate. By 1563, stung by Protestant criticism, even the Catholic Council of Trent caught the wave—and declared that any marriage that had *not* been performed publicly, in front of the parish priest, was invalid. So there!

Small and sensible as those rules may now sound, the change was revolutionary. For the first time in history, individuals and families no longer had the power to say who was married. And the real winners in this marriage battle—the nation-states—didn't hold back as much as religious authorities might have in using their power over marriage. Rather, they quite enthusiastically took up marriage regulation, control, and even surveillance. The French king, outraged that the Catholic Church did not invalidate clandestine marriages, in 1579 set the *legal* age of marriage without parental consent at twenty-five for women and thirty for men. The longer the states had power over marriage, the more widely they were tempted to use that power. In 1739, Prussian states forbade noblemen to marry peasants, artisans to marry before completing apprenticeships, students to marry before graduation, and cripples or blind persons to marry at all. The French revolutionaries, like all revolutionaries, saw changing marriage as a way to break down the old order, made mandatory a civil ceremony and registration, and officially decreed that the State married you—not you yourselves, and certainly not God. Private power was banished, replaced by the state. As historian Nancy Cott writes, "one of the principal means that the state can use to prove its social existence—to announce its sovereignty and its hold on the populace—is its authority over marriage."

The marriage revolution took a lot longer in the English-speaking countries. England's established church had merely fired the pope without much changing Catholic marriage theology. Unlike the Continental Protestants, the Anglicans kept the idea that private vows were the sacrament that created a marriage: if you said you were married, married you were. Writes historian Lawrence Stone, "England was full of people like Robert Davies of Northwich and Elizabeth Madson of Whitegate 'who say they are married together, but 'tis not known whether nor how nor when they were married.' " Of course, people had been marrying for millennia without official recognition—but not in the brave, mobile, urbanizing new world of capitalism. Now that the village and ecclesiastical systems had collapsed, the newly organizing state had to pick up the business of tracking contracts, fiscal or marital. With neither local community supervision nor proper bureaucratic records, British marriage was a disaster zone. Comments Stone, "The judges were exasperated by having to deal with cases of inheritance, bigamy, incest, etc. in which the evidence was nothing better than a grubby private marriage register kept by some down-at-heel clerk or shifty woman in an alehouse in the Fleet, and full of false erasures, insertions, and back-dating."

Why couldn't Britain just pass a law that regularized marriage? Easy to say, but not so easy to do in a democratic system. Trying to change civil laws about marriage—that institution that touches everybody's family, spiritual, emotional, financial, and public lives —gets everybody pretty darn touchy. There were some venal concerns, such as who got to keep all those licensing fees, and whether there would still be enough marriage litigation to keep certain barristers in business. But the really controversial questions had to do with the definition of marriage—such as whether it was a public and secular institution that the state had the right to regulate, or whether it was a sacrament privately administered and acknowledged only afterwards. The Anglican bishops who sat in the House of Lords were particularly worried about whether it could possibly be moral for the secular state to invalidate a marriage that two people—and presumably therefore God—had brought into being. The various bills that attempted to order the public institution of marriage "aroused strong passions" and "debates were extremely long and bitter; one of the debates in the Commons . . . lasted until half past three in the morning."

After a century or so, they managed it. In 1753, the powerful Lord Hardwicke forced members to sit through endless sessions during fetid August heat until they agreed on and passed some basic marriage regulations: licensing, public and daylight ceremonies, registries signed and dated by spouses and witnesses, parental consent up to age twenty-one. Anything else was to be annulled and ferociously punished; ministers who performed clandestine marriages or falsified marriage registries could be transported to the colonies or executed. (The Quakers, who refused to take public vows, and the Jews, those resident foreigners with their own peculiar laws, were exempted and allowed to run their own marriages.) Finally, in England as on the Continent, the definition of marriage had been transformed from a private sacrament to a publicly authorized contract.

Things were a little less simple on the other side of the Atlantic, in the British colonies, where the definition of marriage varied from region to region. The Puritan colonies had, like their Protestant brethren, outlawed the scandal of clandestine marriages, while the Southern colonies had marriage laws as messy and uncertain as mother England's. But by the nineteenth century, the courts decided that private marriage was a necessity, not a scandal, and invented an entirely new form, "common-law marriage," even when they had to overrule existing statutes to do so. According to influential nineteenth-century judges, Americans were so mobile and scattered around the frontier that if you acted as if you were married, or said that you were married, then you *were* married—in life and in court. Faced with the dilemma of widows who said they had been married but could show no proof, one judge in 1809 ruled that times had changed and that upholding private promises would be better than defying them. A host of judges followed, using the new "common-law" invention. Some legislatures joined in, as when an 1843 Indiana statute insisted that "no particular form of ceremony shall be necessary, except that the parties shall declare . . . that they take each other as husband and wife." Cohabitation, anyone?

Early nineteenth-century American marriage, in other words, was made by the couple themselves, and recognized only afterward by law. Not vows, not registration, but behavior made a marriage: as one South Carolina chancellor insisted, "it is the agreement itself, not the form in which it is couched which constitutes the contract." When one woman tried to deprive her dead brother's widow of his estate because there'd been no wedding or registration, a New York court ruled for the widow: "Society would not be safe for a moment, in this, the most sacred of its relations, if an open and public cohabitation as man and wife for ten years, continued with all the conventional usages of married life, and followed by the procreation of children, could be overturned." The judge's wording is entertaining, since this is precisely the view that today makes the family-values people shudder: *cohabitation* is sacred, and gets all the legal benefits of marriage, simply because you *treat* each other as married?

And the family-values folks of the era *did* shudder. By the 1870s a marriage reform movement erupted, part of what one historian has called a "moral panic." Publicity, formal ceremonies, registration—all the things made unnecessary by the very existence of common-law marriage—were demanded by organizations such as the National League for the Protection of the Family. Common-law marriage, one writer thought, was "suspiciously near the borderland of illicit intercourse." Some courts kept honoring the claims of long-established couples even if they had no formalities behind them. But by the nineteenth century's end, for the most part marriage in the United States had also become a public, state-regulated status—bestowed by a central authority, hedged by registries, licenses, fees, and witnesses.

So had the Protestants and the nation-states won a complete triumph over the marriage rules, sweeping all competitors off the field? Perhaps—for awhile. But just as state power over marriage peaked in the nineteenth century, there came an upswelling of civil disobedience against externally imposed marriage rules. Just when every civilized Victorian had come to believe that the regulation of marriage and family life was not merely essential to State order but had always and would always exist, that publicly bestowed marriage was the *only* kind of marriage, there arose a romantically rebellious movement insisting that individual spirits, and *not* the family, church, or state, are what create and legitimate each marriage. "Free love"—the idea that the heart made its own marriages, that any law enforcing or policing it was a spiritual travesty—swept not just the poor folks who had long ducked church or state marriage regulation, but the educated classes.

One needn't be a Marxist to see how easily "free love" could bubble up from the contradictions within the industrializing democracies. On the one hand, the capitalist states needed and glorified the individual and his (yes, his) imagination and conscience, freed from parental control to run the new economy. On the other hand, as a kind of seatbelt against the new economy's rollercoaster of social change—as if controlling marriage were more important than controlling *laissez faire* robber barons—those states were strapping people more tightly into marriage than ever before. Some couldn't stand the contradiction.

The Victorian free-lovers were fierce moralists, taking seriously the romantic rhetoric on which they'd been raised. Because they believed that the heart makes and unmakes marriages, they insisted that marriage law actually worsened and coarsened spouses, enforcing sin by keeping them legally bound once they disliked each other—and, not coincidentally, legally turning women into helpless maidservants and men into tyrants. Their fervent theories often came from painful conflict with state-enforced marriage. In the 1840s, for instance, when Mary Gove Nichols fled a husband who beat her, she also lost the legal battle to contact her children, as was common for wives who rebelled against the vow to obey. And so when she and her new "husband" Thomas Nichols—husband in life, though not in law—described the situation of a modern wife, their list of legal facts was illumined by her experience:

> Married, she becomes his property, and may become his victim, his slave. She must live where he wishes her to live; she must submit to his embraces, however loathsome; she must bear his children, whether she wish to do so, or not; her property, her liberty, her comfort, her person, her life, are all in his power. He will probably be punished for an outright murder by poison or steel, but there are many ways of killing, which she has no power to resist. The subject of his caprices, the victim of his lusts, starved in her sympathies ... this human being has but one duty, and that is *obedience*.

The free-lovers took the radical idea at the heart of Catholic marriage theology—the idea that mutual consent is the sacrament—to its logical limit, insisting that "what the law calls fornication, when it is the union of mutual love, may be the holiest action two human beings can engage in ... as it is sanctified by a mutual sentiment and attraction to which no law or ceremony can impart any additional sanction." And they went farther, insisting, "It is marriage, and the license which it gives, which debauches, enervates, degrades, and pollutes society!"

You can imagine the socially shocking consequences. As the notorious free-lover, feminist, spiritualist, and general hell-raiser Victoria Woodhull thundered from her pulpits, "Who will dare say that love should not be a precedent to marriage? But when this is affirmed, the legitimate corollary is not seen: that, since marriage should not begin without love it should cease when love is gone."

Wives should be able to say no when their husbands wanted sex; marriages should dissolve when affection failed; husbands and wives should be equal in private and in law; and no imprimatur should be needed for sexual relations beside the heart and God. In other words, once the pendulum had swung so sharply toward an understanding of marriage as a *publicly* bestowed status, the free-lovers wanted to define it again as an internal state. And now, back to the *verba!*

The orderly Victorians, with their newly apotheosized family, were appalled: common-law marriage was one thing; open *defiance* of marriage was quite another. Leo Miller was arrested and jailed when he left his wife and openly moved in with his lover, declaring their opposition to marriage in a local free-love paper. Mary Gove Nichols was stripped of her children when she fled her abusive husband and ended up among the free-lovers. "Free love" was an imprecation hurled (often accurately) at all sorts of radicals, from Margaret Sanger to Emma Goldman, as a hint that clean-minded Americans should recoil from the sexual filth that lurked beneath any putatively high-minded movement.

And of course, "free love" won.

Yes, it won. The nineteenth-century free-lovers' agenda now runs Western codes of sexuality and marriage (that is, if you leave out the item on the agenda that calls for the institution's complete destruction). The ability to dissolve marriage when love dissolves; the freedom to form sexual relationships based on affection, without state sanction or intervention; equality between spouses in everything from property ownership to divorce; the idea that affection and companionship are marriage's main goals: the free-lovers' demands have been absorbed into our laws. Or to put it differently, although the nation-states are still registering and tracking marriage, our society has begun moving back to the old and honorable idea that marriage is something made by the couple, not by any outside authority—and has integrated some radically modern ideas about sexual equality and individualism.

The free-love triumph has happened in daily life, in marriage statutes, and in court. In the 1960s, the Western nation-states, which had launched their control over marriage with such comprehensive absolutism, started pulling out of the business of regulating intimate life—freeing love from law, and in very dramatic language striking down such restrictions on marriage as race, debt, imprisonment, and employer approval. "The right to marry is an individual right *d'ordre public* which cannot be restricted or alienated; . . . the freedom to marry should in principle be safeguarded," wrote the highest French court in 1968, deciding—in a radical break with historical precedent—that an employer could not terminate an employee for marrying. In the United States, *Loving v. Virginia* was written up in similarly freedom-touting language, saying, "The freedom to marry has long been recognized as one of the vital personal rights essential to the orderly pursuit of happiness . . . one of the 'basic civil rights of man' . . . and cannot be infringed by the State." Or as comparative legal scholar Mary Ann Glendon writes, in the middle of the twentieth century Western courts—all at once—started "sloganizing" about marriage. As if out of nowhere, "the idea of a basic individual right to marry has emerged. . . . a banner has been raised over the slowly shifting minutiae of marriage law. The banner is one of the gaily-colored pennants of the pursuit of happiness, and the words inscribed on it are 'Freedom to Marry' and 'Marriage—A Basic Human Right.'"

It is firmly within the main current of this triumphing marriage ideology that Madeline and I stand. We say we are married—and so we are, in all but law. If the inner life is what makes a marriage, who could have the hubris to judge the quality and commitment of mine? When the state has been sweeping away all shackles on marriage except the heart's bond, how can it, in justice, refuse to recognize ours?

To which definition do you subscribe? Do you believe you are married when you pledge yourself to your spouse, or when the state writes you into its registries? For most people the public vows and the state's acknowledgment are simultaneous—although that's not always so, as when Richard and Mildred Loving were refused recognition by Virginia. If you define marriage as the inner, immanent state, then perhaps you recognize that Madeline and I already *are* married. If you accept the more recent definition of marriage as something conferred by public authority, then perhaps you'll recognize that it has been changing since it first gained the field, and that we belong under its widening twentieth-century "Freedom to Marry" banner.

Living Together: Is It Marriage Yet?

The question of whether it is the state's sanction or one's internal decision that makes a marriage—or to put it differently, *is* the marriage—affects far more people than just same-sex couples. Just as Western judges were pronouncing their new freedom-to-marry slogans, many people began deciding that they were *so* free to marry that they needn't even inform the state. Some live happily outside the legal institution's strictures, recognized only by family and friends, explicitly preferring a social to a state marriage. Other state-marriage dissenters want their private marriage to be semi-public so that they can gain a few of the more useful rights that come with state marriage, like shared health insurance benefits and the right to each other's pensions—but without sacrificing their independence from the state institution. The debate over how legally to treat these relationships is taking place worldwide. For instance, the United States hosts an ongoing debate over "domestic partnership" benefits and registration; Australia has a comprehensive intermediate status called De Facto Relationships that recognizes unmarried heterosexual partners in inheritance, property division when splitting up, wrongful death suits, running family businesses, and more; France is considering legalizing "civil solidarity pacts," or as one magazine calls it, *"mariage light,"* to recognize the more than two million couples, straight and gay, outside legal marriage. But while lesbian and gay couples, on the one hand, and unmarried heterosexual couples, on the other, are often treated as interchangeable in this debate, they raise two separate questions. Lesbian and gay couples *cannot* marry and are seeking entry to the full existing institution; unmarried heterosexual couples want simultaneously to refuse the state's authority over marriage *and* to have their bond treated with full respect and public benefits. One movement wants to widen an existing institution; another wants—although it is never put precisely this way—to invent or rediscover an intermediate marriage, a demi-marriage that lives by custom rather than law, picking and choosing which authorities and statutes it will accept and which it will reject.

Of course, an intermediate marriage class is nothing new. The Romans and many of the nations with civil codes based on the Romans'—the seventeenth-century Dutch, for instance—allowed women to choose between two kinds of marriages: marriages in which she transferred from her own family into her husband's, took his status, lived under his power—essentially changing her subcitizenship from her own family to his—or marriages in which she kept her birth family's name and status, not to mention the right to buy, own, sell, contract, sue, and make wills.

Perhaps more surprising to us is the most common demi-marriage: the long blurry time between betrothal—a formal and financially binding contract—and wedding vows, a time that could last from many months to years. Until the Protestants got out their brooms in the sixteenth century, the intendeds often lived together, or at the very least got to know each other sexually. Italians might betrothe girls as early as age five and send them to live with their future husbands until the age of twelve, when they could say their final vows: one poor girl who'd been betrothed but "widowed" three times before the age of fourteen worried that the Catholic Church's antagonism toward widows remarrying meant she would spend her adolescence and adulthood alone. Several historians consider today's "consensual unions" to be a return to an older and more realistic habit of easing into marriage, a refusal of the legally sensible but emotionally absurd idea that "at quarter to one, you are not married; at quarter after one, you are."

The Western world *is* once again slowly crafting a state of demi-marriage, an intermediate status, that confers some but not all the benefits and responsibilities of the full form. "Crafting" probably implies far too much intention: bit by bit, here and there, demi-marriage is poking holes into social consciousness. Here and there a company has "domestic partnership benefits," offering unmarried partners a few of the benefits it offers married ones. Here and there a nation—Australia, and soon perhaps France—insists that unmarried heterosexual couples who've demonstrated commitment in life if not in law must be treated as coupled. Here and there a nation—Israel, South Africa, Brazil—insists that a lesbian widow or gay male widower must receive her or his dead partner's military pension. Here and there an American state allows an unmarried couple to adopt together, while its neighboring state does not. What society and authorities are being forced to recognize— piecemeal, sometimes grudgingly, sometimes with alarm—is that millions of Western couples *are* both married and un- at the same time, depending on whether you squint at them from the privately-agreed or the publicly-bestowed definition.

But having considered what lesbian and gay couples and demi-married straight couples have in common, look again at what separates them. The heterosexual demi-marrieds have (presumably) made a choice to enter their demi-married state rather than take the plunge into full *conubium,* or legal marriage; lesbian and gay couples are barred from *conubium,* with no legal right to enter the full institution, and so like Roman slaves are defined into *conterbernium* by the state. And being banned from legal marriage is vastly different from rejecting it: it's a sign of lower status, a banner saying your heart is beneath the notice of the society and the law.

But in either case—whether the demi-married-by-default lesbians and gay men, or the demi-married-by-choice heterosexuals— demi-marriage forces Western law once again into the position of Roman judges attempting to judge *affectio maritalis* or fourteenth-century ecclesiastical courts trying to define whether the couple really did say those *verba* and pronounce the sacrament. How can a court, post-hoc, define what was in two partners' minds—especially if they now squabble over what they intended, or if one partner is dead? How can you tell the consensual couples who *want* to be exempted from breakup or inheritance rules from those in which, for instance, a powerful man is yeah-yeah'ing a woman into concubinage, accepting her services as housemaid and hostess and mistress by promising to marry her until, just as her upper arms and thighs start to sag—what a coincidence!—he finds someone new? Without some accepted social form, society must repeatedly, case by case, untangle the complicated question of whether married-by-heart couples should be treated as married-by-law. Or to put it differently, whenever there are disputes, society has to play sorcerer and find a way to divine private intentions. How is a probate judge (or hospital administrator, or rent-control supervisor) to know whether you two really are or were living in *affectio maritalis*—that the woman who *says* she was your beloved spouse really was, that you didn't consider her just a nurse or a sleazy adventuress or a lunatic roommate? We are returning, in other words, to the conundrum that one historian noted in medieval marriage: "The real hurdle for the courts was the persistent idea that people could regulate marriage for themselves."

Which brings us back to where this chapter began. There would be no need for the public institution of marriage—whether by custom or law—if human beings always treated each other with perfect justice. But as Mary Ann Glendon paraphrases Max Weber, "Deregulation in the name of freedom ... means leaving the realm abandoned by the law to be governed by the play of private power relations." Without *some* supervision—whether that's sending your heavily armed brothers to demand your dower from your dead husband's clan, or having the state instruct landlords to let a widowed spouse stay in his apartment of twenty years although it was listed in his dead husband's name—disputes are won not by justice but by strength. Although imperfect by any standard, the centuries' accretion of marriage laws are, today, society's painstakingly hammered consensus on how a couple should justly be treated.

While some of us might abjure *any* governing authority, the triumph of the secular state over religions, families, and tribes means that individual choice in marriage for the first time officially overrides any class, religious, ethnic, or other group allegiance. And rightly so. Some social commentators have suggested dis-

solving state registration and supervision of marriage entirely, returning marriage to the various religions. But who then would
intervene in the children's custody if, as recently happened in a
custody case in Massachusetts, a formerly agnostic married couple
divorced after one converted to evangelical Christianity and the
other to Hassidic Judaism—two fundamentalisms whose world-
views and marriage rules are deeply at war? Who would decide
questions of alimony if a wife found her husband intolerable after
their Southern Baptist Convention endorsed the idea that a wife
should "submit" to her husband, after she left both the faith and
him? In a state committed to equal justice under law, it's hard to
swallow the idea of consigning individual marriages to the supervision of warring gods. The baggy pluralism of civil marriage
law—big enough to swallow up every religious interpretation—is
fundamental to the West's contemporary public philosophy and
capitalist economy.

And yet law remains a gross, blunt, and tremendously limited
instrument: it cannot recognize the nuances of every human relationship, from which sibling you've refused to speak to for twenty
years to which friend you urgently want in charge of your hospital-
ized care. Most of human life rightly takes place outside the radar
of the law—whether that's the three-times-weekly call to your best
friend or the intimate coworker bringing food every night when
you're wheelchair-bound after a car accident. What the law *can* do
is recognize the single most important relationship most human
beings throughout history have had: the one in which we share our
bodies and our daily lives. Perhaps for today's dissenters there
should be some less-demanding marriage form, one that offers
fewer benefits and fewer restrictions, a signature that lets people register their intentions in the eyes of the law, writing their
own private marriage contract—or perhaps that too easily lets the
stronger take advantage of the weaker, and we should bring back
common-law marriage, with all its faults. Whichever way the West
decides to recognize the growing category of demi-marriage, it will
be returning to something more traditional than today's standard-
ized marriage rules.

As society tries to come to a new consensus, it may be important to remember the history of perpetual dissent over the demi-married, the common-law couples, the *verba*-vowed, the *affectio maritalis*'d. "There are more problems in the world than solutions," writes Israeli social commentator and novelist Amos Oz. "I must stress that I do not mean that there are many unsolved problems *at the moment,* but that *in the nature of things* there are more problems in the world than solutions." That seems particularly true in the marriage wars. The question that has been fought over for millennia is not yet, and never fully will be, resolved: what is *the* just, or proper, or moral consensus on what counts as a marriage? Society's task is always to find a way of enforcing that consensus, according to the social conditions of the time. And though there may not be solutions to every problem, marriage is always key political territory, critical to the individual who wants her or his life choices fairly observed—and critical to society as well, which wants individuals cared for fairly and property moved in an orderly way. State intervention in marriage—not to mention the state's particular ideas about dividing up responsibilities and property—may offend, but what other authority could we possibly invoke to adjudicate disputes: religions, say, or clans?

Lesbian and gay couples and our families are neither better nor worse than our heterosexual siblings: we too squabble over inheritance, epitaphs, hospital decisions, and breakups. Although one hopes that every marriage lasts happily ever after, we all know that's a myth, whatever the sexes. When we—we humans, that is—break up we can do it so furiously that we willfully, angrily distort who owes what to whom. And although every happily married couple's most fervent wish is to die simultaneously, few manage it: the one who's left must suffer through the imperfect human fact that their beloved may have died without leaving clear signs about the bond, allowing landlords or siblings or parents to shove you out, no matter your twenty years of faithful arguments and caring.

So what is marriage for? The public institution of marriage, in Western democracies, is for applying a just consensus to private disputes, a consensus to treat each individual bond with respect and equality. Given that all human beings occasionally need such Solomonic intervention, same-sex couples belong.

Remember the Ladies: Who Runs the Marriage?

One of the charges levied persistently against marriage is that its most fundamental purpose is to put men in charge and keep women down—that marriage officially transforms them into servants or slaves. Is it true? Has marriage always and inevitably, to quote William Congreve's *The Way of the World,* made her "dwindle into a wife" while he is "enlarged into a husband"? Or are there particular laws, customs, and rules that reshape husbands and wives into pairs that reflect the general public consensus on how to keep social order: owner and owned; autocrat and subject; separate but equal; best friends and genuine peers?

Of course, we can never actually know how particular husbands and particular wives treated each other under different regimes.

ARTICLE 40 copy!

)n we will investigate the slow rise of the ₂ or not in practice—of equality between ₁at reigns today.

; always a disparity between marriage in public ge in private practice. Every contented long- about the fact that marriage is an intimate lit- :, with each one wrestling for the upper hand :iendly and sometimes painful. Will we go to for Thanksgiving? Will we buy the city town- : the suburban single-family that you want? ly *not see* how filthy the bathroom is? Maybe ₇e learn the inner story of marriage's power e only in a biographical study like Phyllis which opens with her comment that "Every pon some understanding, articulated or not,

about the relative importance, the priority of desires, between its two partners. Marriages go bad not when love fades—love can modulate into affection without driving two people apart—but when this understanding about the balance of power breaks down, when the weaker member feels exploited or the stronger feels unrewarded for his or her strength."

Those struggles are scarcely limited to different-sex couples—don't get me started—and are far from identical among every heterosexual pairing. But what heterosexual couples do that same-sex couples cannot is generalize their own personal marriage battles into the famous "battle of the sexes," happily accusing the entire other sex of every possible sin. What's the difference between St. Jerome's "If you find things going too well, take a wife" and Henny Youngman's "Take my wife, please"? In the medieval *Ballad of the Tyrannical Husband,* the husband insists that what his wife calls exhausting work—nursing all night, milking at dawn, making butter and cheese, feeding the poultry, taking the geese to the green, baking and brewing, carding, spinning, and beating flax—is easy and that she really spends her day at the neighbors' gossiping. When he takes over for her for a day, she wins the argument—an argument that's still going on today in debates about women's double shift. From Chaucer to Thurber to *Roseanne,* each sex can seem frustrated with the other's intractable refusal to see reason—i.e., to see things their way.

Wives' complaints do have some extra oomph. Since the husband has always been elevated by official marriage ideology, he has usually had an incredible advantage in the personal battle for marital power—whether he knows it or not. Think about the difference between the 1950s housewife expected to pick up and follow her husband and today's two-career couple commuting between, say, Boston and D.C. If you or any of your married friends ever got an incredible job offer out of town, how did the debate go? Did they just assume that the woman should follow her man, or was there argument and earnest discussion, maybe punctuated by shouting and tears? If she followed because his work earns more, can we really say that theirs was a personal choice, given that women in general make some two-thirds of what men do? Each marriage may well be its own private civilization, but general social norms loom behind every argument.

In other words, acheiving husband-wife equality in practice has been easier and harder in various eras, regions, and classes. The surprise is that the history of women's position within marriage is anything but a straight line of progress from utter subjection to complete equality: it dips and rises unevenly across ages and regions and classes. Sometimes wives' official position has been a nightmare—such as Athenian women confined to the *gyna-ceum* and given no legal or social power to run their own lives, or medieval clans' daughters swapped for land, or Anglo-American nineteenth-century women living under Blackstone's infamous formula that in law "husband and wife are one person, and the husband is that person." In other times and places, the wife's position has not been as bad.

Let's take just the variations in her financial position, since earning power gives you domestic power—negotiations within marriage go better for the spouse who's got her own wallet. From this point of view, medieval wives were better off than Victorian wives. In thirteenth-century Sienna, for instance, married and unmarried women were free of male guardianship and could inherit, own, buy, sell, lend, contract, sue, and generally practice the full range of commercial obligations—which made them at least somewhat independent of their husbands' purses. Merchant and upper-class medieval and pre-modern women might have property settled so firmly on themselves and their children that their husbands could not touch it. Dutch law allowed seventeenth-century New Amsterdam women to be wealthy business powerhouses—but once they became New Yorkers under British law, those same women owned less and less. Historians agree that "A woman of 1200, even if she was unmarried or widowed, would have had no cause to envy a woman of 1700, and even less one of 1900."

And yet, whatever the economic variations, until the nineteenth century, husbands and wives have *officially* been portrayed as alpha and beta, number one and number two, in every Western system on record. So any discussion of marital equality brings us quickly to two age-old ideas: first, the idea that women and men are innately, immutably, essentially different (sometimes expressed as she's lesser, and sometimes as separate-but-equal), and second, that—from Adam on—men are destined to rule by either nature or the creator (same difference, as my grade-school fellows would have said).

Such rule was at least politically consistent when *all* public order ran by hierarchy, when nearly everyone was subject to someone one rung above. "During most of Western history only a minority of grown-ups ever achieved [social and political] independence," explains historian John Boswell. "The rest of the population remained throughout their lives in a juridical status more comparable to 'childhood,' in the sense that they remained under someone else's control—a father, a lord, a master, a husband, etc." And if the general social and political order is hierarchical, it will seem natural if, within marriage, the husband is officially in charge. For instance, in the world of Aristotle—where male heads of households actually ran their own little fiefdoms, coordinating things in the polis as if they were a neighborhood association—a wife was never to expect her husband's love: "it is the part of a ruler to be loved, not to love, or else to love in another way." Old Testament patriarchs treated women as semihuman, their wombs property to be traded among men, with the biblical rules for marriage contracts listed with the rules for purchasing servants, oxen, and cattle. Although the early Christians tried to launch an ideal of everyone's spiritual equality, they accepted *political* inequality, whether the rule of masters over slaves or husbands over wives; and so Paul enshrined his contemporaries' idea that just as "the head of every man is Christ, the head of a woman is her husband." In a world in which people usually saw themselves as belonging somewhere in a great chain of authority, seeking the favor of their "natural" superiors (whether owner or ruler, Caesar or Medici), wives were naturally slotted somewhere below the patriarchal top of the line.

Enlightenment political theorists, when arguing that the radical new ideal of democratic rule should overturn the divine authority of kings and aristocracies, got very defensive about the charge that destroying the divine right of kings would also destroy the rule of husbands. In one famous debate about democracy, Locke had to argue that a husband's power over his wife was not political at all, but rested rather in the capitalist's right to rule his own property: "to order the things of private Concernment in his Family, as Proprietor of the Goods and Lands there, and to have his Will take place before that of his wife." Some women recognized the injustice in the argument that the new egalitarian ideals were for everyone but them. "Passive Obedience you've transferred to us," wrote one poet in 1701, "That antiquated doctrine you disown, / 'Tis now your scorn, and fit for us alone." Or as a later Englishwoman wrote, "If all men are born free, how is it that all women are born slaves?"

But it took several hundred years before the conflict between the new egalitarian political theory, on the one hand, and the vestigial divine right of husband-rule, on the other, was fully exposed. As the general political order changed, quite a few other things were also happening to marriage. For one, the Protestants were preaching their belief in "holy matrimony," with its sacred affection. At first the Protestants' phrase "holy matrimony" meant companionable *rule*. But slowly it melted into a new theory of companionate marriage, a marriage of "mutual esteem, mutual friendship, mutual confidence," in which husbands treated wives not as "domestic drudges, or the slaves of our pleasures, but as our companions and equals."

Equals! It was a subversive word—and in tune with the other changes taking place in the new capitalist democracies. By the nineteenth century, all legally imposed marital subordination—in property ownership, child custody, and the "separate spheres"—had become anachronistic, vestigial as an appendix, an irritation that flared into political battles across the Western world. The divine right of kings—once the obvious model for husband-rule and wifely obedience—had become such a distant nightmare that the only political comparison left for husband-rule was—can you guess?—slavery. Feminists of all stripes rhetorically exploited the comparison as fully as they could, rampantly and vehemently using the word. Wrote one in 1876, "The bondage of the wife is clearly evident from the circumstance that if she elope, the husband may seize upon her by law and take her home, as fugitive slaves were wont to be restored to their masters." John Stuart Mill pointed out, "The law of servitude in marriage is a monstrous contradiction to all the principles of the modern world . . . Marriage is the only actual bondage known to [English] law." Writes historian Nancy Cott, "Although historians have usually highlighted the demand for the vote in the women's rights conventions . . . in fact complaints about wives' unjust subordination *within marriage* and demands for greater parity between spouses were far more central." A wife's ability to take a job, own land, buy a hat, or refuse sex—without asking her husband's permission—were far more immediate and practical needs than casting a ballot.

And so some radicals began repudiating the marriage contract. In one famous 1855 marriage ceremony, feminist and physician Lucy Stone and Henry Blackwell declared:

> While we acknowledge our mutual affection, by assuming the sacred relationship of husband and wife, yet . . . we deem it a duty to declare that this act on our part implies no sanction of, nor promise of voluntary obedience to, such of the present laws of marriage as refuse to recognize the wife as an independent rational being, while they confer upon the husband an injurious and unnatural superiority, investing him with legal powers which no honorable man would exercise, and which no man should possess. . . . marriage should be an equal and permanent partnership, and so recognized by law.

Such language outraged right-thinking folk: *everybody* knew that God and nature had made woman to obey, and that any change would mean—by now, can we all say this together?—disease and the collapse of marriage, the family, children, Christian morality, and civilization itself. One representative tract insisted, "She is not the equal of man; she is not his superior. She was taken out of him; she belongs to him; . . . she is nothing but a shadow, or an image in a mirror, without him." A late nineteenth-century pope, Leo XIII, thundered, "The husband is the ruler of the family and the head of the wife, the woman ... is to be subordinate and obedient to a husband."

Naturally, emancipated women (and their children) were threatened with disease and plagues, since women were violating their own "natural" limits. For instance, an influential physician wrote that serious education for women, that accompaniment to the cry for marital equality, "by deranging the tides of her organization ... divert blood from the reproductive apparatus to the head" and brought on "dysmenorrhea, chronic and acute ovaritis, prolapsus uteri, hysteria, neuralgia and the like," quite possibly leaving women sterile or unable to nurse. Others emphasized that women's "unnatural" behavior (such as getting an education or treating their husbands as equals), that "crime before God and humanity," would not only violate the sanctity of marriage but would lead to the collapse of civilization. As one writer explained, "Any attempt to improve the condition of women ... must result in *disaster to the race* ... So far as human life in the world is concerned there can be no improvement which is not accomplished in accordance with the laws of nature." Another emphasized that violating the centuries-honored submission of wives would have horrifying repercussions, since any such proposal "criticizes the Bible ... degrading the holy bonds of matrimony into a mere civil contract ... striking at the root of those divinely ordained principles upon which is built the superstructure of society."

But even shorn of jeremiads, it's illuminating to read the arguments against female marital equality, seen as—like female suffrage, another outrageous proposal based on the idea that women and men are equals—one of the patently ridiculous items on the militant feminist agenda. One writer baldly caricatured all this reform by asking readers to picture where it would end:

> every post, occupation, and government service is to be thrown open to woman; she is to receive everywhere the same wages as man; male and female are to work side by side; and they are indiscriminately to be put in command the one over the other. Furthermore, legal rights are to be secured to the wife over her husband's property and earnings. ... *Nor does feminist ambition stop here.* It

> demands that women shall be included in every advisory commit-
> tee, every governing board, every jury, every judicial bench, every
> electorate, every parliament, and every ministerial cabinet; fur-
> ther, that every masculine foundation, university, school of learn-
> ing, academy, trade union, professional corporation, and scien-
> tific society shall be converted into an epicene institution—until
> we have everywhere one vast cock-and-hen show. . . . Wherever we
> look we find aversion to compulsory intellectual cooperation with
> woman. Practically every man feels that there is in woman . . . an
> element of unreason which, when you come upon it, summarily
> puts an end to purely intellectual intercourse.

The horror! How could society offend men's sensibilities so—forcing them to override their "natural" aversion and to deal with
women in the home (or may I add, gay men in the military) as
equals?

How? Because in a world that ran now by individual effort rather
than hierarchical obedience, male supremacy could no longer be
justified. And so the husband-rule argument lost—if not at every
hearth, then at least in public philosophy.

For instance, at the beginning of the nineteenth century, the social consensus about who ruled marriage had been explicitly written into the French Civil Code, thus: "The husband owes protection to his wife, the wife obedience to her husband. . . . The wife is
obliged to follow him wherever he judges it appropriate to reside;
the husband is obliged to receive her and to furnish her with all
that is necessary." That ideology became untenable as women began stepping out of the political and economic basement. As early
as 1945, one French commentator wrote that "The notion of a head
of the family is contrary to good sense and contrary to reality." By
1970 the French parliament agreed, replacing the old strictures
with a new provision that "the spouses together assure the moral
and material direction of the family." Similarly, the German civil
code gave the husband the right to "decide all matters of matrimonial life" until 1976—when the law was changed to read, "the
spouses conduct the running of the household by mutual agreement." By the late 1980s, one of the last strongholds of the male-
ownership model of marriage—the idea that a woman's body was

her husband's sexual property—was erased as feminists invented and wrote into law the concept of "marital rape," the radical (and once oxymoronic) idea that a woman owns her own body even after she marries. In England, legal decisions now include such declarations as "both spouses are the joint, co-equal heads of the family" or "husband and wife are . . . partners—equal partners—in a joint enterprise." And why not? How could marriage be the only employment left (except physical combat) that requires the sexes to fulfill their "naturally" separate roles?

In other words, not so long ago Isadora Duncan may have been justified in saying, "Any intelligent woman who reads the marriage contract, and then goes into it, deserves the consequences." But by the late 1980s, almost everything about marriage to which Lucy Stone and Henry Blackwell had once objected had been dismantled—legally, at least. Real household equality may not yet have arrived, but—and this is one reason it's possible even to *discuss* same-sex marriage—equality *has* triumphed as our operating theory and social ideology.

Which brings us to our current question: same-sex marriage. Once the theory of white supremacy had been toppled, interracial marriage could no longer fairly be barred. In just the same way, once the theory of male supremacy and female inferiority was dismantled—the theory that man must rule and woman must serve —there is no longer any justification for barring marriage between two women or two men.

In other words, much of the fight over same-sex marriage is a fight-by-proxy over one of the last strongholds of *gender* supremacy: the idea that a man rules a woman, that a woman without a man is missing something essential, that a man who seeks another man is degrading himself by turning into a woman. Lynn Wardle, a Brigham Young University law professor, insists, "the union of two persons of different genders creates a relationship of unique potential strength and inimitable potential value to society"—a belief that, since it can't be substantiated, he merely repeats, adding, "The essence of marriage is the integration of a universe of gender differences (profound and subtle, biological and cultural, psychological and genetic)." David Frum agrees in *The Weekly Standard,* writing that "there are important differences between men and women the law must respect and honor." Well, of course. But Frum and company actually want something quite different than respect and honor: they want courts to *enforce* differences between men and women—even if that means outlawing the differences in how individual folks actually *experience* being male or female. Such social enforcement of a supposedly natural difference is the last gasp of a supremacy ideology—as when judges insisted that people of African and European ancestry actually *couldn't* marry each other biologically, their bodies, talents, and capacities being "naturally" different, which not coincidentally helped prop up the segregation that kept whites officially in charge.

As John Stuart Mill wrote in *The Subjection of Women,* "So true it is that unnatural generally only means uncustomary, and that everything which is usual appears natural." If "female" can mean only one narrow thing, how do Frum, Wardle, and fellows explain what "female" essence is held in common by temporary Miss America Vanessa Williams, career invalid Alice James, Princess Diana, Gertrude Stein, and WNBA star Sheryl Swoopes? Can we consider the possibility that there are many ways to be female or male—to be *human*—and that a truly egalitarian society makes room for those differences? Can we recognize that there is no difference between a girl who loves mathematics and a girl who loves girls—that each girl violates the socially invented rules of "nature" by following her own inner nature? Frum doesn't think so. He ventriloquizes his own opinions onto the sensible masses, who, he says, "feel—they are right to feel—anger and outrage when it's proposed to them to abolish marriage and *replace it with a new unisex partnerhood.*"

And so we discover what *really* outrages Frum and fellows: female equality, or feminism. Which is precisely what excites me about same-sex marriage: a "new unisex partnerhood" sounds thrillingly like what feminists have been battling toward for centuries. When same-sex couples enter the existing institution, not some back-of-the-bus version called "domestic partnership" or "queer marriage," marriage and divorce law will have to become even more gender-blind. When marriage is guided by the idea of two equal companions joining together in love, women's rights more firmly anchors its laws. Lesbians and gay men have long known that two women or two men together invent themselves outside society's gender expectations: who cooks and who mows the lawn, who takes care of the kids and who earns a living, are chosen personally rather than socially imposed. That vision may be difficult to offer to pairs who come "pre-gendered." But once we can marry, jurists will have to decide every marriage, divorce, and custody question (theoretically, at least) for a pair of equal partners, neither having more historical authority, their lives defined by their actions. Just as the right wing correctly fears, our entrance might rock marriage toward its more egalitarian shore.

I am *not* suggesting that every marriage *must* be gender-equal. Some women even today believe that God wants them to serve their husbands, or that having men in charge is convenient. Each couple should feel free to argue through their own decisions about whether to sign up for the male-supremacy model of marriage, and to extol that model's virtues in such public forums as op/ed columns and radio talk shows. But should those people be able to force me to live by their separate-but-(not-quite)-equal ideology, or should I be free to live by the gender-neutral ideology that rules the rest of today's public philosophy and marriage law?

Nor would I suggest that male and female are precisely alike: obviously there are differences in biology and psychology, or I would not have spent my life falling so powerfully in love with women, drawn to men only as friends. But it's easy for some heterosexuals to confuse their own *personal* differences from their spouses with god-given, sex-based universal differences between *every* pair of spouses—as if only sex-based differences lead people to the maturity and compassion and joy that so many of us find in marriage's intimate and stubborn struggles. William Bennett writes, "marriage ... is an honorable estate based on the different complementary natures of men and woman—how they refine, support, encourage, and complete one another." But Bennett can only speculate—he cannot know—that the way he and his wife "refine, support, encourage, and complete one another" is so *un*like the way Madeline and I do, that her and my very different "natures" cannot be "complementary" in any "honorable" way. Or to put it differently, Bennett cannot know for certain that his marriage is so entirely *like* every other male/female marriage: Marabel Morgan's saran-wrapped obsequies, Franklin and Eleanor Roosevelt's joined independences, Victoria and Albert's regal domesticity, Virginia and Leonard Woolf's astringent intimacy, John and Yoko's passionate friendship, Ike Turner's brutality toward Tina, Bill and Hillary's unfathomable bond. Can Bennett possibly believe that every happy family must be happy in the same way? And even if he does, why should our society allow only one model, a model based not on our inner lives but on our genitals?

I would like to suggest that men and women are equal for the purposes of carrying out marriage's contemporary duties: caring for each other lifelong, in sickness and in health, for richer or poorer, till death do us part. Which is my life's most fundamental hope and goal: to do precisely that for the woman I adore. And if caring by two officially equal partners (however different their characters and gifts) is what marriage is for, then same-sex couples belong.

SIX:

Heart

___

Nothing can be more cruel than to preserve by violence a union, which at first was made by mutual love, and is in effect dissolved by mutual hatred. . . . I had my choice, 'tis true, of my prison; but this is a small comfort, since it must still be a prison.

—JOHN MILTON, "The Doctrine and Discipline of Divorce" (1643)

[N]othing is more dangerous than to unite two persons so closely in all their interests and concerns as man and wife, without rendering the union entire and total. . . . How many frivolous quarrels and disgusts are there . . . which would soon inflame into the most deadly hatred, were they pursued to the utmost under the prospect of an easy separation?

—DAVID HUME, "Of Polygamy and Divorces" (1742)

Since Marriage was instituted for the purpose of promoting the happiness of individuals and the good of society and since the attainment of those objects depends entirely on the Domestic harmony of the parties connected and their living together in a perfect union of inclinations, interests, and affections, when it becomes impossible for them to remain longer united . . . the good of Society no less than the well-being of individuals requires that it should be dissolved and that the parties should be left free to form such other domestic connections as may contribute to their felicity.

—American divorce petition (1791)

Love is moral without marriage, but marriage is immoral
without love.

—ELLEN KEY (1915)

PRESS MOST WESTERNERS ON WHY THEY THEMSELVES
married—pushing past those jokes about toasters or dental
insurance, and leaving behind beliefs about the institution's
origins—and they'll almost certainly tell you they fell in love. If
they've been married a long time they might explain that today
"love" means something different than when they first met; if
they've been divorced or in therapy they might talk for a long
time about their mistakes; if politically or academically inclined,
they might launch into a dissertation about love as an illusion by
which society justifies power imbalances; if religious, they may
talk about the prayer and belief involved in keeping love alive.
But almost all will consider "love" to be *the* acceptable justification for getting or staying married. A loveless marriage strikes
most contemporary Westerners as a travesty, a great sadness, an
emptiness at your life's center. As a result, it's easy to despise or
pity or be frankly baffled by the aging CEO marrying a trophy wife
and the young social climber who accepted him; by the widow remarrying for security; by the faintly antagonistic couple who stay
together for the children; or by anyone—from southern Asians to
Moonies—assigned in marriage to a virtual stranger. Romantic
love is a kind of spiritual breath each of us was raised on, hopes for,
dreams of, and expects in our lives. Those of us who have it can
scarcely imagine life without it, as if we'd suffocate for lack of
oxygen.

But wasn't it *always* so? If this is new, as I've been suggesting
throughout this book, why is literature so full of love—for instance, this perfect little sixteenth-century quatrain that so many
English lit majors have by heart:

> Westron wind, when will thou blow?
> The small rain down can rain:
> Christ, if my love were in my arms,
> And I in my bed again!

You can surely tot up your own mental examples, beginning with Ovid's metamorphosing lovers; Jacob falling in love at the well with Rachel; Cleopatra and Marc Antony; Tristan and Isolde; most of Shakespeare's sonnets and plots.

Yes, of course, premodern folks could and did *feel* love—ranging from companionable affection to passionate desire—and even sometimes felt it for their spouses. But in this book we've discussed something different: the coronation of romantic love as the monarch of *marriage*. That's what's new: love as marriage's public philosophy, displacing everything from finances to babies.

This chapter looks at two radical consequences of the falling away of all other purposes or social justifications of marriage. One is the idea that marriage can dissolve when love fades. The other is the idea that has led most specifically to our debate today over same-sex marriage: the idea that not your parents but you yourself should consent to and even (gasp!) choose your own spouse.

The shifting histories of both consent and dissent, of marriage's entrance and exit rules, are just as contentious as everything else about marriage—in other words, far more than most of us might suppose. Marriage today is presided over by the cultural deity of intimate love yet is constantly tugged apart by the centrifugal forces of work and school and daily life. That conflict has been punditized widely and will scarcely be resolved soon. But it does bring us to a painful consequence of the shift in marriage's public philosophy: divorce. Once emotional expectations rise, once marriage's inner life *is* the marriage, mustn't the death of love undo the marriage? And if marriage is immoral without love, then mustn't a moral society change the rules of—and expect a dramatic rise in —divorce?

Dissent: Untying the Knot, or When Can You Say "I Don't"?

It is a truth universally acknowledged that the more marriage is about property, the harder it is to break off. Equally true is the converse: when individuals and the economy can function without stable couples, society frees us to make and break marriages based not on our outer but our inner fortunes. But there is also a third truth, which many commentators have noted over the years: if society respects marriage, it must allow divorce.

And so we come to the penultimate section of this book, which is, appropriately, about an event that is—for many contemporary Americans—very likely to be the last act of the marriage. Every society's battle about divorce rules is really a battle over this book's question: what is marriage for? One 1920s witticism had it that marriage was necessary because without it you couldn't get divorced. More seriously, if marriage is for having sex, then impotence undoes the marriage. If marriage is for love, then love's loss undoes the marriage. Asking when, why, and how various societies let you divorce, in other words, lets us end with a rearview mirror survey of the long, winding, and very bumpy road that has been Western marriage.

Since Romans' marriages existed simply because of *affectio maritalis,* or the intention of being married, the disappearance of that intention meant the disappearance of the marriage. Romans could divorce as privately as they married, simply by saying (with or without witnesses) this legal formula: *Take back what is yours* (him) or *Keep what is yours* (her). The words needn't be pronounced in person. All she had to do was move out; all he had to do was drop her a letter saying things were over. How commonly those formulae were used, however, varied dramatically. On the one hand were the bone-tired farmer/senators of the early farm-based Republic, with an economy based on the couple's labor. Since these working marriages couldn't afford to come apart, the early Romans rarely divorced, and then only for extreme offenses like her adultery or his attempt to murder her. On the other hand were the later Empire conquerors, living on trade and gorged on plenty, who *could* get along financially without each other—and so felt free to divorce early and often, for no other reason than irritation. These folks shifted alliances like software programmers, although without necessarily losing any of the bonds they'd earlier made, since repudiating a spouse was no insult. Roman divorce didn't create the

kind of legal smash-ups we find in our own time, since those pragmatic aristocrats wrote exit rules into every marriage contract—
and since everyone knew that he always got the children, while she
always got her dowry back. If marriage was a private agreement
whose purpose was to make legitimate offspring and to pass on
property—and if no one imagined children needed the presence of
both parents—why should it be anybody's business (besides, of
course, their families) whether the pair stayed together?

The Christians changed the history—indeed, the *definition*—of
marriage with the famous phrase: "What God has joined together,
let no man put asunder." According to one theological historian,
that sentence shocked Jesus's listeners, "for instead of answering
the question he had been asked about the *grounds* for divorce, he
simply ruled out divorce altogether." No divorce? Not at *all*? How
could that be possible?

The good answer is that the Church was trying to protect
women, preventing powerful men from discarding wives as soon
as a marriage stopped being politically convenient or as soon as
they lost their youth. The bad answer is the Church's belief that
marriage merely, as one ninth-century bishop put it, "designate[s]
the use of the genitals." Rejecting one set of genitals and selecting
a new set to consort with was, in the Church's view, polygamy: why
should anyone get more than one living sexual playmate? If marriage was a necessary outlet for the always-sinful sexual impulse,
then nothing but impotence should dissolve the marriage.

And yet that theory was put in practice only for about three hundred years. Or to put it differently, today's infamous cascade of annulments actually brings the Church back to its *traditional* approach to marriage. In its early years the Church hadn't enough
clout to keep marriages together. Early medieval Germanic divorce
decrees, for instance, include such "Christian" attitudes as this:
"as between X and Y there is no charity according to God, but dis-
cord . . . they have decided that each of them should be free to enter
the service of God in a monastery or to contract a new marriage."
And many early Church theologians *did* allow divorce: in the 700s,
according to various Church canons, you could divorce your

spouse if he or she got leprosy, attempted or plotted your murder, was captured or sold into slavery, or entered a religious order. If marriage was for sexual relations, then circumstances that prevented sex dissolved the marriage.

So when did the Church actually, and sternly, banish divorce? Probably just about the same time the Protestant Reformation reclaimed it: in the sixteenth century.

We've already seen that the Protestants' middle-class moral uprising tried to sweep away the Catholics' gap between theory and practice, its cobwebby accommodation of human frailty. No more sex before the wedding! Priests and ministers had to marry like anyone else! Will everyone (as Comstock later said) please *behave!* The Catholic marriage sacrament rested on the idea that your consent, once given (whether in words or by having sex), changed your soul's status forever, merging you with your spouse—and could never be undone. The practical Protestants felt, instead, that marriage was a contract for companionship, and that it was not consent upon entering but living up to that contract that made marriage holy. If you violated your contract, you shattered the marriage.

And so, for the Protestants, the key question was: what was the essence of the marriage contract, or to put it differently, what behavior made matrimony holy? The answer varied from one reformer to another—but for none was it the emotional intimacy we venerate today. As one preacher wrote, "Anyone can be idolatrous, a heretic, impious, and yet remain a valid husband: but no one can be an adulterer and a husband, that is to be one flesh of two kinds." Loss of affection was not a problem: committing a sexual sin was. And so many of the new Protestant communities pulled together marriage courts that delved into whether one of you had fallen (or had pushed the other). Did you both commit adultery? You were stuck with one another for life. Did your spouse refuse to have sex with you? Divorce granted. Did your husband beat you, refuse to let you attend church, humiliate you in public? Too bad. If marriage was an oasis of sexual righteousness, only sexual misbehavior canceled the marriage.

The Catholics bristled at the Protestants' heretical idea that marriage could be unmade by misbehavior and at their stinging accusations that Catholic sexual and married life was wormy and rotten with loopholes. And so in 1563 the Catholic Church went on a new-broom sweep of its own. It tightened up its marriage rules in a host of ways—including finally writing into canon law the doctrine that marriage could never, ever, ever be dissolved. Never. Certainly not for any of those flimsy Protestant excuses, like "heresy, or irksome cohabitation, or the affected absence of one of the parties," or "the adultery of one of the married parties." After 1500 years of Christian history, the Catholic church was finally and seriously enforcing marriage as a lifetime, no-exit deal.

In our era, the difference in *practice* between sixteenth-century Catholic and Protestant positions on divorce may seem thin indeed. Very few people did manage to divorce, under either regime, and those who did were socially notorious. But the Protestants had introduced a key, subversive, and now familiar concept: the idea that a crime against the marriage undoes the marriage. Once opened that little crack, marriage's exit door got pushed open wider and wider. Especially as the Protestants preached more and more about holy matrimony's honorable innards, as the industrial economy pried apart the couple's need for each other's land and labor, the inner life increasingly edged onto the divorce stage. And as re-publicanizing nations divorced their kings, they also began calling for the right to divorce their spouses. The philosophical center of marriage, its definition and purpose, started migrating to that third and Protestant-nominated purpose: to "conforte, maintayne, helpe and counsaill"—or as William Bennett might paraphrase it, "refine, support, encourage and complete"—one another. A new social understanding—that since marriage was for affection, incompatibility of various kinds should dissolve it—kept making itself felt in law, a widening wedge in the divorce door.

When did the shift happen from divorce only for marital crimes to divorce when love died? Apparently not in the 1960s, as today's social commentators like to accuse, but in the mid-eighteenth century—just as capitalism seriously took root. One historian looked at Catholic petitions for annulments in one French town and found that in suits spread across classes of workers, bourgeois, and nobles, "only 9% before 1770 cited emotional attachment as a reason for marriage, while 41% after 1770 did so." Similarly, historian Nancy Cott looked into a century of Massachusetts divorce records, which included everyone from heiresses to ex-slaves, and found that people seeking a divorce "never named loss of conjugal affection among their grievances in 58 petitions between 1736 and 1765." Then there's a big shift in the emotional weather, and "more than a tenth of 121 suits between 1766 and 1786 . . . contained complaints such as 'her affections were thereby alienated from him,' 'all conjugal affection has fled,' 'he lost all affection for her,' her actions 'opposed nuptial happiness,' he 'ceased to cherish her,' she had 'almost broken his heart.'" Welcome to the land of Oprah! Even if people had tried to divorce earlier based on loss of love, they hadn't felt it respectable to talk that way. Suddenly, in the eighteenth century, it was more and more acceptable to insist publicly that a marriage be fulfilled not just in its outward duties but in its heart. By 1849, Connecticut passed a (then notorious) law allowing divorce for "any such misconduct as permanently destroys the happiness of the petitioner and defeats the purpose of the marriage relation."

This seems so obvious to us that we might not grasp how radical it was. Imagine telling a judge that you should be freed of your employment contract or military services, with no penalties, because you no longer loved your coworkers or officers. You'd be laughed out of court. Nobody says you'll always *enjoy* fulfilling your duties, but society would dissolve if every contract could be enforced based only on its signers' feelings—which is how the love-is-gone attitude toward divorce struck our predecessors. But as the traditional marriage economy collapsed—the economy in which two workers were dependent on each other for life—marriage's heart was left as its main justification.

And yet in this new and escalating romance lay a painful paradox: both before and after they married, these new husbands and wives—who expected *more* from marriage than their ancestors—might actually intersect *less* in their daily lives than the farmers or shopkeepers or tanners from whom they descended. Their educational and occupational gap was actually wider. Now that the shop was off the premises and many goods bought in the market, father and son went off to earn wages and learn trades while stay-at-home mother and daughter were in charge of—what? Overseeing the servants and doing the marketing, buying the things they used to make. And so, despite a surge of romantic letters and diaries that recount swelling, bleating, blending, and beating hearts, a nineteenth- or twentieth-century married pair actually had *less* chance to know each other well, both before and after marriage, than did the far less sentimental married medieval peasants (although perhaps more than married medieval aristocrats—but then, aristocrats' behavior had always been notoriously immoral, at least in Protestant terms). No wonder intimacy, romance, and parenthood became subjects fit for a hymnal, whether the Protestant hymnal of the nineteenth century or the pagan one of the twentieth: with the work partnership gone, what else—besides feelings and sex—is left for a married couple to share? And no wonder divorce spiked dramatically.

And so in the nineteenth century, battle was joined: between those who believed that marriage without affection was foul, and those who insisted that society would collapse if marriage's definition was so fundamentally altered—from a permanent state to a temporary contract, dissolved at will. On one side was an 1845 English judge who scathingly opined on his country's lack of a divorce law as he sentenced a man convicted of bigamy:

> Prisoner at the bar, you have been convicted before me of what the law regards as a very grave and serious offence: that of going through the marriage ceremony a second time while your wife was still alive. You plead in mitigation of your conduct that she was given to dissipation and drunkenness, that she proved herself a curse to your household while she remained mistress of it, and that she had latterly deserted you; but I am not permitted to recognize any such plea. . . . [Y]ou ought first to have brought an action against your wife's seducer if you could have discovered him; that might have cost you money, and you say you are a poor working man, but that is not the fault of the law. . . . You must then have

gone, with your verdict in your hand, and petitioned the House of Lords for a divorce. It would cost you perhaps five or six hundred pounds and you do not seem to be worth as many pence. But it is the boast of the law that it is impartial, and makes no differences between the rich and the poor. . . . It is my duty to pass upon you such sentence as I think your offence deserves, and that sentence is, that you be imprisoned for one day . . . you will be immediately discharged.

On the other hand was a Tory Lord who argued that "the lower classes, whose morals are more corrupt and whose principles on these subjects are more lax than those of the higher classes, will be continually applying for divorces . . . [which] will increase the immorality of adultery, and indeed give encouragement to the commission of that offence." Most people, in other words, will get away with whatever they can. Even John Stuart Mill acknowledged that

most persons have but a very moderate capacity of happiness; but no person ever finds this out without experience, very few even with experience: and most persons are constantly wreaking that discontent which has its source internally, upon outward things. Expecting therefore in marriage a far greater degree of happiness than they commonly find: and knowing not that the fault is in their own scanty capabilities of happiness—they fancy they should have been happier with some one else . . . but if they remain united, the feeling of disappointment after a time goes off, and they pass their lives together with fully as much happiness as they could find either singly or in any other union, without having undergone the wearing of repeated and unsuccessful experiments.

Of course, both were right. Allowing people to leave *does* undermine marriage's sense of security, absolute commitment, and willingness to compromise—and not allowing *anyone* to leave means some people will strangle inside what Milton called "the empty husk of an outside matrimony, as undelightful and unpleasing to God as any other kind of hypocrisy." So which definition of marriage should the state endorse? The one that ensured an intact marital house, or the one that voted for the integrity of the individual choice? The answer was the one that fit the rising philosophy.

Free choice for the individual, our new Western political philosophy, had to apply equally to the economy, to marriage's entrances,
and to its exits. In 1857, Britain passed a divorce law. Catholic
France did the same in 1884. By 1886, only six American states refused to accept cruelty as grounds for divorce. The heart had begun
to triumph—in law as in life.

But it had only just begun (to paraphrase the pop song) its triumph. Exactly how narrowly or broadly those divorce laws would
be framed was still up for grabs. And so began a century of jurisdic-
tional shopping that made courts, legislators, and individual citizens crazy. In the United States it began in 1850, when Indiana's
state legislature (passing a law written by free-lover and state legislator Robert Dale Owens) ushered in the purest incarnation of the
idea that *sans* love, marriage should simply and freely unravel. Under this divorce law—the loosest the nation had ever known—
judges could grant divorce for any reason at all, and more important, *to* anyone at all. A New Yorker who wanted to escape his wife
could check into an Indianapolis hotel for an hour to establish residence, go to court, run ads in an Indianapolis paper "notifying"
his wife of the divorce, and come home with an incontestable decree—all while his wife had no idea what was going on, and no
chance even to argue for custody or property settlement. The great
idea—that when love is gone the marriage simply dissolves—
turned out to be immensely complicated. *Who* decides that love is
gone? What if the other spouse disagrees: doesn't he or she have
any say? Who gets and supports the children? Must a man compensate a woman for the years she devoted to his care, and if so how?
Should she be punished (and if so, more than he would be?) for being sexually adventurous, or a bad housekeeper, or an uncompliant
wife? Who decides?

Indiana's new statute became a national scandal. In 1858, the *Indiana Daily Journal* complained, "We are overrun by a flock of ill-
used, and ill-using, petulant, libidinous, extravagant, ill-fitting
husbands and wives as a sink is overrun with the foul water of the
whole house." But when the Hoosier state tightened its residence
requirement, other frontier territories quickly took its place, vying

for divorce infamy: Illinois, Utah, South Dakota, North Dakota, Oklahoma, Wyoming, and finally Nevada, which courted the divorce trade so assidulously that it developed a gambling and entertainment industry to occupy those who had nothing to do while waiting to establish residence. Lawyers in these various states advertised prominently in the New York, D.C., and San Francisco press, "Have You Domestic Trouble? Are You Seeking DIVORCE? Do You Want Quick and Reliable Service? Send for My Booklet."

This blatant solicitation for divorce horrified those concerned with the goodness and righteousness of the American family. *The Nation* opined in 1893:

> One does not need to take a high view of the sacredness of marriage, or a low view of divorce, to pronounce all this demoralizing and shocking. . . . Where, out of savagery, could such sights be witnessed as are said to be common in Sioux Falls hotels, where a divorced husband may be seen introducing his new wife to his old one, who, in her turn, presents her new husband, while the bewildered children involved in this scandalous mixture wander about in disconsolate uncertainty as to their identity and relationships? This is the very chaos of marriage. . . . the whole country [cries] out against these laws that encourage what is practically polygamy.

The question of whether states had to recognize each other's divorces reached the Supreme Court—repeatedly. Over and over, for 150 years, the Supreme Court returned 5–4 verdicts that sometimes favored the out-of state-divorce . . . and sometimes did not. Depending on which way the unpredictable Court needle wavered, individuals were remarried or jailed for bigamy; gained or lost custody; were legitimate children or disinherited bastards. By 1948, one U.S. Supreme Court Justice was so frustrated at once again facing the divorce question that he wrote, "If there is one thing that the people are entitled to expect from their lawmakers, it is rules of law that will enable individuals to tell whether they are married, and if so, to whom."

It is, perhaps, too much to ask courts to definitely solve contentious questions on which society still has not made up its mind. So long as the West's consensus on marriage's definition—was it "so long as we both shall *live*" or "so long as we both shall *love*"?—was shifting, determined people would travel across borders to change the borders of their marriages. But the direction was clear. Since the language of love had become the monarch of marriage, divorce was going to triumph. Dissenters could remain in their own marriages if they chose; and England allowed its ministers to refuse to celebrate remarriages they believed to be, essentially, polygamy. But divorce became a decision as individual as marriage.

The language of the antidivorce activists will sound very familiar—because it's the same language used, variously, against any proposed change in the marriage rules, whether granting married women the right to own property, legalizing contraception, allowing interracial marriage, or condoning same-sex marriage. In 1816, Yale President Timothy Dwight warned that Connecticut's divorce law would have dire consequences: "Within a moderate period, the whole community will be thrown, by laws made in open opposition to the Laws of God, into general prostitution. . . . To the Eye of God, those who are polluted in each of these modes [divorce and prostitution] are alike, and equally impure, loathsome, abandoned wretches; and the offspring of *Sodom* and *Gomorrah*." Horace Greeley wrote in his *New York Tribune* that divorce violated marriage's very definition (you could read it in the dictionary!): joining two people for life. "There may be something better than Marriage; but nothing *is Marriage* but a solemn engagement to live together in faith and love *till death*," he wrote, offering to let divorce proponents have their way so long as they would "give their bantling a distinctive *name,* and not appropriate ours." Please—do what you like, just so you don't profane *my* institution by calling *yours* a "marriage."

In Britain, socialists' views on consensual divorce were blasted as "wicked, unchaste, disgusting, and beastly." New Zealand politicians fought local divorce proposals by warning that American states had already shown that it led to "successive polygamy." But once such rhetoric hits the streets, the debate is over, and the "traditional" advocates have lost. Appeals to an older morality never mean that morality itself is dying, but rather that a new morality is being born—a morality that justifies sex and marriage in a way that fits contemporary reality.

After England passed a divorce law in 1857, its number of divorces a year suddenly jumped from four to between two and three hundred. In France, after the 1884 bill, divorces jumped to seven thousand, twice the annual number of official "separations of bed and board" there had been before 1884. In the United States, divorce climbed at rates that caused predictions of civilization's immediate demise: "Between 1867 and 1929, the population of the United States grew 300 percent, the number of marriages increased 400 percent, and the divorce rate rose 2,000 percent." The death of the family was predicted when, during World War I, divorce ended one marriage in six. By then attitudes had changed so dramatically that even in New York—where the only ground for divorce was adultery—everyone knew that you could get a divorce simply by having your picture snapped lying on a hotel bed with a co-respondent-for-hire. Law could not keep flying in the face of social reality.

So what caused the jump in divorce rates? Perhaps the most fundamental reason, as almost every sociologist today recognizes, was economic. Once women could get an education and make a living, they were free to refuse someone they'd discovered to be a tyrant. One 1909 professor wrote, "If marriage is a failure, she does not face the alternative of endurance or starvation. . . . She is no longer compelled to accept support or yield to the tyranny of a husband whose conduct is a menace to her health and happiness." Many commentators note that the only way to reduce the divorce rate would be to ban women (not just mothers but all women) from working—an option that no longer seems enforceable or even moral. The economy made the choice for all of us: the individual is now our banner.

The debates over same-sex marriage and divorce are not, of course, precisely comparable. As many have pointed out, liberal divorce laws can, unless checked, leave the weaker—usually wives and children—in a position to be abandoned, exploited, and hurt.

Divorce's questions for social policy are exceptionally complex and well beyond the scope of this book: as every society has recognized, marriage's exit rules must be carefully crafted and overseen, or marital bullies take all. But when my bond with Madeline is recognized, no one will be harmed, abandoned, or left bereft. And so what *is* comparable is the underlying debate over what a marriage is for. Once happiness is publicly accounted as marriage's purpose and measuring stick, how dare a democratic state decide for its citizens whether they may leave—or enter?

"One of the paradoxes of modern western society is the simultaneous popularity of marriage and divorce," one historian writes. Finally we can see that this is not a paradox but a necessary link. If marriage is defined by love, then lovelessness is by definition a marital crime. And it is precisely this that makes both marriage and divorce so popular: although people may want guidance or breach-of-contract rules on their financial or social interests, everyone is an authority on their inner lives. And once individuals' decisions about their own happiness governs something so fundamental as marriage's exit rules, how can society base its entrance rules on anything else? How dare the state presume to deny the value or integrity of my spiritual life? Or to argue (as debaters say) for the affirmative, if marriage is for love, affection, and companionship—then same-sex couples belong.

Consent: Tying the Knot, or Who Can Say "I Do"?

This book began with money and ends with heart—as it should, since that's the story of marriage in Western history. Capitalism's long untangling of personal finances from matrimony is the central event in the history of marriage, the one that has led to the twentieth century's coronation of love. Which means that the patient reader has been led through this story more than once during this book. While there are still an endless number of historical facts, twists, and turns in the history of consent—do you or your father get to propose and say yes?—we've really been telling that story throughout. Oh, there are a few peculiar or noteworthy points in the history—and for a few pages we'll look at those. But a chapter titled Heart is also a kind of reward—an excuse to tell a marriage story that's just a bit more personal.

First, a little leapfrogging through history. When making a marriage, who has the right and obligation to say yes? You might smile at the question itself. But take the Romans. Their weddings included pledges exchanged by—are you sitting down?—the groom and his *father-in-law*. In the standard upper-class Roman ceremony, the groom said, "Do you promise to give your daughter to me to be my wedded wife?" The bride's father answered, "The gods bring you luck! I betrothe her." She said not a word. Because legal marriage was such a dynastic arrangement, an upper-class way of arranging alliances and inheritances, marriage had of course been arranged among the families—so much so that even the son's consent could be quite superficial. According to the Roman Digest, or code of laws, "If a son marries a woman on the order of his father, that marriage is valid, although one cannot be forced to marry against one's wishes: however, it will be presumed that he chose to accept." *Presumed that he chose to accept:* that doesn't sound much like our active courtships, does it? But at least the groom had to open his mouth. The bride—well, "a daughter who does not openly resist her father's wishes is assumed to have consented." After all, who would have stood up for her individual choice, given that her family or clan *was* the all-powerful civil authority, the law under which she lived?

A thousand years after the birth of Christ, one pope decided to insist that the rules had changed. When a powerful French noble, Jourdain, married off his daughter against her vehement objections, the pope annulled the marriage—a decision as shocking and urgent in its time as, say, *Loving v. Virginia*. The pope won. Within two centuries, the Church had turned the standard wedding ceremony topsy-turvy. Now the girl, and not her father, had to say—out loud—"I do." Now it was she, and not her father, who gave away the rights in herself: he might still walk her down the aisle, but he no longer literally placed her hand in her husband's; she did that herself. As one theologian explained, "where there is to be union of bodies there ought to be union of spirits." After reading about centuries in which men traded off their daughters' wombs like cattle—and often *for* cattle—you want to give three big cheers for the Church.

In practice, among the late medieval and early premodern upper classes, the children's consent was still assumed: it would have taken extraordinary willfulness for a twelve-year-old girl and a fourteen-year-old boy to stand up against her or his parents (without, remember, school pals or MTV to cheer on her rebellion). One thirteenth-century English archbishop outlawed adolescent marriages, but since local bishops gave dispensations freely—or rather, for a reasonable price—who cared?

When the sixteenth-century Protestants sided with the parents, outlawing secret marriages and requiring parental consent, it was because they refused the idea that marriage was a private affair. *Everyone's* interests had to be consulted, with parents and "friends" (sibs, uncles, godparents, interested others) proposing, and with marriageable adults thinking seriously about the suggestions of those who cared about their welfare. Oh, the Protestants did believe that, at a certain age—between, say, twenty-two and twenty-five—you were old enough to marry without your parents' consent. But until then it was common sense that your parents knew better than you did, that marriage based on "such ephemeral factors as sexual attraction or romantic love was if anything *less* likely to produce lasting happiness than one arranged by more prudent and mature heads." Consider the first marriage of Hermann von Weinsberg of Cologne, a sixteenth-century burgher whose "parents suggested he consider marrying his neighbor Weisgin Ripgin, the proprietor of a wool and yarn shop, recently widowed after sixteen years of marriage." His response: "Because you and my mother so advise me, and because I know her well and trust God, I shall be a happy man if the woman also desires me." Hermann's father proposed and within a week: married! Sure, both Hermann and Weisgin each had the opportunity to say *no*—but the philosophy they were following was closer to *reasonable, re-sponsible, appropriate, duty* than to our era's profound training in *passion, delight, uniqueness, love.*

And yet, as we saw in *Dissent*, despite themselves the Protes-tants' emphasis on "holy matrimony," combined with the Cath-olics' insistence on consent, eventually exploded into today's emphasis on love. The startling concept of "holy matrimony" ex-ploited a contradiction in Catholic theology: if consent and the in-dividual will were so spiritually important, wasn't the marriage bond itself—its inner life—holy as well? Of course, some of the preaching about "holy matrimony" was done by now-married priests who had to justify to their consciences and congregations their own fall from celibacy. But things also worked the other way around: with the preacher-men now married, they started to see marriage, that difficult and daily attempt to treat each other well, could be a spiritual act that pleased God.

Following the law of unintended consequences, the meaning of the phrase "holy matrimony" grew larger and more explosive as time went on. At first, it encompassed the idea that Hermann and Weisgin, in fulfilling their duty by marrying, were doing a holy thing. But over the centuries "holy matrimony" expanded to mean that marriage's inner life was actually *more* important than its forms—that the souls must meet *before* marriage, that the *inner* life must guide you to your spouse. Where once you had only veto power—your parents would nominate, and you would say yes or no—your feelings now could nominate and run the entire spousal election process.

Exactly when things switched from consent to choice is impossi-ble to pinpoint, since the history of the inner life is notoriously hard to trace. But diaries, letters, and literature suggest to histori-ans and literary scholars that some fairly large earthquake in mar-riage attitudes sent tremors across the eighteenth century. By then even the propertied classes, the ones who traditionally gave their children the least control, began to think that the children should have a say in who they married. The new romantic theories began surfacing in novels like Richardson's weeper *Clarissa*, in which parents' heedlessness of their daughter's heart leads to her ruin and death, or Fielding's *Tom Jones*, in which two young people's apparently mismatched love turns out to be just right. One French traveler to upper-class eighteenth-century England was startled enough by the rise of this remarkable idea of conjugal affection to write home that English girls and boys had an extraordinarily free opportunity to get to know each other before marriage; that "three marriages out of four are based on affection"; and that, even after marriage,

> husband and wife are always together and share the same society. It is the rarest thing to meet the one without the other. The very richest people do not keep more than four or six carriage-horses, since they pay all their visits together. It would be more ridiculous to do otherwise in England than it would be to go everywhere with your wife in Paris. . . . the Englishman would rather have the love of the woman he loves than the love of his parents.

Imagine!

We're still not looking at anything like the standards of today's marriages. One historian writes that "A popular 1779 treatise described the ideal marriage as 'a union of mind and sympathy of mutual esteem and friendship for each other.'" One eighteenth-century Salem schoolteacher told her diary she preferred to "remain in 'single blessedness' than to enter those sacred indissoluble bonds from mere motives of interest." And yet her standards for a suitor would strike us as astonishingly low: "Never have I rejected an individual whose presence gave me equal pleasure to that of his absence." It's not so hard for me to imagine marrying a man if *that* were my measuring stick: Don't care whether or not he's here.

By the late nineteenth century, young people began and managed their own courting, only afterwards allowing their parents a veto—a process that speeded up dramatically in the 1920s, as courtship moved from front porch to backseat.

In other words, for the past four hundred years, young people have steadily moved out from under their parents' thumbs, until today we would be a bit shocked if adults did *not* select spouses for themselves. And since the middle ages, girls and women have steadily been moving forward on the question of *my body, my right to choose:* to choose to marry someone her father proposed; to choose a suitor; to choose whether or not to expose herself to pregnancy every time she had sex; to choose even whether to love a woman or a man.

Or to quote again that twelfth-century theologian, "[W]here there is to be union of bodies there ought to be union of spirits." It is that union of spirits, that insistence on active consent and personal choice, that now rules our marriage ideology—and my own home life. Which brings me, finally, to offer a glimpse of the love story behind this book.

One day in 1991, almost against my will, I knew Madeline and I were going to stand up in front of the people we loved and commit ourselves to each other. Of course, it's ridiculous to say that it was against my will. I decided. Madeline, being distinctly private, wanted just to exchange rings. But an insular suburban life had strangled my childhood and my parents' marriage, so I recoiled: something inside me insisted on a ritual moment in full community view. It took awhile to write a ceremony that meant enough, but not too much. In our dearest friends' living room, we would say a few Jewish prayers, recite four favorite poems, exchange rings, speak our declarations, and, of course, kiss.

All of which we did, semicircles of family's and friends' eyes on us like lamps.

How can I describe what came next? It was nearly a delirium: by accident we'd spilled into something sacred. In that backyard in (yes) June, we kissed madly, actually forgetting we were lesbians, forgetting that the neighbors might be shocked. Madeline forgot to eat or drink. I would have kissed the letter carrier had he walked through. My dryly sarcastic brother cried so hard while making his toast that he could barely complete his sentences. My stepfather, who once squirmed at hearing I was queer, announced his pride in me and my friends. My mother led the blessings, cut the challah, and charmed all my friends. To poke fun at the ceremony's earnestness, we brought out a cake topped with two brides—laughing so hard that we brought down the house. To our utter surprise, the ceremony did bring us closer, pulling an invisible cloak around us that has warmed us during difficult times. We'd thought ourselves as committed as any couple could be: how else could we have exposed ourselves to the world's ridicule? But now even the most subtle traces of doubt dissolve instantly, chased away by the memory of that day when we made our declarations so publicly, placing our love in the hands of God and everyone we knew.

Today, after nearly a dozen years together, each morning when I wake up and find Madeline beside me, I still feel—if you'll excuse me for lapsing into poetry—surprised by joy: "and then my state / Like to the lark at break of day arising / From sullen earth sings hymns at heaven's gate." I am one of those former lit majors who has whispered the "westron wind" quatrain to my love over the phone when far away. In front of that roomful of family and friends, before vowing to care for her lifelong, I spoke to her that most famous Shakespearean sonnet, that determined lifetime promise—"Let me not to the marriage of true minds / Admit impediments. Love is not love / Which alters when it alteration finds." And I've repeated it to her, alone at home, when one or another of us is disconsolate, as age slowly creeps up on us, to remind her that, "Love's not Time's fool, though rosy lips and cheeks / Within his bending sickle's compass come; / Love alters not with his brief hours and weeks / But bears it out, even to the edge of doom."

Our marriage, in other words, has been bought and paid for with our society's common cultural currency: love. I adore her: I want to stand by as her perfect skin mottles and browns, as her dark brown hair grays, as her sweet eyelids sag. I want to calm her panic when she's ill, cry in her arms when my life goes wrong, and argue over our different driving styles until we're in the grave. I cry at others' weddings because I was so happy at—and am still so happy *with*—my own. With great good fortune, I was old enough—even under the French king's age of consent rules—when I made my choice to have made the right one, one that seems an ongoing fountain of joy.

If our society believes in letting two people choose their life's partner from a sea of particular and unique individuals—if each of us is free to choose a spouse based on our own hopes for companionship, affection, friendship, and love—then how dare anyone tell me I have chosen wrong? If marriage is for, as Archbishop Cranmer wrote in 1547, "mutual society, help and comfort, that the one ought to have of the other, both in prosperity and in adversity," Madeline and I belong.

Conclusion

> Will marriage as we have known it survive even to the next
> generation? *Can* it survive?
>
> —FELIX ADLER, *Marriage and Divorce* (1905)

And so we return, full circle, to the question with which I began
this book: What is marriage for? In one form or another, answering that question has preoccupied many a theologian and political
philosopher, aristocrat and politician, church court and peasant
jury. And finding the answer has never been simple, because so
many competing interests have always been at stake. Even the simple question, "Is John married to Mary or to Anne (or neither,
or both)" might be answered differently depending on whether
you believe marriage is made by their own private consent or by
a parentally approved public ceremony; whether it's a marriage
or a brothel if they have sex while trying to prevent conception;
whether it's a marriage or a barnyard if they marry across tribal
lines; whether they can or cannot exit if they despise each other—
to name only a few of marriage's many conundrums. *What is marriage for?* turns out to be a question about many things: about
which families will be allies in trade and politics, which will rise
and fall in the coming generation's economic competition; about
the right use of the body and the meaning of sex; about which
tribes count as political and social equals; about which child
starves and which inherits a prospering farm; about sexual equal-

ity, about farm life versus urban capitalism, about feudalism, theocracy, democracy, and much, much more.

What is marriage for, in other words—like most serious political or social questions—is a question about what it means to be fully human. Throughout this book we've seen arguments among the Romans, Jews, and early Christians; among the sixteenth-century Protestants and Catholics; between eighteenth-century democrats and monarchists; between the nineteenth-century purity brigade and the free-love forces; between feminists and male supremacists. The argument is always conducted by people with passionate beliefs about how to live a moral and responsible life, debating how to put the human body and spirit to good, joyous, productive use. And with such a large question behind it, the marriage battles are sometimes in the foreground, and sometimes in the background, but always with us.

If the question of whether John is married to Mary has been fraught with so many tensions and beliefs, we can hardly expect the question of whether John is married to Martin, or whether Mary is married to Anne, to be less contentious. And yet today's arguments about what constitutes a moral life—and a moral marriage—are treated as if they are unusually shocking, at least in what the United States calls the culture wars. As always, the conservatives want to hold onto the incarnation of marriage that won the last century's battle, anachronistically calling that version "traditional" and "time-honored"; the progressives want to bring marriage into step with how people actually live today; the utopians want to banish marriage entirely.

Yet marriage is a much hardier institution than either the doomsayers or the utopians ever seem to recognize. We can get a better perspective on today's marriage debates by remembering that although each apparently revolutionary proposal to change the marriage rules has shocked the conservatives of any given era, when such proposals surface in public debate the underlying economic and social changes have already happened.

So which side should win today's marriage battle, and why? The reader surely knows my opinion by now. But it might still help to reprise briefly what *our* era has concluded marriage is for—and how the intertwined rise of capitalism and egalitarian democracy transformed it. Marriage ceased to be a way to assign clan wealth or to choose your working partner—and turned into a way to share and shore up one's dearest companion's well-being and inner fortunes. Marriage stopped being justified only by making babies—and became justified by enriching the couple's happiness and intimacy. The family stopped being seen as your main work group, in which the child obeyed when her labor was assigned out—and started to be seen as a careful and nurturing nest for the vulnerable young, a nest in which men and women are equally qualified to serve as financial protector or personal nurturer or both. Making kin stopped being quite so critical to marriage, letting the pair themselves choose, free of family permission. Social order does remain one of marriage's key purposes: the legal institution attempts to apply a just social consensus to private disputes.

Or to put it more simply, Western marriage today is a home for the heart: entering, furnishing, and exiting that home is your business alone. Today's marriage—from whatever angle you look—is justified by the happiness of the pair. When combined with the West's root commitment to officially treating the sexes as equal, that marriage philosophy makes it possible—no, necessary—to recognize the marriages of two people of one sex. Our society has endorsed what some of us think of as the most *spiritual* purpose of marriage, the refreshing of the individual spirit. And if we are to respect that spirit, same-sex couples belong.

Naturally, conservatives are dragging out the rhetoric that has been hurled against every marriage change, as we've seen. Allowing same-sex marriage would be like allowing married women to own property, "virtually destroying the moral and social efficacy of the marriage institution." Or it would be like legalizing contraception, which "is not what the God of nature and grace, in His Divine wisdom, ordained marriage to be; but the lustful indulgence of man and woman. . . . Religion shudders at the wild orgy of atheism and immorality the situation forebodes." Or it would be like recognizing marriage between the races, a concept so "revolting, dis-

graceful, and almost bestial" that it would lead directly to "the father living with his daughter, the son with the mother, the brother
with his sister, in lawful wedlock"—and bring forth children who
would be "sickly, effeminate, and . . . inferior." Or it would be like
making wives the legal equals of their husbands, a proposal that
"criticizes the Bible . . . degrading the holy bonds of matrimony
into a mere civil contract . . . striking at the root of those divinely
ordained principles upon which is built the superstructure of society." Or it would be like allowing divorce, "tantamount to polygamy," thereby throwing "the whole community . . . into a general
prostitution," making us all "loathsome, abandoned wretches, and
the offspring of Sodom and Gomorrah."

Such warnings are usually based on the idea that changing a
given rule changes the very *definition* of marriage. And of course,
they're right: define marriage as a lifetime commitment, and divorce flouts its very definition. Define marriage as a vehicle for legitimate procreation, and contraception violates that definition.
Define marriage as a complete union of economic interests, and
allowing women to own property divides the family into warring and immoral bits. Define marriage as a bond between one
man and one woman, and same-sex marriage is absurd. But define
marriage as a commitment to live up to the rigorous demands of
love, to care for each other as best as you humanly can, then all
these possibilities—divorce, contraception, feminism, marriage
between two women or two men—are necessary to respect the human spirit.

That's the reason that same-sex marriage is being accepted or actively debated in every postindustrial country (including, at this
count, the Netherlands, Sweden, Norway, South Africa, Finland,
France, Luxembourg, Belgium, Germany, and Hungary, as well as
several American states). If you count the slower incursions of recognizing same-sex partners for specific purposes like immigra-
tion or child custody or alimony or pension benefits, then the list
includes Canada, Israel, Brazil, Argentina, Spain, England, Australia, Switzerland, Namibia, and Slovenia.) The law follows rather
than leads, trying to catch up with contemporary social realities.

Today's civil courts are *already* forced to adjudicate disputes about same-sex couples, over all the same questions that they adjudicate with different-sex pairs: custody and inheritance, pensions and divorce settlements.

Peculiarly, I sympathize with those anxious about what will happen when civil marriage opens to include Madeline and myself. Belief in love, belief in the integrity of the individual conscience, is profoundly unsettling. Putting same-sex couples into marriage law will endorse the changes in marriage that have been growing since 1800. It will insist yet again that each individual should—no, *must*—be free to choose his or her life course rather than following a path laid out by tradition. The fight over same-sex marriage is so rhetorically violent, so upsetting to so many, for the same reason as so many other debates in the past two hundred years have been: it insists that each of us matters, and that each of us must choose for ourselves how to live. Living in a pluralist nation is a fundamentalist's nightmare, a reminder that a democratic society keeps its institutional doors open wide. Same-sex marriage will inscribe personal sexual and emotional choice firmly into our laws and social codes—but remember, it's already here.

And yet same-sex marriage does make even more visible a difficult fact of contemporary life: that every commitment—to job, spouse, community, religion, and more—must be invented from the inside out, tested and confirmed as we go. Making lesbians and gay men more legally visible will neither solve nor complicate anyone else's daily commitments. And yet it *will* insist on something that is quite unnerving to acknowledge: that we must each pay rigorous attention to—and believe in—each individual spirit.

Notes

One: Money

Sections about dowry, dower, and marriage as a working partnership are
drawn chiefly from Anderson, *Sociology of the Family;* Ariès and Duby,
A History of Private Life, vols. 1–4; Burguière et al., *A History of the Fam-
ily,* vols. 1 and 2; Cott and Pleck, *A Heritage of Her Own;* Dickemann,
"Women, Class, and Dowry"; Dixon, *The Roman Family;* Epstein,
The Jewish Marriage Contract and *Marriage Laws in the Bible and the
Talmud;* Gies and Gies, *Marriage and the Family in the Middle Ages;*
Goode, *The Family;* Goody and Tambiah, *Bridewealth and Dowry;* Hana-
walt, *The Ties That Bound;* Hufton, *The Prospect Before Her;* Kaplan,
The Marriage Bargain; Lévi-Strauss, *The Elementary Structures of Kin-
ship* and *"The Family";* Mintz and Kellogg, *Domestic Revolutions;*
Molho, *Marriage Alliance in Late Medieval Florence;* Stone, *FSM.*

"marriage for love has traditionally been assumed": Hanawalt, 202.

"It did not matter that anyone of good society": Burguière and Lebrun,
in Burguière et al., vol. 2, 91.

"Many marriages have been": de La Roncière in Ariès and Duby, vol. 2,
162.

"marriages must be free": Molho, 302.

". . . that women should have secure dowries": Dixon, 66.

Charitable contributions to dowry funds discussed in Gies and Gies, 173.

Information about Florence's Monte delle Doti in Molho, 262.

Spanish legislative attempts to limit dowry in Hufton, 67.

Data about unmarried sons and daughters of various aristocracies during
periods of dowry inflation in Stone, *FSM,* 37–42, and Hufton, 67–68.

"hath since Easter": Quoted in Stone, *FSM*, 130.

"Marriages would in general be as happy": Johnson, quoted in Stone, *FSM*, 129.

"The arranged marriage works far less badly": Stone, *FSM*, 82.

"For the shoemaker, the cooper, the fishmonger": Gies and Gies, 149.

"The farmer's wife generally tended": Hufton, 156.

"Whatever sadness a man experienced": Hufton, 223.

"In English villages up to 80 per cent:": Hufton, 123.

"They get married out of financial interest": Quoted in Hufton, 127.

"One cannot take one's vineyard": Quoted in Burguière et al., vol. 2, 84.

"A son who inherited a third of a house": Ibid, 63.

"We are neighbors": Ibid, 84.

"Dresse the Victualls": Quoted by Carr and Walsh, in Cott and Pleck, 40–41.

"Medieval literature does not contain the same": Hanawalt, 10.

"As one judge put it": Grossberg, 130.

"A Roman would have found it": Veyne, in Ariès and Duby, vol. 1, 62.

"Slave marriage was not recognized": Gies and Gies, 22.

"Saturday night the roads": Gutman, 136–137.

"To guard against such a heart rending": Quoted in Burnham, 210.

"The relation between slaves": Quoted in Grossberg, 131.

"What surprises one": Quoted in Gutman, 361.

"a serf could not contract": Phillips, 26.

"unless the being on whom [life]": Mill, *On Liberty*, 108.

"rejects as preposterous Sarah's request": Glendon, 8–9.

"an almost total lack of change": Hufton, 9,13.

"the landed elite would marry": Stone, *RD*, 126, 127, 321.

"What is the peculiar character of the modern world": Mill, *On Liberty*, 134.

"Children are so much the goods": Quoted in Stone, *FSM*, 128.

"the limit of a parent's authority": Defoe, quoted in Stone, *FSM*, 185.

"There is always need of persons": Mill, *On Liberty*, 64.

Except where otherwise noted, information in this section about the financial position of married women in the nineteenth century and about the married women's property acts comes from Backhouse, "Married Women's Property Law in Nineteenth-Century Canada"; Basch, *In the Eyes of the Law*; Biemer, *Women and Property in Colonial New York*; Chused, "Late Nineteenth Century Married Women's Property Law" and "Married Women's Property Law: 1800–1850"; Grossberg, *Governing the Hearth*; L. Holcombe, *Wives and Property*; Lazarou, *Concealed Under Petticoats*; Stone, *FSM;* and Shammas, "Re-Assessing the Married Women's Property Acts."

Married women did not have the same economic status in every European country. Dutch, French, and Spanish laws adapted the Roman system that allowed her a separate legal personality—able to contract, sue, buy, sell, and inherit.

"still depended on mutual trust and personal associations": Basch, 39.

"In 1800 Richard Cadbury": Hall, in Ariès and Duby, vol. 3, 64–74.

The invention of the "servantless" kitchen noted in Mintz and Kellogg, 124.

Wealthy families' safeguards for their daughters' estates described in Chused, 1386.

"infidelity in the marriage bed": Quoted in Basch, 146.

Quotes from British members of Commons and *The Times* of London in L. Holcombe, 89, 153.

"Criminals, Idiots, Women, and Minors": Quoted in L. Holcombe, 144. This classification is very much like a current apples-and-oranges list: prostitutes, child molesters, adulterers, and homosexuals.

"Millicent Garrett Fawcett had her purse snatched": L. Holcombe, 3.

"the complexity and fragility of marriage as a social institution": Basch, 154.

"contrary not only to the law": Quoted in L. Holcombe, 93.

"set at defiance the experience of every country": Quoted in L. Holcombe, 93.

"It may startle a good many lawyers": Quoted in Backhouse, 237, 241.

"of doubtful propriety": Quoted in Lazarou, 37–38.

"require women to leave the work force": D. Popenoe, 536, 554.

"the intrusion of work": Blumstein and Schwartz, 154.

"courting couples may discuss": Ibid., 51.

"It is unacceptable": Letter to the editor, *New York Times Magazine*, April 27, 1997.

"the right to marry": French high court decision quoted in Glendon, 78.

"Labour must be performed": Max Weber, *The Protestant Ethic and the Spirit of Capitalism*, trans. Talcott Parsons (Routledge, 1992), 62.

"The spouses are mutually obliged": German civil code quoted in Glendon, 114–115.

U.S. Bureau of the Census, 1990 Vital Statistics, Table no. 54: "Unmarried Couples, 1970 to 1988"; U.S. Bureau of the Census, 1997 Vital Statistics, Table no. 66: "Households, Families, Subfamilies, Married Couples, and Unrelated Individuals."

"People are actually producing goods and services": Goode, 10.

Couples' money management styles discussed in Blumstein and Schwartz, 53.

"the moral implications of a long-shared life": Chambers, 485.

The statistical information and conclusions about marriage and health are drawn primarily from Waldron, Hughes, and Brooks, "Marriage Protection"; Waldron, Weiss, and Hughes, "Marital Status Effects on Health"; Trovato and Lauris, "Marital Status and Mortality in Canada"; Wyke and Ford, "Competing Explanations for Associations Between Marital Status and Health"; Rogers, "Marriage, Sex, and Mortality"; Hahn, "Marital Status and Women's Health"; Joung et al., "Differences in Self-Reported Morbidity by Marital Status"; Rodrigue and Park, "General and Illness-Specific Adjustment to Cancer"; Burman and Margolin, "Analysis of the Association Between Marital Relationships and Health."

"Marriage is a healthy state": Quoted in Ebrahim et al., 834.

Two: Sex

Except where otherwise noted, information on Rome in this section and throughout the book comes from Brown, *The Body and Society*; Dixon, *The Roman Family*; Rousselle, "Fathers as Citizens of Rome, Rome as a City of Fathers"; Thomas, "The Family Under the Roman Empire"; articles and personal communications from Treggiari, including "Women as Property in the Early Roman Empire"; and Veyne, "The Roman Empire," in Ariès and Duby, *A History of the Family*, vol. 1.

"Unchastity in a freeborn person": Treggiari, "Women as Property in the Early Roman Empire," 20–21.

"he invited scorn in metaphorically abdicating": Boswell, *CSTH*, 75. Or as Andrew Wallace-Hadrill writes in his review-essay "Love Among the

Romans," *TLS*, June 12, 1998, 3–4, "one cannot get very far in Roman culture without recalling the violence that underpins it."

Here and throughout this chapter, unless otherwise noted, information about Jewish laws and attitudes toward sexuality comes from Alvarez-Pereyre and Heymann, "The Desire for Transcendence: The Hebrew Family Model and Jewish Family Practices," in Ariès and Duby, eds., *A History of the Family*, vol. 1; Boyarin, *Carnal Israel*; Brown, *The Body and Society*, and "Person and Group in Judaism and Early Christianity," in Ariès and Duby, eds., *A History of Private Life*, vol. 1; Epstein, *The Jewish Marriage Contract*, and *Sex Laws and Customs in Judaism*; Feldman, *Marital Relations, Birth Control, and Abortion in Jewish Law*; Katz, *Tradition and Crisis*; Pagels, *Adam, Eve, and the Serpent*; and Wegner, *Chattel or Person?*

Throughout this chapter, material about the early Christians is drawn primarily from Brown, *The Body and Society*; Pagels, *Adam, Eve, and the Serpent*; and Noonan, *Contraception*.

"By refusing to act upon the youthful stirrings": Brown, 32.

"Even today, an adolescent who takes time": Pagels, 80.

"This man . . . denigrates marriage": Brown, 5.

"the mists of slimy lust of the flesh": Augustine, in Clark, ed., 12–15.

Except where otherwise noted, here and throughout this book information about medieval sexual and family life comes from Ariès and Duby, *A History of Private Life*, vols. 1–4; Burguière et al., *A History of the Family*, vols. 1 and 2; Gies and Gies, *Marriage and the Family in the Middle Ages*; Goody, *The Development of the Family and Marriage in Europe*; Hanawalt, *The Ties That Bound*; Herlihy and Klapisch-Zuber, *Tuscans and Their Families*; Hufton, *The Prospect Before Her*; Ingram, *Church Courts, Sex, and Marriage in England, 1570–1640*; Laslett, *The World We Have Lost*; Laslett, Oosterveen, and Smith, eds., *Bastardy and Its Comparative History*; Rotberg and Rabb, eds., *Marriage and Fertility*.

"I do not see what other help woman": Quoted in Noonan, 129.

The Catholic Church's licensing of prostitution: Private communication from Rita Nakashima Brock, Bunting Institute Director, October 2, 1998.

Church fee schedule for priests' concubines and bastards: Ozment, *Reformation in the Cities*, 20.

"I dare to say that either the wife": Augustine's comments and other informa-

tion and quotes about early Church attitudes toward contraception come from Noonan, 119–139 and throughout.

Unless otherwise noted, information about the history of contraception in this section comes from Bennett, *Anthony Comstock*; Brodie, *Contraception and Abortion in Nineteenth-Century America*; Broun and Leech, *Anthony Comstock, Roundsman of the Lord*; Chesler, *Woman of Valor*; Dienes, *Law, Politics, and Birth Control*; Fryer, *The Birth Controllers*; Gordon, *Woman's Body, Woman's Right*; McCann, *Birth Control Politics in the United States, 1916–1945*; McLaren, *Birth Control in Nineteenth-Century England*; Noonan, *Contraception*; Owen, *Moral Physiology*; Roraback, "Griswold v. Connecticut: A Brief Case History"; and Stopes, *Married Love*.

"It is better for a wife to permit herself": Quoted in Noonan, 261.

"Of 1000 marriages, I believe": Theologians' quotes in this paragraph from Noonan, 225–227.

Except where otherwise noted, information here and throughout the book about marriage and family life during the Reformation comes from Burguière et al., *A History of the Family*, vol. 2; Hillerbrand, *The Oxford Encyclopedia of the Reformation*; Mintz and Kellogg, *Domestic Revolutions*; Ozment, *The Reformation in the Cities* and *When Fathers Ruled*; and Stone, *Family, Sex and Marriage in England, 1500–1800*.

"Thus am I entangled": Ozment, *Fathers*, 6.

"What more natural than when a set of greedy priests": Goody, 146.

"Pope Gregory wanted celibacy established": Pelikan, 239–240.

The ludicrous charges against gays are made by the American Family Association in *Homosexuality in America: Exposing the Myths*, 14. The first "statistics" are listed without citing the responsible researcher, study, or publication, if any; the lesbian death statistics come from a methodologically hilarious "study" by Paul Cameron, whose statistical manipulations have been repudiated repeatedly by professional associations, including the American Psychological Association and the American Sociological Association.

"how the man and the woman should be taught": Pelikan, vol. 4, 222.

Description of and statistics about European life from 1500 to 1800 from Hufton, 11–12.

"for men of independent means": Noonan, 52.

"even if [women] bear themselves weary": Ozment, *Fathers*, 100.

I write "some Jews" because, since Jewish theology and commentary was and is a constantly evolving discussion that includes dissent in its canon, it's impossible to issue a blanket statement about sexual attitudes that holds from 2500 C.E. to now.

The ascetic rabbi here is Eliezer, whom, according to Boyarin, held an extreme position that was explicitly rejected by other rabbis. The more welcoming interpretation of sex grows from the biblical phrase that "they become one flesh. Rav Yosef cited a tannaitic tradition, Flesh: This means the intimacy of the flesh, namely that he should not behave with her in the manner of the Persians, who make love while dressed." Boyarin, 48.

"To rejoice his wife": Quoted in Feldman, 72.

"Had he believed that one God created the world": Quoted in Feldman, 99.

"One might say: inasmuch as jealousy": Quoted in Feldman, 82.

For a more thorough examination of diary-keeping and the growth and encouragement of the inner life, see especially Ariès and Duby, *A History of Private Life*, vols. 3 and 4.

Unless otherwise cited, information about the free-love movement in the United States comes from D'Emilio and Freedman, *Intimate Matters*; Forster, *Sex Radicalism*; Nichols and Nichols, *Marriage: Its History, Character, and Results*; Sears, *The Sex Radicals*; and Stoehr, *Free Love in America*.

"Marital rape" was considered an oxymoron until a feminist campaign during the 1960s and 1970s changed most state laws to allow a wife to withhold her consent; until then, the marriage contract was a license to have sex.

"She is his slave, his victim, his tool": In Stoehr, 267.

"I presume it would be impossible to find": In Stoehr, 287.

"The complete act of union": Stopes, 75–76.

Drop in eighteenth- and nineteenth-century French birth rate reported in Noonan, 388.

American childbearing statistics from Gordon, 48.

"so foule and so hidous that [it] scholde not be nampned": Noonan, 268.

"so notorious in reputation that the inventor": Chesler, 36.

"It seems as though we were living": Quoted in Broun and Leech, 28.

"rubber articles for masturbation": Dienes, 37.

"challenges the permanence of the State": Dublin, 191–192.

"a criminal against the race": Theodore Roosevelt's anti-contraception quotes in Fryer, 199.

"This pernicious sensualism": Noonan, 440.

"Are we to have homes or brothels?": Dienes, 47.

Information about Margaret Sanger comes primarily from Chesler, *Woman of Valor.*

"Sexual congress is thus rendered but a species of self-abuse": Fryer, 120.

"spattering the country with its slime": Chesler, 255.

"The downright perversion of human cooperation": Chesler, 212.

Seventy-five percent of Americans believe health insurance should under-write contraception: Figure from Planned Parenthood advertorial, July 1, 1998, *New York Times,* A27.

"accepted by many as a legitimate exercise": Roraback, 396.

"the wife lying on her back": Explicitly Christian marriage counseling books quoted in Ehrenreich et al., 147.

"the acts of a husband and wife": Finnis, 1068. Homosexuality, heterosexual oral sex, and contraception are morally equivalent: In the original, the addendum about contraception is in a footnote. The author makes clear, however, that he sees contraception as the moral equivalent of homosexuality because it prevents the "real goods" of marriage, but is "omit[ted] from the list in the text only because it would no doubt not now be accepted by secular law as preventing consummation—a fail-ure of understanding."

"men using one another as women": Podhoretz, 41.

"Once a man assumes the role of homosexual": Chauncey, 351.

"fears we now felt of widespread militant": Bryant, 15, 26.

"a carefully disguised attempt to break down": D'Emilio and Freedman, 42.

"Vaginal intercourse is the only kind": Family Research Council, "Domestic Partnerships."

"Homosexuality is not what God intends": American Family Association, *Homosexuality in America.*

Three: Babies

"a civil contract whereby a man": Burguière et al., vol. 2, 108.

"The intent of matrimony is not": Stone, *FSM,* 69.

"Marriage is an institution created": Wilson, 36.

See Goode's discussion of the idea that society never deals with individuals but with families, chapter 1, especially pages 3–4.

"The Romans rarely used it to mean family": Dixon, 2.

The Roman patriarch's legal authority to kill his family members was used mostly for newborns; there were social limits on his right to kill his family's adults, although the symbolic threat could be usefully wielded. Dixon, 36, and Treggiari, personal communication.

"in some ways resembled kinship": Dixon, 114.

"clearly wanted to treat [Patronia] as a daughter": Dixon, 113.

"A citizen of Rome did not 'have' a child": Veyne, "The Roman Empire," in Ariès and Duby, vol. 1, 9.

For fuller discussions of the frustrating plasticity of "the family" (and therefore the impossibility of defining it and studying it as a single phenomenon), see, for instance, Dixon, chap. 1; Gies and Gies, introduction; Burguière and Lebrun, "The One Hundred and One Families of Europe," in Burguière et al., vol. 2, 1–39; Cherlin, 85–87; Stone, *FSM*, 37–66; Laslett, Oosterveen, and Smith, introduction; and de La Roncière, "Tuscan Notables on the Eve of the Renaissance," in Ariès and Duby, vol. 2, 157–170.

"Before the 18th century no European language": Gies and Gies, 4.

"Most households included non-kin": Stone, *FSM*, 28. For illuminating glimpses of demographic and family historians straining to determine which "servants"were or were not biological children, see, for instance, Laslett, Oosterveen, and Smith, and Rotberg and Rabb.

"The want of affection": Hanawalt, 157.

Tuscan wetnursing statistics given in de La Roncière, in Ariès and Duby, vol. 2, 220.

The Catholic Church commissioned "pictures of the Madonna suckling the Child, a representation that must have stood as a perpetual reproach to those mothers, not only from the richer households, who had their children breast-fed by others, a practice that the Church had tried to stop as far back as the eighth century . . . .": Goody, 154.

"Less than half of the children": Stone, *FSM*, 50.

Seventeenth-century French stepchildren: Burguière and Lebrun, in Burguière et al., vol. 2, 59.

British premodern children in stepfamilies: Stone, *FSM*, 46–50.

U.S. Bureau of the Census, 1992, "Marriage, Divorce, and Remarriage in the 1990s," quoted in D. Popenoe, 127.

Fourteenth-century and contemporary British family homicide rates: Hanawalt, 208, and Stone, *FSM*, 77.

Limited demographic history for the nuclear family: Howard V. Hayghe, Division of Labor Force Statistics, "Family members in the work force," *Monthly Labor Review*, March 1990, 14–19. Presumably demographers' change to using the nuclear family as a census standard came as sprawling rural families became fewer, and as fewer urban families kept servants or boarders.

"The irony remains, however": Gaunt and Nyström, in Burguière et al., vol. 2, 486–487.

Much of the bastardy discussion is based on Laslett et al., *Bastardy*.

"Consider of what importance to society": Johnson, quoted in Laslett et al., *Bastardy*, 214.

"is plainly a great discouragement": Blackstone, quoted in Laslett, Grossberg, 198.

"because he was born before the marriage": Hanawalt, 72.

Statistics on pregnant English brides from Laslett, in Laslett et al., *Bastardy*, 23.

Figures for postcolonial American pregnancies before marriage from Wells, in Laslett et al., *Bastardy*, 353.

Scandinavian "out of wedlock" birthrates from Laslett et al., *Bastardy*, 56, 329, 330; and Gaunt and Nyström, "The Scandinavian Model," in Burguière et al., vol. 2, 488.

"If two parties, living together": (italics in original) Laslett et al., 11.

In the *Michael H v. Gerald D* case, "the state invoked the existence of a marriage to actually *sever* the link between procreation and child-rearing." Brief filed by Robinson, Murray, and Bonauto, for the Supreme Court of the State of Vermont, *Baker v. Vermont*, Spring 1998, 28 and 32.

Information about various child custody expectations comes from the sources previously given for each historical period. More particularly, information about child abandonment and adoption comes from Boswell, *The Kindness of Strangers*. The historical break from father-right to mother-custody comes from Mason, *From Father's Property to Children's Rights*, and Grossberg's explanation of the "best interests of the child" doctrine in *Governing the Hearth*, esp. chap. 7. Information about the invention of modern adoption in the United States comes from Zainaldin and from Presser.

"Be sure then to establish the authority": John Locke, "Some Thoughts Concerning Education."

"An orphan in colonial America": Mason, 18.

Mothers worthy of heaven: American black, immigrant, and working-class mothers may have been extolled by their own families and groups, but they were generally accused of vice and ignorance and blamed for their families' poverty. American black women especially were left out of the idealization of "women" and "mothers"—a contradiction Sojourner Truth's "Ain't I A Woman?" speech exploited so powerfully.

"Well may we exclaim THE MOTHER!": Quoted in Coontz, *Social Origins*, 230.

"notwithstanding the father's natural right": Mason, 14.

"denial of the father's right": Grossberg, 241.

"We are informed by the first elementary books": Einhorn, 132.

"nothing less than an assumption of power": Quoted in Einhorn, 126.

"weaken the ties of marriage": Quoted in Grossberg, 245.

"If women had the guardianship": Quoted in Grossberg, 247.

"The love of the mother for her child": Quoted in Grossberg, 253.

"A Plymouth court severely rebuked": Mason, *From Father's Property*, 39, 18.

"surrendered his rights over the child": Zainaldin, 1081–1083.

Critic of Massachusetts' "irrevocable" adoptions: Presser, 457–461.

The breakthrough concept of "psychological parenthood," widely cited in custody decisions and law journals ever since, was delineated by three child custody experts, Goldstein, Freud, and Solnit, in 1979.

"the family, long supposed to be the best anchored": Ernest Groves, *Marriage* (New York: Henry Holt, 1933), 3.

"distinctly antisocial, for it enables": Dublin, 186–194.

"A little child is a strongly uniting bond": F. B. Meyer, *Love, Courtship, and Marriage* (London: S. W. Partridge and Co., 1899).

"From their offspring the parents": P. Popenoe, 161.

"Which way happiness?": Merle Bombardieri, *The Baby Decision: How to Make the Most Important Choice of Your Life* (New York: Rawson, Wade Publishers, 1981), 117.

"The essence of adultery": Judicial decisions equating donor insemination with adultery (*Orford v. Orford* and *Doornbus v. Doornbus*) are discussed in Katherine Arnup, "Finding Fathers: Artificial Insemination, Lesbians, and the Law," *Canadian Journal of Women and the Law* 7 (1994): 97–115.

Catholic theologians who wanted to outlaw DI: Juliette Zipper, "What Else Is New? Reproductive Technologies and Custody Politics," in *Child Custody and the Politics of Gender*, ed. Carol Smart and Selma Sevenjuijsen (New York: Routledge, 1989).

"One who consents to the production of a child": People v. Sorenson, 68 C.2d 280; 66 Cal.Rptr. 7, 437 P.2d 495.

DI now accounts for eight to ten times more births than all other types of reproductive technology combined. Wallach and Zacur, *Reproductive Medicine and Surgery* 782 (1995), cited p. 33, Appellants' Reply Brief, Baker v. Vermont, May 1998.

The "divorce effect": Cherlin, 87–88. "As might be expected, the children whose parents divorced showed more behavior problems and scored lower on reading and mathematics tests than did the children whose parents stayed together. But when we looked backward through the records to the start of the study—before anyone's parents had separated or divorced—we found that the children whose parents would later divorce *already* were showing more problems and doing worse in reading and mathematics."

This book cannot give a thorough account of the effects on kids of divorce versus death. For an investigation of single parenthood, see McLanahan and Sandefur.

"while an absent father might": P. Cohen, *New York Times*, July 19, 1998, A13–15.

Much of the material on children and fathers in this chapter comes from Lamb, *The Role of the Father in Child Development*, and Stevenson and Black, "Paternal Absence."

Study controlling for mother's age and the family's poverty reported by Lewis, in Lamb, ed., 137: "When [the mother's] age and the family's poverty are controlled for there appear to be no unique contributions to the child's development made by the father's presence or absence."

The question of how to measure masculinity and femininity, traits whose manifestations vary from one culture to the next, is complex. Psychological researchers have not yet come up with a scale upon which they all agree. Some scales measure such things as whether you rate yourself independent, forceful, ambitious and aggressive . . . or affectionate, compassionate, warm, and gentle. But people who rate, on such scales, as more "masculine" are also rated as better adjusted; perhaps these scales are simply measuring the things that our culture values, rather than some "masculine" or "feminine" essence. Other scales try to measure things that happen to cluster among males or females— whether you prefer to take a shower or a bath, for instance—as if those measured something essential, not simply current cultural expectations. (A sixteenth-century lady of the chamber who liked to wear stockings, for instance, would have been considered masculine.) For more discussion about measuring masculinity and femininity, see Golombok and Fivush, *Gender Development*, 1994.

On influence of fathers on boys' behavior and "masculinity" ratings, see Stevenson and Black, and Lamb, throughout.

Fathers encourage sons to *"play with sex-typed toys"*: See Lewis, in Lamb, ed., 126.

"tended to provide staccato bursts": Lamb, in Lamb, ed., 111-112.

Pregnancy risk for girls in father-custody reported in Warshak, 133.

"In sum, very little about the gender": Lamb, in Lamb, ed., 10, 13.

"If there are differences": Lewis, in Lamb, ed., 141-142.

Right-wing critiques of studies of children of divorced lesbians and gay men regularly charge that researchers refuse to compare lesbians' and gay men's children with children of "normal, intact" families. They have misunderstood—perhaps intentionally—the fact that researchers used divorced families because they were, in psychology-speak, "controlling for other variables."

All studies of children of lesbians and gay men through 1991 are cited and summarized in Charlotte J. Patterson, "Children of Lesbian and Gay Parents," *Child Development* 63 (1992): 1025-1042.

The longitudinal study on children of divorced lesbian mothers is summarized in the introduction of Tasker and Golombok, *Growing Up in a Lesbian Family*.

Do the children of gay parents grow up to be gay? See Patterson, and Tasker and Golombok, 107.

What percentage of the population is "gay"? Although defining and measuring who is "gay" is exceptionally difficult, the conservative estimate of 2 or 3 percent, not the "one in ten" figure, strikes me as easier to believe. This is not, however, important in any way for political debate: the size of a minority must not determine how its members should be treated. American Jews, for instance, make up only 1 or 2 percent of the U.S. population.

The newer and more methodologically sound studies of children of lesbians and gay men include A. Brewaey et al., "Donor Insemination"; Golombok, Tasker, and Murray, "Children Raised in Fatherless Families from Infancy"; and Chan, Raboy, and Patterson, "Psychosocial Adjustment Among Children Conceived via Donor Insemination." Tasker and Golombok summarize the research in *Growing Up in a Lesbian Family*.

The latest research is more meticulous: To ensure that its sample was truly random and representative, for instance, one European study included *all* the lesbian couples who used a particular Brussels fertility center within a four-year period, matched to heterosexual couples who used the same center, as well as to non-DI couples with similar characteristics. Others use such standard psychological research techniques as including researchers', parents', and teachers' observations of the child, and having interview results scrutinized by outside experts who are "blind" to the children's families.

"Secure attachments": Explaining attachment theory—the theory of infant and early childhood psychological development upon which most psychological researchers currently rely—is beyond the scope of this chapter. Much of the work in child development over the past fifty years has suggested that strong and secure attachment to at least one adult by the time an infant is six months old is an excellent predictor of healthy psychological development, while insecure or weak attachment prognosticates poorly.

On the variations in studies on children of lesbian moms, see Patterson, 256–257.

Studies of DI children show less pathology: See Kovacs et al.

That children's feelings for biomoms were stronger than for second parent, whether a mom or dad, reported in Brewaeys et al.

Writings that assert that "homosexuals" are a danger to children almost all rely on spurious work by Paul Cameron, who has been expelled from the American Psychological Association for misrepresentations and ethical violations; denounced by the American Sociological Association because he "has consistently misinterpreted and misrepresented sociological research"; chastised by scientists for "distorting their findings in order to promote his anti-gay agenda"; and questioned by judges for fraudulence. He is either self-published or published in obscure journals (ones that rarely reject submitted articles) or vanity journals (to which contributing authors must pay a fee). Since his work uses distorted or sloppy methods to produce invalid "statistics," it is consistently rejected by juried publications for its serious method- ological flaws, such as surveying gay men who attended a VD clinic and using that skewed sample to make generalizations about "homo- sexual" sex practices. He is never cited by legitimate psychologists or sociologists except, occasionally, to dispute his conclusions or object to his misuse of others' work. For more information about Cameron, see Mark E. Pietrzyk, "Queer Science: Paul Cameron, Professional Sham," *The New Republic,* October 3, 1994; Gregory M. Herek, "Myths about Sexual Orientation: A Lawyer's Guide to Social Science Research," *Law & Sexuality* 1 (1991): 133, fn.116, or http://psychology.ucdavis.edu/ rainbow/html/facts_cameron.html.

1998 study of sexually abused boys: "One in Eight Boys of High-School Age Has Been Abused, Survey Shows," A11, *New York Times,* June 26, 1998, reporting on a 1998 study conducted by Louis Harris and Associ- ates done for The Commonwealth Fund.

Denver Children's Hospital study: See Jenny et al.

Is all male/boy sexual abuse committed by men who *are* "homosexuals," even if that's not how those men otherwise identify or behave? Many people interpret it this way. The problem here is with the dual mean- ing of "homosexual"; it's both a coldly clinical adjective for all same- sex sexual contact and a descriptive noun for a personal identity that holds a universe of attractions and emotions—which is why so many of us recoil from the word "homosexual" and prefer "lesbian" or "gay" as wide enough for our hearts and minds and lives.

Study of 175 Massachusetts men imprisoned for child sexual assault: See Groth and Birnbaum.

Roughly 20 percent of adult women report having been sexually abused as children: See Finkelhor.

Vets' feelings for their "warbabies" and later children discussed in Griswold, 177–184. One returning World War II vet said about his second child, "When she got out of her crib to look around and become a member of the family, I was there and she adjusted to me and I adjusted to her." Another veteran told a psychologist, "Alma [the firstborn] and I had a hard time. Now I can see it . . . it was so different with Pauline [second child]. I saw her from the beginning. If you want to put it in a nutshell, you could say it like this. I was never home with Alma when she was lit- tle and helpless."

How we know who is "ours": J. Goldstein et al. set the standard that has been cited in custody and policy questions ever since: "For the child, the physical realities of his conception and birth are not the direct cause of his emotional attachment. . . . Whether any adult becomes the psychological parent of a child is thus based on day-to-day interaction, companionship, and shared experiences" (17, 19).

"We know for certain that men can be competent": Kyle Pruett, quoted in Warshak, 38.

"Under the magic of family responsibility": P. Popenoe, 175–176.

"Young men say that they gave up certain deviant": D. Popenoe, 75.

Adult children of divorced lesbian moms spoke more proudly of their families: See Tasker and Golombok, 65.

"The offspring of these unnatural": Washington, 86.

"for Christmas I don't really want": In re Pearlman, 15 Fam. Law Rep. 1356.

"When one reflects on the seemingly limitless parade": In re K. [1995] 23 OR (3d) 679 Ontario Court (Provincial Division).

Pepper Schwartz's testimony that letting same-sex couples marry would be better for the kids quoted in Hawaii Judge Kevin Chang's opinion, issued December 3, 1996, Circuit Court of the First Circuit, State of Hawaii, Civil Case No. 91–1394.

Four: Kin

"since he could not have the eldest daughter": Burguière and Lebrun, in Burguière et al., vol. 2, 139.

White supremacists' use of biblical verse: "Terrorists in the Name of God and Race: Phineas Priests use religious arguments to justify their violent crimes," *Klanwatch Intelligence Report*, August 1996, no. 83, 1–5, Southern Poverty Law Center.

Enslaved Africans and indentured Irish held in equal contempt: See Johnston, 184.

Except where otherwise noted, the account of interracial marriage laws is drawn from Fowler, *Northern Attitudes Towards Interracial Marriage*; Grossberg, *Governing the Hearth*, 126–140; Johnston, *Race Relations*; Pascoe, "Miscegenation Law"; Roberts, "Black-White Intermarriage in the United States," in Johnson and Warren, eds., *Inside the Mixed Marriage*; Sickels, *Race, Marriage and the Law*; J. D. Smith, ed., *Racial Determinism*; and Wallenstein, "Race, Marriage, and the Law of Freedom."

"has English blood in him, and therefore was born free": Quoted in Johnston, 167.

"The account he has given of himself": Roberts, in Johnson and Warren, 27.

"*If we would allow the negroes any kind of equality*": Quoted in Fowler, 159.

"*if the statute against mulattoes is*": Quoted in Wallenstein, 373.

"*persons who marry take each other*": Quoted in Grossberg, 128–129.

"*What was at first a law for the servant class*": Friedman, 192.

"*under certain conditions, Negro virus*": Lindley Spring, quoted in Smith, 16.

New Orleans cashier who transfused himself: See Johnson and Warren, 29.

"*the marriage matter*": Gunnar Myrdal, *An American Dilemma: The Negro Problem and Modern Democracy* (New York, Harper & Brothers Publishers, 1944), 60–61.

"*to prohibit such intermarriage would be*": Du Bois, quoted in Washington, 83.

"*There it is for anyone to see*": Herman Eugene Talmadge, *You and Segregation* (Birmingham, AL: Vulcan Press, 1955), 33.

"*One can usually take for granted*": Goode, 50.

The most notorious expression of community opposition to black/white pairings, of course, is the Southern lynching. But Northern riots in response to imagined or suspected black/white pairings took place in New Haven in 1831; New York in July 1834; Columbia, PA, in 1834; and other cities, as reported in Fowler.

"*to hold a superior race*": Lindley Spring, in Smith, 291.

"*intermixture of the two races*": Lindley Spring, in Smith, 272.

"*to permit persons of the same sex to marry is to declare*": Richard Posner, quoted in Duncan, 599.

"*the newfound concept of 'social justice'*": Florida Supreme Court decision in *McLaughlin v. Florida*, 1964, reported in Sickels, 101.

"*If the Federal Government can determine*": Quoted in Sickels, 79.

"*distinctly woolly*": William Benjamin Smith, in Smith, 100–102.

"*segregation . . . is and always has been*": Tennessee and Florida decisions quoted in Sickels, 49–50.

"*we might have in Tennessee the father living with his daughter*": Quoted in Sickels, 48.

"*hybrids are never healthy or vigorous*": William Benjamin Smith, in Smith, 105.

"*the offspring of these unnatural*": Washington, 86.

More than 95 percent of Americans marry heterosexually: Cherlin, 67.

Statistics on marriage from Ozment, *When Fathers Ruled*, 1; Wells, in Cott and Pleck, 90, 91; and Stone, *FSM*, 40–41.

Father can use, sell, or give daughter away: See Wegner's chapter, "The Minor Daughter."

"all the marriageable girls they could possible know": Flandrin, Jean Louis, *Families in Former Times* (New York: Cambridge University Press, 1979), 24.

Church incest rules changed the West: "The early medieval system of exchange is one of the most complex that has ever existed . . . it does force the groups . . . to extend and loosen their network of alliances. The sociopolitical game becomes more open. This system in effect marks a transition between that of archaic societies, in which each man's mate is more or less designated in advance, and that of modern society, in which the range of choice open to both man and woman is very wide." Barthélemy, in Ariès and Duby, vol. 2, 119.

"is an unclean thing": A Treatise on the Unlawfulness of Marrying a Brother's Wife (Hartford: Peter B. Gleason and Co., 1813).

"prohibitions of natural law": Quoted in Grossberg, 111–113.

"were most amazingly interwed": Gutman, 89.

"if each small biological unit": Lévi-Strauss, introduction to Burguière, vol. 1. See also his *Elementary Structures of Kinship* and "The Family."

One well-known Carolingian lord: Gies and Gies, 53.

"can be considered as no less than a social revolution": Goody, 76.

Except where otherwise noted, the account of Joseph Smith and the Mormons in this section is taken from Foster, *Religion and Sexuality*, chapters 4 and 5.

"restore the ancient gospel spirit": Foster, 123–124.

"polygamy would allow men to reassert": Foster, 176.

"let the wives and the children": Muncy, 132.

"at the deepest level, [polygamy] was a fundamental protest": Foster, 139.

"pleased to see [her husband] when he came in": Foster, 212.

"If a woman's husband has four wives": Foster, 214.

"was related by blood or marriage": Foster, 151.

"incompatible with civilization, refinement, and domestic felicity": Grossberg, 121.

"women shall be wives in common": Book V, *Plato's Republic*, trans. G. M. A. Grube (Indianapolis: Hackett Publishing Co., 1974), 119 and 125.

"Jesus commanded his followers to forget": Pagels, 15.

"hate his own father and mother": Luke 14:26, quoted in Pagels, 15.

"anxiety for those he loves": Quoted in Pagels, 83.

"a sermon for bachelors": Mount, 28.

Discussion of nineteenth-century utopians draws from Foster, *Religion and Sexuality*; W. Goldman, *Women, the State, and Revolution;* Holloway, *Heavens on Earth;* Mandelker, *Religion, Society, and Utopia;* Muncy, *Sex and Marriage;* and Weisbrod, *The Boundaries of Utopia.*

Noyes preached *"communism in love"*: Noyes' quotes from Foster, 81 and 83.

"Free love with us": Foster, 72.

"Between 1848 and 1869, . . . at most 31 births": Foster, 95.

"in abolishing civil and juridicial marriage": Bakunin, quoted in Khoren Arisian, *The New Wedding: Creating Your Own Marriage Ceremony* (New York: Vintage, 1973), 96.

"she does not let out her body": Friedrich Engels, "The Origin of the Family, Private Property, and the State," 1884.

"based solely on mutual affection": Ibid.

"They screamed at us": Quoted in W. Goldman, 191.

"Then who will decide what is marriage?": W. Goldman, 234.

Information and data about the kibbutzim are from Ben-Rafael, *Crisis and Transformation: The Kibbutz at Century's End.*

"the human condition in its continuity": Oz, 129–130.

"after some years of quiet householding": Quoted in Muncy, 11–12.

"the desire to marry in the lesbian and gay community": Polikoff, "We Will Get What We Ask For," 1536.

"monogamous airlock": Edmund White, "What Century Is This Anyway?" *The Advocate,* June 23, 1998.

"I advocate complete freedom": Woodhull, in Stoehr, 364.

Five: Order

In one 1998 custody battle that went to the North Carolina Supreme Court, a woman who left her two sons in the care of their father went back to court because their father had discovered he was gay and settled into a regular and happy monogamous relationship. She won because, the court wrote, the father—who was working two jobs, one at a GE plant and one at Home Depot, to provide for his sons—was engaging in illegal "activities such as the regular commission of sexual acts in the home by unmarried people."

Marriage as a publicly policed institution and marriage as an inner experience: I am indebted to Jay Harris for his discussion and emphasis of this distinction.

"regard each other as man and wife and behave accordingly": Reynolds, 21.

On Church debates over marriage see Pagels, *Adam, Eve, and the Serpent;* Reynolds, *Marriage in the Western Church;* Goody, *The Development of the Family;* Gies, *Marriage and the Family in the Middle Ages;* Burguière, vol. 1, esp. 397–465; and Noonan, *Contraception.*

"It is clear that this attempt to impose order": Toubert, in Burguière, vol. 1, 398.

"broken the back of aristocratic resistance": Fossier, in Burguière, vol. 1, 415.

The stories of the fifteenth-century family the Pastons are from Gies and Gies, 255–267.

"under an ash tree, in a bed, in a garden": Helmholz, 29.

The *verba*'s murkiness: The particular marriage litigation cases referred to in this paragraph are discussed in Helmholz and in Stone, *RD.*

"of 101 unions mentioned in the register": Goody, 149.

Up to one-third to one-half of European adults in the sixteenth century officially unmarried: See Ozment, *When Fathers Ruled,* 41–42.

"The real hurdle for the courts": Helmholz, quoted in Goody, *The Development of the Family,* 150.

"when two young people secretly": Ozment, *When Fathers Ruled,* 28.

Nation-states enthusiastically took up marriage regulation: Mount, 32, and Glendon, *The Transformation of Family Law,* 32–33.

"one of the principal means that the state": Nancy Cott, talk given at Radcliffe College's Schlesinger Library, May 8, 1997, manuscript on file with the author.

"England was full of people like Robert Davies": Stone, *RD,* 105.

"The judges were exasperated": Stone, *RD,* 120.

"aroused strong passions": Stone, *RD,* 127.

Things were a little less simple on the other side of the Atlantic: Historians' quotes and information about American marriage are drawn from Grossberg, 67–79.

"Married, she becomes his property": Nichols, *Marriage*, 75.

"what the law calls fornication": Nichols, *Marriage*, 114.

"Who will dare say that love": Woodhull, in Stoehr, 354.

"the idea of a basic individual right": Glendon, *Transformation*, 76.

shared health insurance benefits: This demand could be taken care of if the United States would join the civilized world and decouple health benefits from marriage through single-payer healthcare—a subject beyond the scope of this book.

In 1998, France began debating a legal status called *pactes de civil solidarité (PACS)*.

"at quarter to one": Laslett, quoting Ariès, *Bastardy*, 14. The Gies quote James Brundage similarly: "Thus the emergence in the late twentieth century of informal conjugal living arrangements as a prelude or substitute for marriage may be seen historically as a long-delayed response to a problem created by the Reformation and Counter-Reformation" (300–301).

"The real hurdle for the courts": Helmholz, quoted in Goody, 150.

"Deregulation in the name of freedom": Glendon, *Transformation*, 145.

"There are more problems in the world than solutions": Oz, 130.

"Every marriage is based upon some understanding": Rose, 7.

Ballad of the Tyrannical Husband: In Ozment, *When Fathers Ruled*, 52.

"A woman of 1200, even if she was unmarried": Fossier, in Burguière, 426.

"During most of Western history only a minority": Boswell, *Kindness*, 27.

"it is the part of a ruler to be loved, not to love": Quoted in Susan Moller Okin, *Women in Western Political Thought* (Princeton, NJ: Princeton University Press, 1979), 87–89.

"to order the things of private Concernment": This debate is referenced and quoted in Carole Pateman, *The Sexual Contract* (Stanford, CA: Stanford University Press, 1988), 23, 52–53.

"Passive Obedience you've transferred to us": Quoted in Stone, *FSM*, 164–165.

"If all men are born free": Ibid.

"domestic drudges": Quoted in Kellogg and Mintz, 46.

"*The bondage of the wife*": Miller, in Stoehr, 297.

"*The law of servitude in marriage*": J. S. Mill, "The Subjection of Women."

"*Although historians have usually highlighted the demand*": Nancy Cott, unpublished talk given at Radcliffe College's Schlesinger Library, May 8, 1997, manuscript on file with the author.

"*While we acknowledge our mutual affection*": Stoehr, 270.

"*She is not the equal of man*": William H. Holcombe, M.D., *The Sexes, Here and Hereafter* (Philadelphia: J. B. Lippincott & Co., 1869), 174.

"*by deranging the tides of her organization*": The quotes in this paragraph are from Dr. Edward Clarke's *Sex in Education, or, A Fair Chance for Girls* (1873), quoted in Cott, *Root of Bitterness*, 330–333, and Rosalind Rosenberg, *Beyond Separate Spheres: Intellectual Roots of Modern Feminism* (New Haven and London: Yale University Press, 1982), 12.

"*every post, occupation, and government service*": Sir Almroth Wright, M.D., F.R.S., *The Unexpurgated Case Against Woman Suffrage* (London: Constable and Company Ltd., 1913), 61.

"*the husband owes protection to his wife*": French and German civil codes quoted in Glendon, *Transformation*, 89–93.

Now that the *theory* of male supremacy and female inferiority has been dismantled, there is no longer any justification for barring marriage between two women or two men: See Hunter, "Marriage, Law, and Gender," and Koppelman, "Why Discrimination Against Lesbians and Gay Men Is Sex Discrimination."

"*the union of two persons of different genders*": Wardle, 52.

"*there are important differences between men and women*": Frum, 12.

"*feel—they are right to feel—anger*": Ibid.

"*marriage . . . is an honorable estate*": William Bennett, "Gay Marriage? A Man and a Woman needed for the 'Honorable Estate,' " St. Louis Post-Dispatch *Commentary*, Thursday, May 23, 1996.

Six: Heart

"Westron wind": This version found in J. B. Trapp, ed., *The Oxford Anthology of English Literature: vol. 1, Medieval English Literature* (New York: Oxford University Press, 1973).

Information about the history of Western divorce is drawn, unless otherwise noted, from Blake, *The Road to Reno;* Burguière, *A History of the Family,* vols. 1 and 2; Epstein, *Marriage Laws;* Freid, ed., *Jews and Divorce;* Gillis, *For Better, for Worse;* McCabe, *The Influence of the Church on*

Marriage and Divorce; May, *Great Expectations*; Pagels, *Adam, Eve, and the Serpent*; Phillips, *Putting Asunder* and *Untying the Knot*; Reynolds, *Marriage in the Western Church*; Riley, *Divorce*; Stone, *Road to Divorce*; and Ariès and Duby, eds., *A History of Private Life*, vol. 1.

"for instead of answering the question": Pagels, xxii.

"designate[s] the use of the genitals": Hincmar of Reims, quoted in Gies, 137.

"as between X and Y there is no charity": List of grounds for divorce in Gies, 56–57.

"Anyone can be idolatrous": Phillips, *Putting Asunder*, 56.

French petitions for annulments before and after 1770: Phillips, *Untying the Knot*, 108.

Divorce petitions in eighteenth-century Massachusetts: Cott, in Cott and Pleck, 123.

"Prisoner at the bar": Quoted in Phillips, *Putting Asunder*, 417.

"the lower classes, whose morals are more corrupt": Quoted in Stone, *Road to Divorce*, 365.

"most persons have but a very moderate capacity": J. S. Mill, quoted in Rose, 108.

"the empty husk of an outside matrimony": Milton, 1643, *The Doctrine and Discipline of Divorce*, 39 (reprinted London: Sherwood, Neely, and Jones, 1820).

"We are overrun by a flock": Blake, 299.

"Have you domestic trouble?": Phillips, *Putting Asunder*, 475.

"One does not need to take a high view": "Divorce in South Dakota," *The Nation* 56, no. 1439 (1893): 60–61.

"If there is one thing that the people are entitled": Blake, 187–188.

"Within a moderate period, the whole community": Quoted in Blake, 59.

"There may be something better than marriage": Greeley, quoted in Blake, 90–91.

British and New Zealand accusations about divorce: See Phillips, *Putting Asunder*, 485 and 464.

Jump in divorce rates in England and France: See Riley, *Divorce*, 5.

"Between 1867 and 1929, the population": May, 2.

"If marriage is a failure": James P. Lichtenberger, Ph.D., *Divorce: A Study in Social Causation* (London: P. S. King & Son, 1909), 169–70.

"One of the paradoxes of modern western society": Phillips, *Untying the Knot,* ix.

"Do you promise to give your daughter to me": Gies, 23.

"a daughter who does not openly resist": Dixon, 61.

"where there is to be union of bodies": Gratian, quoted in Gies, 98.

"such ephemeral factors as sexual attraction": Stone, *FSM,* 128.

"parents suggested he consider marrying": Ozment, *When Fathers Ruled,* 74–79.

"husband and wife are always together": Duc de La Rochefoucauld, quoted in Stone, *FSM,* 214, 220.

"A popular 1779 treatise described the ideal": Rothman, 32–33.

"remain in single 'blessedness'": Ibid.

Selected Bibliography

ADLER, FELIX. *Marriage and Divorce.* New York: McClure, Phillips, and Co., 1905.

ANDERSON, MICHAEL, COMP. *Sociology of the Family: Selected Readings.* Harmondsworth, England; Penguin, 1971.

ANSON, OFRA. "Marital Status and Women's Health Revisited: The Importance of a Proximate Adult." *Journal of Marriage and the Family* 51 (February 1989): 185–194.

ARIÈS, PHILIPPE, AND GEORGES DUBY, EDS. *A History of Private Life.* Volumes 1–4. Trans. Arthur Goldhammer. Cambridge, MA: Belknap Press of Harvard University Press, 1987–1991.

AUSTIN, JOHN MATHER. *A Voice to the Married: Being a Compendium of Social, Moral, and Religious Duties, Addressed to Husbands and Wives.* New York: Kiggins and Kellogg, 1857.

BACKHOUSE, CONSTANCE B. "Married Women's Property Law in Nineteenth-Century Canada." *Law and History Review* 6 (Fall 1988): 211–257.

BAILEY-HARRIS, REBECCA. "Property Division on Separation: Will the Married and the Unmarried Pass at the Crossroads?" *The University of New South Wales Law Journal* 8 (1985): 1–20.

BASCH, NORMA. *In the Eyes of the Law: Women, Marriage, and Property in Nineteenth-Century New York.* Ithaca: Cornell University Press, 1982.

BENNETT, DE ROBIGNE MORTIMER. *Anthony Comstock: His Career of Cruelty and Crime.* 1921. New York: Da Capo Press, 1971.

BEN-RAFAEL, ELIEZER. *Crisis and Transformation: The Kibbutz at Century's End.* Albany: State University of New York Press, 1997.

BERNSTEIN, FRED A. "This Child Does Have Two Mothers . . . and a Sperm Donor with Visitation." *New York University Review of Law and Social Change* 22, 1 (1996): 1–58.

BIEMER, LINDA BRIGGS. *Women and Property in Colonial New York: The Transition from Dutch to English Law, 1643–1727*. Ann Arbor, MI: UMI Research Press, 1983.

BLAKE, NELSON MANFRED. *The Road to Reno: A History of Divorce in the United States*. New York: Macmillan, 1962.

BLUMSTEIN, PHILIP, AND PEPPER SCHWARTZ. *American Couples: Money, Work, Sex*. New York: William Morrow, 1983.

BOOTH, ALAN, AND DAVID R. JOHNSON. "Declining Health and Marital Quality." *Journal of Marriage and the Family* 56 (February 1994): 218–223.

BOSWELL, JOHN. *Christianity, Social Tolerance, and Homosexuality: Gay People in Western Europe from the Beginning of the Christian Era to the Fourteenth Century*. Chicago: University of Chicago Press, 1981.

———. *The Kindness of Strangers: The Abandonment of Children in Western Europe from Late Antiquity to the Renaissance*. London: Penguin, 1989.

———. *Same-Sex Unions in Premodern Europe*. New York: Villard Books, 1994.

BOYARIN, DANIEL. *Carnal Israel: Reading Sex in Talmudic Culture*. Berkeley: University of California Press, 1993.

BREWAEYS, ANNE, ET AL. "Donor Insemination: Child Development and Family Functioning in Lesbian Mother Families." *Human Reproduction* 12, 6 (June 1997): 1349–1359.

BRODIE, JANET FARRELL. *Contraception and Abortion in Nineteenth-Century America*. Ithaca: Cornell University Press, 1994.

BROUN, HEYWOOD, AND MARGARET LEECH. *Anthony Comstock, Roundsman of the Lord*. New York: A. and C. Boni, 1927.

BROWN, PETER. *The Body and Society: Men, Women, and Sexual Renunciation in Early Christianity*. New York: Columbia University Press, 1988.

BRUCE, MARTHA LIVINGSTON, AND KATHLEEN M. KIM. "Differences in the Effects of Divorce on Major Depression in Men and Women." *The American Journal of Psychiatry* 149 (July 1992): 914–918.

BRYANT, ANITA. *The Anita Bryant Story: The Survival of Our Nation's Families and the Threat of Militant Homosexuality*. Old Tappan, NJ: Revell, 1977.

BURGUIÈRE, ANDRÉ, CHRISTIANE KLAPISCH-ZUBER, MARTINE SEGALEN, AND FRANÇOISE ZONABEND, EDS. *A History of the*

Family. Volumes 1 and 2. Trans. Sarah Hanbury Tenison, Rosemary Morris, and Andrew Wilson. Cambridge, MA: Belknap Press of Harvard University Press, 1996.

BURMAN, BONNIE, AND GAYLA MARGOLIN. "Analysis of the Association Between Marital Relationships and Health Problems: An Interactional Perspective." *Psychological Bulletin* 112 (July 1992): 39–63.

BURNHAM, MARGARET A. "An Impossible Marriage: Slave Law and Family Law." *Law and Inequality* 5 (July 1987): 187–225.

CHAMBERS, DAVID L. "What If? The Legal Consequences of Marriage and the Legal Needs of Lesbian and Gay Couples." *Michigan Law Review* 95 (November 1996): 447.

CHAN, RAYMOND W., BARBARA RABOY, AND CHARLOTTE J. PATTERSON. "Psychosocial Adjustment Among Children Conceived Via Donor Insemination by Lesbian and Heterosexual Mothers." *Child Development* 69 (April 1998): 443–458.

CHAUNCEY, GEORGE. *Gay New York: Gender, Urban Culture, and the Makings of the Gay Male World, 1890–1940.* New York: Basic Books, 1994.

CHERLIN, ANDREW J. *Marriage, Divorce, Remarriage: Social Trends in the United States.* Rev. ed. Cambridge, MA: Harvard University Press, 1992.

CHESLER, ELLEN. *Woman of Valor: Margaret Sanger and the Birth Control Movement in America.* New York: Simon and Schuster, 1992.

CHUSED, RICHARD H. "Late Nineteenth-Century Married Women's Property Law: Reception of the Early Married Women's Property Acts by Courts and Legislatures." *The American Journal of Legal History* 29 (January 1985): 3–35.

————. "Married Women's Property Law: 1800–1850." *The Georgetown Law Journal* 71 (June 1983): 1359–1425.

CLARK, ELIZABETH, ED. *St. Augustine on Marriage and Sexuality.* Washington, D.C: Catholic University of America Press, 1996.

COHEN, PATRICIA. "Daddy Dearest: Do You Really Matter?" *The New York Times,* July 11, 1998, A13–A15.

COHEN, SHAYE J. D., ED. *The Jewish Family in Antiquity.* Atlanta, GA: Scholars Press, 1993.

COLTRANE, SCOTT. "Father-Child Relationships and the Status of Women: A Cross-Cultural Study." *The American Journal of Sociology* 93 (March 1988): 1060–1096.

COONTZ, STEPHANIE. *The Way We Never Were: American Families and the Nostalgia Trap.* New York: HarperCollins, 1992.

————. *The Social Origins of Private Life: A History of American Families 1600–1900.* London and New York: Verso, 1988.

COTT, NANCY F., ED. *Root of Bitterness: Documents of the Social History of American Women.* 2d ed. Boston: Northeastern University Press, 1996.

COTT, NANCY F., AND ELIZABETH H. PLECK, EDS. *A Heritage of Her Own: Toward a New Social History of American Women.* New York: Simon and Schuster, 1979.

DALY, MARTIN, AND MARGO WILSON. "Evolutionary Psychology and Marital Conflict," in *Sex, Power, Conflict: Evolutionary and Feminist Perspectives,* ed. David M. Buss and Neil Malamuth. New York: Oxford University Press, 1996.

D'EMILIO, JOHN, AND ESTELLE B. FREEDMAN. *Intimate Matters: A History of Sexuality in America.* New York: Harper and Row, 1988.

DICKEMANN, MILDRED. "Women, Class, and Dowry." *American Anthropologist* 93 (December 1991): 944–946.

DIENES, C. THOMAS. *Law, Politics, and Birth Control.* Urbana, IL: University of Illinois Press, 1972.

DIXON, SUZANNE. *The Roman Family: Ancient Society and History.* Baltimore: Johns Hopkins University Press, 1992.

DUBLIN, LOUIS I. "The Fallacious Propaganda for Birth Control." *The Atlantic Monthly,* February 1926.

DUNCAN, RICHARD F. "Homosexual Marriage and the Myth of Tolerance: Is Cardinal O'Connor a 'Homophobe'?" *Notre Dame Journal of Law, Ethics and Public Policy* 10 (1996): 587–607.

EBRAHIM, SHAH, ET AL. "Marital Status, Change in Marital Status, and Mortality in Middle-aged British Men." *American Journal of Epidemiology* 142, 8 (1995): 834–842.

EHRENREICH, BARBARA, ELIZABETH HESS, AND GLORIA JACOBS. *Re-Making Love: The Feminization of Sex.* Garden City, NY: Anchor Press/Doubleday, 1986.

EINHORN, JAY. "Child Custody in Historical Perspective: A Study of Changing Social Perceptions of Divorce and Child Custody in Anglo-American Law." *Behavioral Sciences and the Law* 4, 2 (1986).

EPSTEIN, LOUIS M. *The Jewish Marriage Contract: A Study in the Status of the Woman in Jewish Law.* New York: Jewish Theological Seminary of America, 1927.

———. *Marriage Laws in the Bible and the Talmud.* Cambridge, MA: Harvard University Press, 1942.

———. *Sex Laws and Customs in Judaism.* New York: Bloch Publishing Co., 1948. Reprint, New York: Ktav Publishing House, 1967.

ESKRIDGE, WILLIAM N., JR. *The Case for Same-Sex Marriage: From Sexual Liberty to Civilized Commitment.* New York: The Free Press, 1996.

ESKRIDGE, WILLIAM N., JR., AND NAN D. HUNTER. *Sexuality, Gender, and the Law.* Westbury, NY: The Foundation Press, 1997.

ESTRICH, SUSAN. Counterpoints Column, *USA Today,* Thursday, May 30, 1996, A18.

FABRÈGUES, JEAN DE. *Christian Marriage.* Trans. Rosemary Haughton. New York: Hawthorn Books, 1959.

FALK, ZE'EV WILHELM. *Jewish Matrimonial Law in the Middle Ages.* London: Oxford University Press, 1966.

FASS, PAULA S. *The Damned and the Beautiful: American Youth in the 1920's.* New York: Oxford University Press, 1977.

FELDMAN, DAVID. *Marital Relations, Birth Control, and Abortion in Jewish Law.* New York: Schocken Books, 1974.

FINKELHOR, DAVID. "Current Information on the Scope and Nature of Child Sexual Abuse." *The Future of Children* 4 (Summer/Fall 1994).

FINNIS, JOHN. "Law, Morality, and 'Sexual Orientation,' " *Notre Dame Law Review* 69 (1995): 5.

FLANDERS, STEVEN. "The Benefits of Marriage." *The Public Interest* 124 (Summer 96): 80–87.

FOSTER, LAWRENCE. *Religion and Sexuality: Three American Communal Experiments of the Nineteenth Century.* New York: Oxford University Press, 1981.

FOWLER, DAVID HENRY. *Northern Attitudes Towards Interracial Marriage: Legislation and Public Opinion in the Middle Atlantic States of the Old Northwest, 1780–1930.* New York: Garland, 1987.

FREID, JACOB, ED. *Jews and Divorce.* New York: Ktav Publishing House, 1968.

FRIEDMAN, LAWRENCE MEIR. *A History of American Law.* New York: Simon and Schuster, 1973.

FRUM, DAVID. "The Courts, Gay Marriage, and the Popular Will." *The Weekly Standard,* September 30, 1996, 12.

FRYER, PETER. *The Birth Controllers.* London: Secker and Warburg, 1965.

GIES, FRANCES, AND JOSEPH GIES. *Marriage and the Family in the Middle Ages.* New York: Harper and Row, 1987.

GILDER, GEORGE F. *Sexual Suicide.* New York: Quadrangle, 1973.

GILLIS, JOHN. *For Better, for Worse.* New York: Oxford University Press, 1985.

GLENDON, MARY ANN. *The Transformation of Family Law: State, Law, and Family in the United States and Western Europe.* Chicago: University of Chicago Press, 1989.

GOLDMAN, EMMA. *Marriage and Love*. New York: Mother Earth Publishing Association, 1911.

GOLDMAN, NOREEN, SANDERS KORENMAN, AND RACHEL WEINSTEIN. "Marital Status and Health Among the Elderly." *Social Science and Medicine* 40, 12 (1995): 1717–1730.

GOLDMAN, WENDY Z. *Women, the State, and Revolution: Soviet Family Policy and Social Life, 1917–1936*. New York: Cambridge University Press, 1993.

GOLDSTEIN, ANNE B. "History, Homosexuality, and Political Values: Searching for the Hidden Determinants of Bowers v. Hardwick." *Yale Law Journal* 97 (May 1998): 1073–1099.

GOLDSTEIN, JOSEPH, ANNA FREUD, AND ALBERT J. SOLNIT. *Beyond the Best Interests of the Child*. Orig. ed. 1973. New York: Free Press, 1979.

GOLOMBOK, SUSAN, AND ROBYN FIVUSH. *Gender Development*. New York: Cambridge University Press, 1994.

GOLOMBOK, SUSAN, ET AL. "Families Created by the New Reproductive Technologies: Quality of Parenting and Social and Emotional Development of the Children." *Child Development* 66 (April 1995): 285–298.

GOLOMBOK, SUSAN, FIONA TASKER, AND CLARE MURRAY. "Children Raised in Fatherless Families from Infancy: Family Relationships and the Socioemotional Development of Children of Lesbian and Single Heterosexual Mothers." *Journal of Child Psychology and Psychiatry and Allied Disciplines* 38 (October 1997): 783–792.

GOODE, WILLIAM JOSIAH. *The Family*. 2d ed. Englewood Cliffs, NJ: Prentice-Hall, 1982.

GOODY, JACK. *The Development of the Family and Marriage in Europe*. Cambridge, England: Cambridge University Press, 1983.

GOODY, JACK, AND S. J. TAMBIAH. *Bridewealth and Dowry*. Cambridge, England: Cambridge University Press, 1973.

GORDON, LINDA. *Woman's Body, Woman's Right: A Social History of Birth Control in America*. New York: Grossman, 1976.

GOVE, WALTER R. "The Relationship Between Sex Roles, Marital Status, and Mental Illness." *Social Forces* 51 (September 1972): 34–44.

———. "Sex, Marital Status, and Mortality." *The American Journal of Sociology* 79 (1973–74): 45–67.

GRISWOLD, ROBERT L. *Fatherhood in America: A History*. New York: Basic Books, 1993.

GROSSBERG, MICHAEL. *Governing the Hearth: Law and the Family in Nineteenth-Century America*. Chapel Hill: University of North Carolina Press, 1985.

GROTH, A. NICHOLAS, AND H. JEAN BIRNBAUM. "Adult Sexual Orientation and Attraction to Underage Persons." *Archives Sexual Behavior* 7 (1978): 175–181.

GROVES, ERNEST. *Marriage.* New York: Henry Holt, 1933.

GUTMAN, HERBERT GEORGE. *The Black Family in Slavery and Freedom, 1750–1925.* New York: Vintage, 1976.

HAHN, BETH A. "Marital Status and Women's Health: The Effect of Economic Marital Acquisition." *Journal of Marriage and the Family* 55 (May 1993): 495–504.

HANAWALT, BARBARA A. *The Ties That Bound: Peasant Families in Medieval England.* New York and Oxford: Oxford University Press, 1986.

HELMHOLZ, R. H. *Marriage Litigation in Medieval England.* New York: Cambridge University Press, 1974.

HERLIHY, DAVID, AND CHRISTIANE KLAPISCH-ZUBER. *Tuscans and Their Families: A Study of the Florentine Catasto of 1427.* New Haven: Yale University Press, 1985.

HERMAN, DIDI. *The Anti-Gay Agenda: Orthodox Vision and the Christian Right.* Chicago: University of Chicago Press, 1997.

HILL, REUBEN. "The Returning Father and His Family." *Marriage and Family Living* 7 (May 1945): 31–56.

HILLERBRAND, HANS J., ED. *The Oxford Encyclopedia of the Reformation.* Vol. 1. New York: Oxford University Press, 1996.

HOLCOMBE, LEE. *Wives and Property: Reform of the Married Women's Property Law in Nineteenth-Century England.* Toronto: University of Toronto Press, 1983.

HOLCOMBE, WILLIAM H., M.D. *The Sexes, Here and Hereafter.* Philadelphia: J. B. Lippincott and Co., 1869.

HOLLOWAY, MARK. *Heavens on Earth: Utopian Communities in America, 1680–1880.* 2d ed. New York: Dover, 1966.

Homosexuality in America: Exposing the Myths. Tupelo, MS: American Family Association, 1994.

HUFTON, OLWEN H. *The Prospect Before Her: A History of Women in Western Europe.* New York: Alfred Knopf, 1996.

HUNTER, NAN D. "Life After Hardwick." *Harvard Civil Rights-Civil Liberties Law Review* 27 (Summer 1992): 531–554.

———. "The Sharon Kowalski Case: Sexual Dissent and the Family." *The Nation* 253, 11 (1991): 406–410.

———. "Marriage, Law, and Gender: A Feminist Inquiry." *Law and Sexuality* 1 (Summer 1991): 9–30.

INGRAM, MARTIN. *Church Courts, Sex, and Marriage in England, 1570–1640.* New York: Cambridge University Press, 1987.

JENNY, C., ET AL. "Are Children at Risk for Sexual Abuse by Homosexuals?" *Pediatrics* (1994): 41–44.

JOHNSON, WALTON R., AND D. MICHAEL WARREN, EDS. *Inside the Mixed Marriage: Accounts of Changing Attitudes, Patterns, and Perceptions of Cross-Cultural and Interracial Marriages.* Lanham, MD: University Press of America, 1994.

JOHNSTON, JAMES HUGO. *Race Relations in Virginia and Miscegenation in the South, 1776–1860.* Amherst, MA: University of Massachusetts Press, 1970.

JOUNG, I. M. A., ET AL. "Differences in Self-Reported Morbidity by Marital Status and by Living Arrangement." *International Journal of Epidemiology* 23, 1 (1994): 91–97.

KANDOIAN, ELLEN. "Cohabitation, Common Law Marriage, and the Possibility of a Shared Moral Life." *Georgetown Law Journal* 75 (August 1987): 1829–1873.

KAPLAN, MARION A., ED. *The Marriage Bargain: Women and Dowries in European History.* New York: Institute for Research in History and the Haworth Press, 1985.

KATZ, JACOB. *Tradition and Crisis: Jewish Society at the End of the Middle Ages.* New York: Free Press of Glencoe, 1961.

KATZ, JONATHAN NED. *Gay/Lesbian Almanac: A New Documentary in Which Is Contained, in Chronological Order, Evidence of the True and Fantastical History of Those Persons Now Called Lesbians and Gay Men . . .* New York: Harper and Row, 1983.

KAWASHIMA, YASUHIDE. "Adoption in Early America." *Journal of Family Law* 20, 4 (1981–1982): 677–696.

KINGDON, ROBERT McCUNE. *Adultery and Divorce in Calvin's Geneva.* Cambridge, MA: Harvard University Press, 1995.

KIRKPATRICK, MELANIE. "Gay Marriage: Who Should Decide?" *The Wall Street Journal,* March 13, 1996, A15.

KNIGHT, ROBERT H. *Insight. How Domestic Partnerships and "Gay Marriage" Threaten the Family.* Washington, D.C.: Family Research Council, 1994.

KNIGHT, ROBERT H., AND DANIEL S. GARCIA. *Insight. Homosexual Parenting: Bad for Children, Bad for Society.* Washington, D.C.: Family Research Council, 1994.

KOPPELMAN, ANDREW. "Why Discrimination Against Lesbians and Gay Men Is Sex Discrimination." *New York University Law Review* 69, 2 (May 1994).

KOVACS, ET AL. "A Controlled Study of the Psycho-Social Development of Children Conceived Following Insemination with Donor Semen." *Human Reproduction* 8, 5 (1993): 788–90.

LAMB, MICHAEL E. *The Role of the Father in Child Development.* 3rd ed. New York: Wiley, 1997.

LASLETT, PETER. *The World We Have Lost.* New York: Scribner, 1971.

LASLETT, PETER, KARLA OOSTERVEEN, AND RICHARD M. SMITH, EDS. *Bastardy and Its Comparative History: Studies in the History of Illegitimacy and Marital Nonconformism in Britain, France, Germany, Sweden, North America, Jamaica, and Japan.* Cambridge, MA: Harvard University Press, 1980.

LAVAL, JOHN H. *Marriage, Morals and Mothballs.* New York: Carter, 1939.

LAZAROU, KATHLEEN ELIZABETH. *Concealed Under Petticoats: Married Women's Property and the Law of Texas, 1840–1913.* New York: Garland, 1986.

LÉVI-STRAUSS, CLAUDE. *The Elementary Structures of Kinship.* Trans. James Harle Bell et al. Ed. Rodney Needham. 1949. Rev. ed. Boston: Beacon Press, 1969.

———. "The Family." In *Man, Culture, and Society,* ed. Harry Lionel Shapiro. New York: Oxford University Press, 1956, pp. 261–285.

LINDSEY, BEN BARR, AND WAINWRIGHT EVANS. *The Companionate Marriage.* New York: Garden City Publishing Co., 1927.

McCABE, JOSEPH. *The Influence of the Church on Marriage and Divorce.* London: Watts and Co., 1916.

McCANN, CAROLE RUTH. *Birth Control Politics in the United States, 1916–1945.* Ithaca: Cornell University Press, 1994.

McLANAHAN, SARA, AND GARY SANDEFUR. *Growing Up with a Single Parent: What Hurts, What Helps.* Cambridge, MA: Harvard University Press, 1994.

McLAREN, ANGUS. *Birth Control in Nineteenth-Century England.* New York: Holmes and Meier, 1978.

MACEDO, STEPHEN. "Homosexuality and the Conservative Mind." *Georgetown Law Journal* 84 (December 1995): 261–300.

MANDELKER, IRA L. *Religion, Society, and Utopia in Nineteenth-Century America.* Amherst: University of Massachusetts Press, 1984.

MASON, MARY ANN. *From Father's Property to Children's Rights: The History of Child Custody in the United States.* New York: Columbia University Press, 1994.

MAY, ELAINE TYLER. *Great Expectations: Marriage and Divorce in Post-Victorian America.* Chicago: University of Chicago Press, 1980.

MEYER, F. B. *Love, Courtship, and Marriage.* London: S. W. Partridge and Co., 1899.

MILL, JOHN STUART. *On Liberty; with, The Subjection of Women; and, Chapters on Socialism.* Ed. Stefan Collini. New York: Cambridge University Press, 1989.

MINTZ, STEVEN, AND SUSAN KELLOGG. *Domestic Revolutions: A Social History of American Family Life.* New York: Free Press, 1988.

MOLHO, ANTHONY. *Marriage Alliance in Late Medieval Florence.* Cambridge, MA: Harvard University Press, 1994.

MOUNT, FERDINAND. *The Subversive Family: An Alternative History of Love and Marriage.* New York: Free Press, 1992.

MUNCY, RAYMOND LEE. *Sex and Marriage in Utopian Communities: 19th Century America.* Bloomington, IN: Indiana University Press, 1973.

MURPHY, LAWRENCE R. "Defining the Crime Against Nature: Sodomy in the United States Appeals Courts, 1810–1940." *Journal of Homosexuality* 19, 1 (1990): 49–67.

NATIONAL RESEARCH COUNCIL (U.S.). PANEL ON RESEARCH ON CHILD ABUSE AND NEGLECT. *Understanding Child Abuse and Neglect.* Washington, D.C.: National Academy Press, 1993.

NICHOLS, THOMAS LOW, M.D., AND MARY S. GOVE NICHOLS. *Marriage: Its History, Character, and Results; Its Sanctities, and Its Profanities; Its Science and Its Facts. Demonstrating Its Influence, as a Civilized Institution, on the Happiness of the Individual and the Progress of the Race.* New York: T. L. Nichols, 1854.

NOONAN, JOHN THOMAS, JR. *Contraception: A History of Its Treatment by the Catholic Theologians and Canonists.* Cambridge: Harvard University Press, 1965.

OWEN, ROBERT DALE. *Moral Physiology; or A Brief and Plain Treatise on the Population Question.* 10th ed. New York: G. Vale, 1858.

OZ, AMOS. *Under this Blazing Light: Essays.* Trans. Nicholas De Lange. 1979. New York: Cambridge University Press, 1995.

OZMENT, STEVEN E. *The Reformation in the Cities: The Appeal of Protestantism to Sixteenth-Century Germany and Switzerland.* New Haven: Yale University Press, 1975.

———. *When Fathers Ruled: Family Life in Reformation Europe.* Cambridge, MA: Harvard University Press, 1983.

PAGELS, ELAINE H. *Adam, Eve, and the Serpent.* New York: Random House, 1988.

PASCOE, PEGGY. "Miscegenation Law, Court Cases, and Ideologies of 'Race' in Twentieth-Century America." *The Journal of American History* 83, 1 (June 1996).

PATTERSON, CHARLOTTE. "Children of Lesbian and Gay Parents." In *Advances in Clinical Child Psychology*, vol. 19, ed. T. H. Ollendick and R. J. Prinz. New York: Plenum Press, 1997.

PEDERSON, JAMIE D. *The RCW Project: An Analysis of the Benefits and Burdens of Marriage Contained in the Revised Code of Washington*. For the Legal Marriage Alliance of Washington, September 30, 1997.

PELIKAN, JAROSLAV, ED. *Luther's Works*. St. Louis: Concordia Publishing House, 1986.

PHILLIPS, RODERICK. *Putting Asunder: A History of Divorce in Western Society*. New York: Cambridge University Press, 1988.

———. *Untying the Knot: A Short History of Divorce*. New York: Cambridge University Press, 1991.

PODHORETZ, NORMAN. "How The Gay Rights Movement Won." *Commentary*, November 1996, 32–41.

POLIKOFF, NANCY. "This Child Does Have Two Mothers." *The Georgetown Law Journal* 78 (February 1990): 459–575.

———. "We Will Get What We Ask For: Why Legalizing Gay and Lesbian Marriage Will Not 'Dismantle the Legal Structure of Gender in Every Marriage.' " *Virginia Law Review* 79 (1993): 1535.

POPENOE, DAVID. *Life Without Father: Compelling New Evidence That Fatherhood and Marriage Are Indispensable for the Good of Children and Society*. New York: Martin Kessler Books, 1996.

POPENOE, PAUL BOWMAN. *Modern Marriage: A Handbook*. New York: Macmillan, 1925.

POPOVICH, ROBERT G. "It's All Mine–Or at Least Part of It Is: A California Look at Property Apportionment Between the Families of an Intestate and an Intestate's Predeceased Spouse." *Pepperdine Law Review* 16 (April 1989): 831–870.

POSNER, RICHARD A., AND KATHARINE B. SILBAUGH. *A Guide to America's Sex Laws*. Chicago: University of Chicago Press, 1996.

PRESSER, STEPHEN B. "The Historical Background of the American Law of Adoption." *Journal of Family Law* 11 (1971–72): 443–516.

QUAIFE, GEOFFREY ROBERT. *Wanton Wenches and Wayward Wives: Peasants and Illicit Sex in Early Seventeenth-Century England*. New Brunswick, NJ: Rutgers University Press, 1979.

RAMSEY COLLOQUIUM. "The Homosexual Movement: A Response by the Ramsey Colloquium." *First Things: A Monthly Journal of Religion and Public Life* 41 (March 1994).

REN, XINHUA STEVE. "Marital Status and Quality of Relationships: The Impact on Health Perception." *Social Science and Medicine* 44, 2 (1997): 241–249.

REYNOLDS, PHILIP LYNDON. *Marriage in the Western Church: The Chris-tianization of Marriage During the Patristic and Early Medieval Periods.* New York: E. J. Brill, 1994.

RILEY, J. *Divorce.* New York: Oxford University Press, 1991.

RODRIGUE, JAMES R., AND TRICIA L. PARK. "General and Illness-Specific Adjustment to Cancer: Relationship to Marital Status and Mar-ital Quality." *Journal of Psychosomatic Research* 40, 1 (1996): 29–36.

ROGERS, RICHARD G. "MARRIAGE, SEX, AND MORTALITY." *Jour-nal of Marriage and the Family* 57 (May 1995): 515–526.

RORABACK, CATHERINE G. "Griswold v. Connecticut: A Brief Case His-tory." *Ohio Northern University Law Review* 16 (Summer 1990): 395–401.

ROSE, PHYLLIS. *Parallel Lives: Five Victorian Marriages.* New York: Vintage Books, 1984.

ROTBERG, ROBERT I., AND THEODORE K. RABB, EDS. *Marriage and Fertility: Studies in Interdisciplinary History.* Princeton, NJ: Princeton University Press, 1980.

ROTHMAN, ELLEN K. *Hands and Hearts: A History of Courtship in Amer-ica.* New York: Basic Books, 1984.

RUSSELL, BERTRAND. *Marriage and Morals.* 1930. New York: Liveright, 1970.

SAFLEY, THOMAS MAX. *Let No Man Put Asunder: The Control of Marriage in the German Southwest: A Comparative Study, 1550–1600.* Kirksville, MO: Northeast Missouri State University, Sixteenth Century Journal Publishers, 1984.

SCHIFFREN, LISA. "Gay Marriage, an Oxymoron." *New York Times,* March 23, 1996, A29.

SEARS, HAL D. *The Sex Radicals: Free Love in High Victorian America.* Law-rence: Regents Press of Kansas, 1977.

SHAMMAS, CAROLE. "Re-Assessing the Married Women's Property Acts." *Journal of Women's History* 6 (Spring 1994): 9–31.

SICKELS, ROBERT J. *Race, Marriage and the Law.* Albuquerque: ͟͟ ͟͟ ͟͟ ͟͟er-sity of New Mexico Press, 1972.

SMITH, JOHN DAVID, ED. *Anti-Black Thought, 1863–1925. Volume 8: Racial Determinism and the Fear of Miscegenation Post-1900, Part 2. Race and "The Negro Problem."* New York: Garland, 1993.

SOROKIN, PITIRIM. *The American Sex Revolution.* Boston: Porter Sargent, 1956.

SROUFE, L. ALAN, ROBERT G. COOPER, GANIE B. DEHART, AND MARY E. MARSHALL, EDS. *Child Development: Its Nature and Course.* 2d ed. New York: McGraw-Hill, 1992.

STEIL, JANICE M. *Marital Equality: Its Relationship to the Well-Being of Husbands and Wives.* Thousand Oaks, CA: Sage Publications, 1997.

STEVENSON, MICHAEL R., AND KATHRYN N. BLACK. "Paternal Absence and Sex-Role Development: A Meta-Analysis." *Child Development* 59 (June 1988): 794–826.

STOEHR, TAYLOR. *Free Love in America: A Documentary History.* New York: AMS Press, 1979.

STONE, LAWRENCE. *The Family, Sex and Marriage in England, 1500–1800.* Abridged ed. New York: Harper and Row, 1979.

———. *Road to Divorce: England 1530–1987.* New York: Oxford University Press, 1990.

STOPES, MARIE CARMICHAEL. *Married Love: A New Contribution to the Solution of Sex Difficulties.* 1918. New York: Eugenics Publishing Co., 1931.

STRASSBERG, MAURA. "Distinctions of Form or Substance: Monogamy, Polygamy and Same Sex Marriage." *North Carolina Law Review* 75 (June 1997): 1501–1624.

SULLIVAN, ANDREW, ED. *Same-Sex Marriage: Pro and Con, A Reader.* New York: Vintage, 1997.

TASKER, FIONA L., AND SUSAN GOLOMBOK. *Growing Up in a Lesbian Family: Effects on Child Development.* New York: Guilford Press, 1997.

TREGGIARI, SUSAN. *Papers of the British School at Rome, Volume XLIX.* Hertford, England: Stephen Austin and Sons, 1981.

———. "Women as Property in the Early Roman Empire." In *Women and the Law: The Social Historical Perspective,* vol. 2, ed. D. Kelly Weisberg. Cambridge, MA: Schenkman, 1982.

TROVATO, FRANK, AND GLORIA LAURIS. "Marital Status and Mortality in Canada: 1951–1981." *Journal of Marriage and the Family* 51 (November 1989): 907–922.

UMBERSON, DEBRA. "Gender, Marital Status and the Social Control of Health Behavior." *Social Science and Medicine* 34, 8 (1992): 907–917.

WALDRON, INGRID, CHRISTOPHER C. WEISS, AND MARY ELIZABETH HUGHES. "Marital Status Effects on Health: Are There Differences Between Never Married Women and Divorced and Separated Women?" *Social Science and Medicine* 45, 9 (1997): 1387–1397.

WALDRON, INGRID, MARY ELIZABETH HUGHES, AND TRACY L. BROOKS. "Marriage Protection and Marriage Selection—Prospective Evidence for Reciprocal Effects of Marital Status and Health." *Social Science and Medicine* 43, 1 (1996): 113–123.

WALLENSTEIN, PETER. "Race, Marriage, and the Law of Freedom: Alabama and Virginia, 1860s–1960s." *Chicago Kent Law Review* 70, 2 (1994).

WARDLE, LYNN D. "A Critical Analysis of Constitutional Claims for Same-Sex Marriage." *Brigham Young University Law Review* 1 (1996): 1–101.

WARSHAK, RICHARD ADES. *The Custody Revolution: The Father Factor and the Motherhood Mystique.* New York: Poseidon Press, 1992.

WASHINGTON, JOSEPH R., JR. *Marriage in Black and White.* Boston: Beacon Press, 1970.

WEGNER, JUDITH. *Chattel or Person?* New York: Oxford University Press, 1988.

WEISBROD, CAROL. *The Boundaries of Utopia.* New York: Pantheon, 1980.

WHITMORE, WILLIAM HENRY. *The Law of Adoption in the United States, and Especially in Massachusetts.* Albany: Joel Munsell, 1876.

WILSON, JAMES Q. "Against Homosexual Marriage." *Commentary*, March 1996.

WRIGHT, SIR ALMROTH, M.D., F.R.S. *The Unexpurgated Case Against Woman Suffrage.* London: Constable and Company Ltd., 1913.

WRIGHT, CARROLL DAVIDSON. *Outline of Practical Sociology, with Special Reference to American Conditions.* New York: Longmans, Green, and Co., 1899.

WYKE, SALLY, AND GRAEME FORD. "Competing Explanations for Associations Between Marital Status and Health." *Social Science and Medicine* 34, 5 (1992): 523–532.

ZAINALDIN, JAMIL S. "The Emergence of a Modern American Family Law: Child Custody, Adoption, and the Courts, 1796–1860." *Northwestern University Law Review* 73 (1978–79): 1038–1089.

Acknowledgments

I would like to acknowledge my tremendous gratitude for the many kinds of help this book has received from many sources and directions. Writing this book simply would not have been possible without my time as a Visiting Scholar at Radcliffe College's Schlesinger Library, where I was able to ransack its marvelous collection on the history of women and also had the run of Widener Library and the entire Harvard library system. My endless thanks to Mary Maples Dunn and the incomparable staff of the Schlesinger Library, including Diane Hamer, Wendy Thomas, Ellen Shea, and to the magnificent research assistants Anna Baldwin, Kelly Kinneen, and Julia Soyer. Nor could I have written this book without very different kinds of practical support from Mary Lou Dopart and the New England Development Center, David Graff, Rebecca Graff, Lisa Larson, Susan Meigs, editors Marya van't Hul and Amy Caldwell, and agent and friend Louise Quayle. And my thanks go as well to Katherine Acey and the Astraea Foundation, for all their past and ongoing support.

Others offered their interest, conversation, criticisms, challenges, input, and encouragement, including Suzanne Berne, Mary Bonauto, Chris Chinlund, Karen Cook, Jackie Dirks, Barb and Milton, Cynthia Enloe, Carolyn Goldstein, Ruth E. Hersh, Jeff Howard, Florence Ladd, Susan Miller, the New Words salon, Joni Seager, Joe Shay, Claudia Siegman, Hillary Smith, Andrew Sullivan, and John Wilkinson. Still others generously took time out from their own pressing deadlines to read an early draft and to apply their critical minds in ways that helped me clarify and con-solidate the book's facts and arguments: my tremendous thanks to professors Nancy Cott, Jay Harris, Charlotte Patterson, Susan Treggiari, and Jennifer Wriggins.

The traditional disclaimer more than applies: all errors remain my own.

The most extraordinary critical commitment to this book came from Laura Zimmerman, writing buddy for whom no superlatives are too extreme. And always my love and gratitude go to Madeline Drexler, who breathed life into this book from the first day we met.

Index